The Dead Horse Investigation
Forensic Photo Analysis for Everyone

Colleen Fitzpatrick, PhD

Rice Book Press
Fountain Valley, Ca

Published by Rice Book Press
www.forensicgenealogy.info

Thanks to the Sheboygan Historical Research Center for the use of the Sheboygan Dead Horse Photo for the cover of this book

Cover designed by Kimball Clark.

Library of Congress Control No. 2008903783

ISBN 978-0-976-71605-1

First Printing

Printed in the United States of America

Dedicated to my three favorite people,

Michael, Quinn, and Margaret Fitzpatrick

The children of
Terry Fitzpatrick and Jane Snyder

The grandchildren of
Emmett Fitzpatrick and Marilyn Rice

The great grandchildren of
Thomas Steven Fitzpatrick, Sr. and Loretta Kelly

The great great grandchildren of
John Fitzpatrick and Ellen Flynn

The great great great grandchildren of
Peter Fitzpatrick and Mary Hanlon
Natives of Co. Louth and Co. Wexford, Ireland

Acknowledgements

Many thanks to all the people who made this book possible, especially the loyal Quizmasters who have become our photo-family through the photo-quizzes we post on our website every week at www.forensicgeneaogy.info. I would like to offer a special thanks to Sharon Sergeant for helping with the editing, to John Roberts and the History Posse for the interesting photo mysteries they have shared with me, to Lloyd McGuire, Jr., for his assistance with the photograph of Guthrie, OK, and to Doug Miller for his hints on bringing out faded writing with powder. Thanks also go to Bob Wainwright, the great grandson of Charles Eisenmann, for his generosity in sharing his collection of Eisenmann's photographs, and to Beth Dibble, Director of the Sheboygan Historical Research Center, for allowing us to use the Sheboygan Dead Horse Photo as the cover of this book. Most of all, I'd like to thank Andy for all he has done for me, knowing that no matter what I say, it will not be adequate to cover everything.

Table of Contents

Introduction

Old photographs are part of the legacy that our ancestors have left us. Each person in an unidentified photograph was just as much a human being as you and I, with a name, a personality, a family history, and quirks. Yet many of these people remain unidentified because no one remembered to put their names on the backs of their pictures.

But there is hope that life can be breathed back into these cardboard images with a little bit of ingenuity. The name of a person in a picture may not be lost forever.

This book is meant to develop your photo-detective skills by showing you new ways to look at old photographs. It teaches you that no detail should be discarded, however insignificant it may seem. It might be just the clue you are looking for.

What Is a Photo *Really* Saying?

The first step to becoming a good photodetective is to understand what a picture is trying to tell you. A missed clue can often lead you down the wrong path.

A picture of George and Jane Trollop Clark and their family is shown below. It was taken in Kearney, Nebraska in 1919. In the back row are their children Millie (18 yrs), Rolland (21 yrs), Lester (15 yrs), Sadie (19 yrs), and Ray (16 yrs). In the front are their two children Glen (13 yrs) and Sadie (3 yrs).

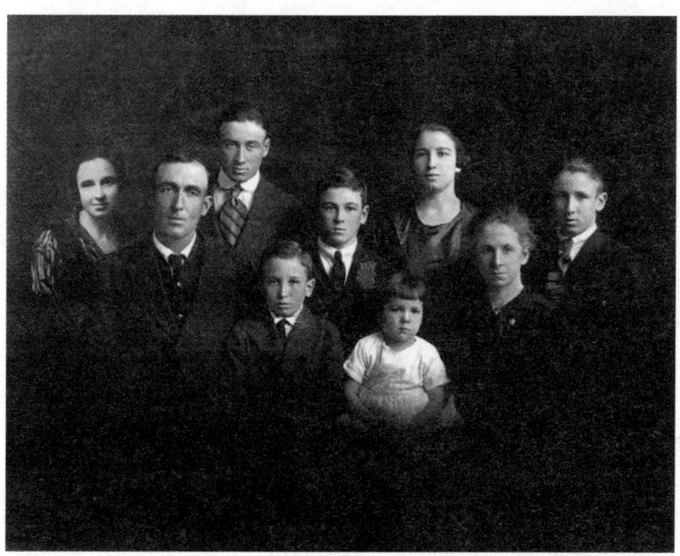

Submitted by C. E. Clark.

At first glance, this seems to be a typical family photograph, a dad and a mom surrounded by their seven children. Yet there is something unusual about it. One of the Clarks was not able to make it to the studio that day with the rest of the family. Who was it?

Take your time and look at the picture carefully. We'll tell you the answer later in the book.

Remember to Look at the Back, the Edges, the Shape, the Paper, the Mat ...

Since we cannot do DNA analysis on the people in a photograph, forensic photo-genealogists need to rely on other clues to analyze a picture. Sometimes clues have nothing to do with the contents of the image itself. Often the best clues are found on the back, or relate to the edges, the shape, the paper it is printed on, or to the type of board it is mounted on.

Remember to Look at the Back!

While many unidentified photos languish in boxes in the attic without a single identifying mark on them, there is the occasional photograph that could be redeemed if only someone would turn it over and look at the back. Valuable clues are often missed because we assume that there's nothing of interest on the "other side".

All kinds of clues that can appear on the back of a picture can help you identify it. A name or a date can provide explicit information. More subtle clues are just as valuable. Some of the most common markings that appear on the backs of photographs are:

- Writing
- Lot numbers
- Print paper logos
- A personal mark by the person who developed the picture
- Another picture

Always remember to turn a photograph over and look at the back. You may be surprised at what you find.

What If You Can't See the Back?

To examine the back of a photo, you must be able to see it! Sometimes this is simply a matter of turning it over and having a look, but in other cases this might not be possible. For example, if a photo has been removed from an album, the back might be hidden by pieces of album page stuck to it.

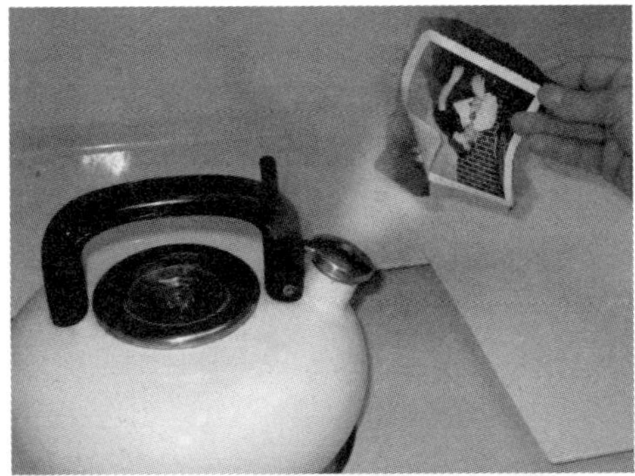

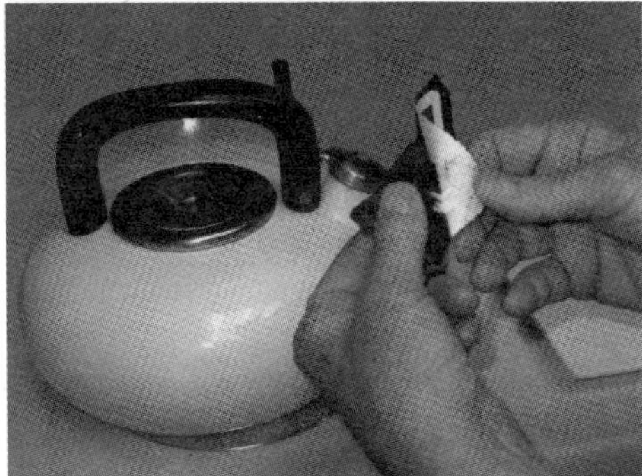

Figure 1. Using a tea kettle to remove album paper stuck to the back of a photograph..

Fortunately, you can remove these residual album scraps without damaging the photo by holding the picture in steam from a boiling tea kettle.

It's easy to do. First heat the water in the tea kettle until there is steam coming out of the spout. Then carefully hold the photo in the edges of the column of steam-just close enough to get the picture warm but not hot and wet. Don't burn your fingers! You may hold it using chopsticks if you like. Gently heating the photograph softens the adhesive that holds the scraps of paper to the picture, but does not affect the picture itself. In a moment, the adhesive will be soft enough for you to gently peel or scrape the shards of paper from the back. See Figure 1.

Sometimes the photo will curl slightly in response to the heat. If this happens, lay it on a horizontal surface with a heavy book on top of it. That will flatten it.

If you are worried that the steam might damage your photograph, try heating a small corner of the picture in the edge of the column of vapor. In my experience, if you are working with snapshots, your photo will not be damaged.

What If The Writing Is There but It Is Hard to See?

The back of the photo in Figure 2 yields important clues about the identities of the two children in the picture. They are apparently the sons of Mary Mackay McLeod, sister of George Mackay of Ingersoll, Ontario, Canada. The story the inscription seems to tell is a sad one-Mary's younger son was drowned in a mill race in Ingersoll. As we will see later in the chapter Relative Amnesia, this is close to the truth, but the inscription is misleading. A

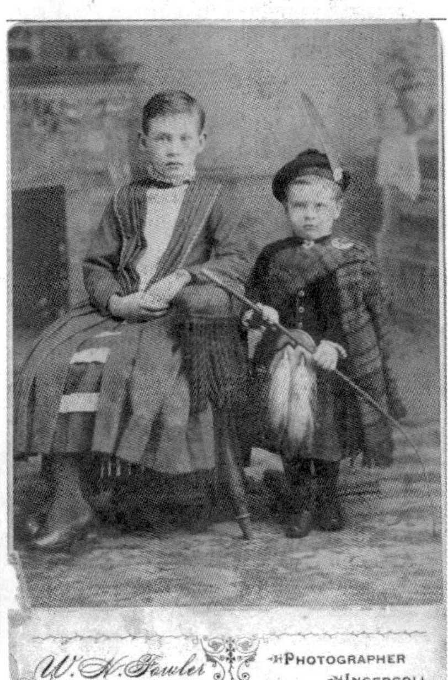

Figure 2. Aunt Mary McLeod sister of George McKay her sons - smallest drowned in mill race at the house in Ingersoll.

Photograph compliments of John Roberts and the History Posse.

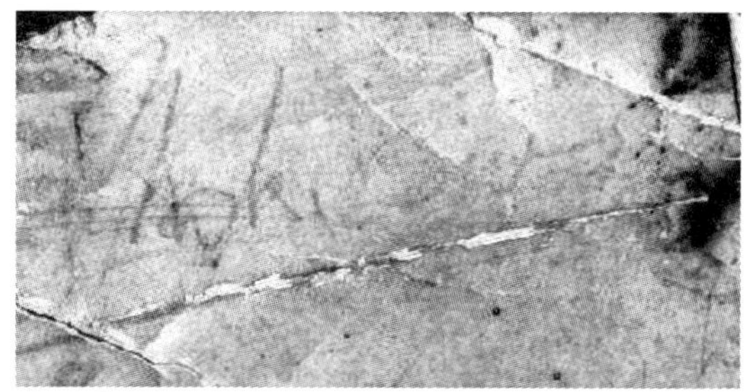

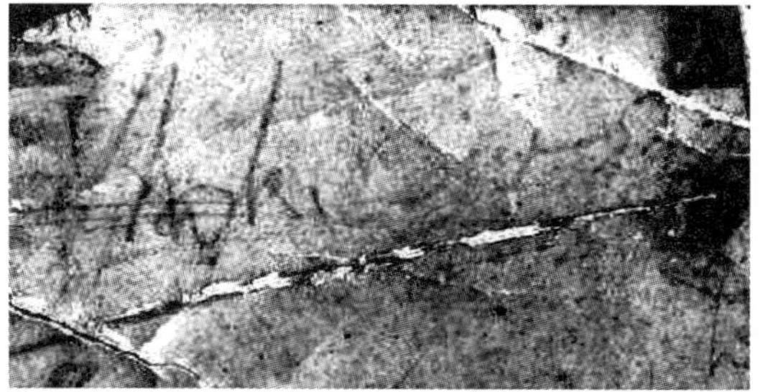

Figure 3. Before and after changing the contrast and brightness.

photo can be inscribed by a well-meaning family member long after the fact, with information that is not quite right but perhaps not too far from the truth. Even so, the information on the back of a photo can be a valuable start for further investigation.

Sometimes when the writing on the back of a photo is faint, it might be necessary to coax out its inscription. There are several ways to do this.

A modern photo detective can use a scanner to make a digital copy of a picture. Then photo-editing programs can be used to alter the contrast and the brightness of both the front and the back of a photo. (Figure 3.) The least complicated and easiest program I have found for this job is called *Irfanview*. It can be downloaded as freeware from www.irfanview.com. It has simple controls to enhance the writing in relation to the background. Of course there are more sophisticated and expensive software packages available with advanced capabilities. For example, *Adobe Photoshop* allows you to manipulate specific areas of a photo while leaving the rest unchanged. However, in my experience, if the writing can be enhanced at all, *Irfanview* is sufficient to do the job with minimal effort.

If your photograph is on a dark-colored mat, you might have trouble reading an inscription, especially if it is in pencil. One very simple thing you can do to increase its visibility is to illuminate your photograph at an angle, either in sunlight or using a flashlight. Pencil marks are usually shiny so that they behave like a dull mirror. If you vary the angle you use to view your photo, you will find a position where the inscription is the most legible. If you use a flashlight, it helps to have the room lights off. See Figure 4.

If an inscription is so faint that it is impossible to enhance electronically or read by using different lighting angles, there might not be enough writing left to see.

But all hope is not lost. A heavy-handed writer, pressing hard enough on his pencil or pen, might have created more than writing on the back of a photo. He could have embossed the mat as he wrote.

The embossing may not be noticeable at first, but you can enhance the visibility by gently rubbing a cotton ball dusted with talcum powder over the surface. Figure 5 shows that gently massaging an inscription in different directions will cause the grooves to fill with powder, creating a white inscription on the dark background of the mat. So even if you can no longer read the original inscription, you might still be able to read the grooves.

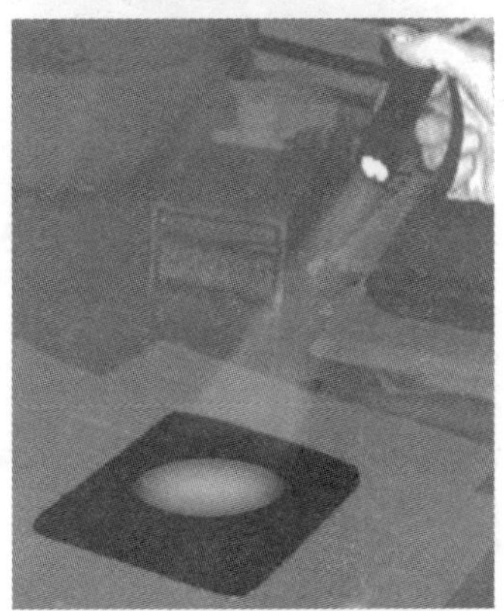

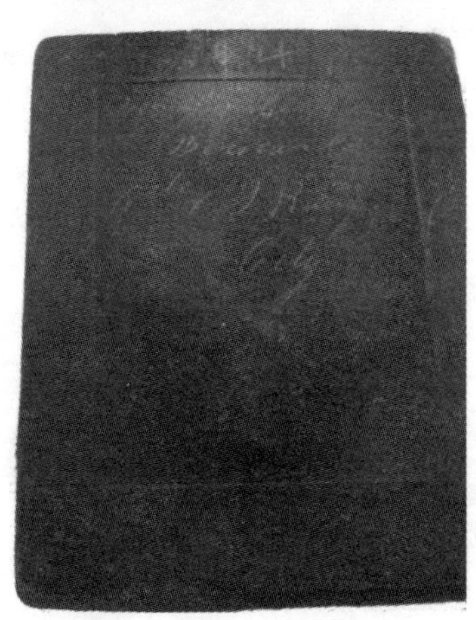

Lot Numbers, Logos, Personal Marks

Besides handwritten notes, photos may carry a marks or a numbers on the back that are helpful. The most common marks are: the lot number of the print paper, the logo of

Figure 4. Illuminating a photo at an angle can enhance the visibility of pencil marks.

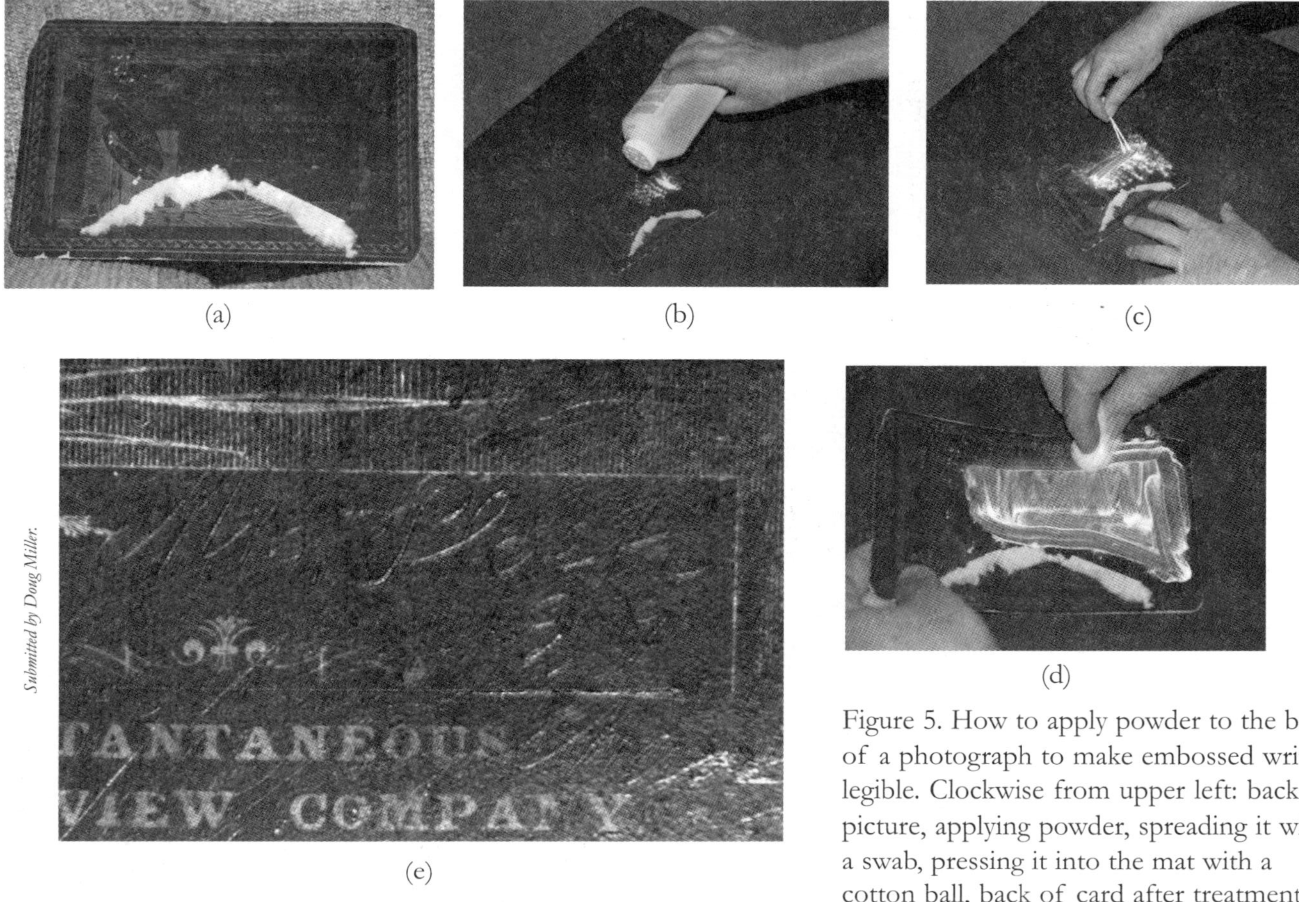

(a) (b) (c) (d) (e)

Figure 5. How to apply powder to the back of a photograph to make embossed writing legible. Clockwise from upper left: back of picture, applying powder, spreading it with a swab, pressing it into the mat with a cotton ball, back of card after treatment.

Submitted by Doug Miller.

the print paper showing its type or manufacturer, and marks made by the developer who processed the film.

As print paper was manufactured a lot number to designate when and where the film was produced was often stamped on the back. By grouping photographs that are marked with the same lot number, as shown in Figure 6, pictures printed on paper from the same lot can be identified. This usually means the pictures were processed at the same time. Information known about one photograph can often provide information on other photographs from that lot.

The second kind of mark that is useful for dating old photographs is the logo of the manufacturer or the name of the specific type of print paper. See Figure 7. For example, sometime between the 1920s and the 1940s, Kodak started marking the back of its photographic paper with the *VELOX* logo[1]. In the early to mid 1950s, the logo was changed to '*Kodak VELOX Paper*'.

At about the same time Agfa made a similar change in its logo. Prior to the 1950s, Agfa used a two part logo, made up of the name *Agfa* followed by the brand name (*Agfa Brovira*, for example). For new products introduced after 1945, and for existing products produced after the mid-1950s, the company dropped the brand

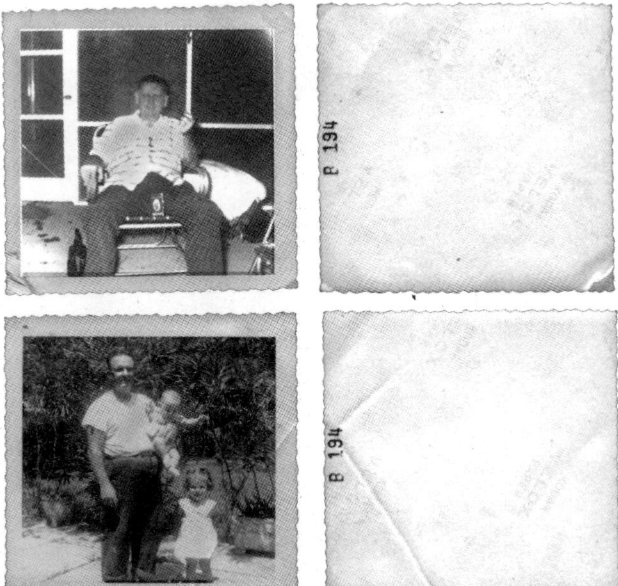

Figure 6. The backs of photos often carry lot numbers that help to identify them.

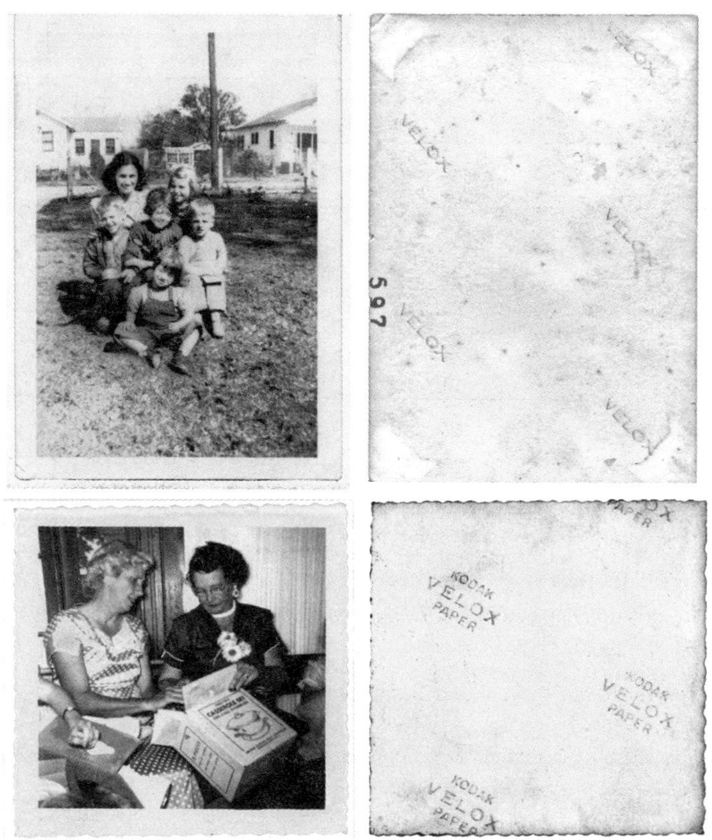

Figure 7. The logo on the back of a photo is an important clue.

name and used the single word *Agfa.* Table 1 provides a guide in using Kodak and Agfa print paper logos to determine an approximate date a photograph was taken. For example, if you have a photograph with a two part Agfa logo, you can be sure it was produced before the mid-1950s[1].

By the way, don't expect to find American photographs from the early - to mid-1940s printed on Agfa paper. Agfa is a German company, and there was a world war going on at the time.

Many old photographs carry a mark made by the darkroom that processed the picture. This kind of mark can be anything from a handwritten number to a stroke with a pencil or a graphite wheel. See Figure 8. If the

Table 1. Kodak and Agfa Logos[1].

Kodak		Agfa	
Logo	**Date**	**Logo**	**Date**
Kodak	Bef early 1950s	Agfa + Product Name	Before 1950s
Kodak VELOX Paper	Aft early 1950s	Agfa	After 1945 or 1950s, depending on product

handwritten numbers are the same on a group of photographs, chances are they came from the same roll of film. If the pencil or graphite stroke appears at exactly the same place on the back of several pictures, chances are they were processed from the same roll of film. If the marking system was automated, it is possible that rolls of film that were developed by the same darkroom at different times will have marks in a similar position, but it is highly unlikely that they will appear in exactly the same place.

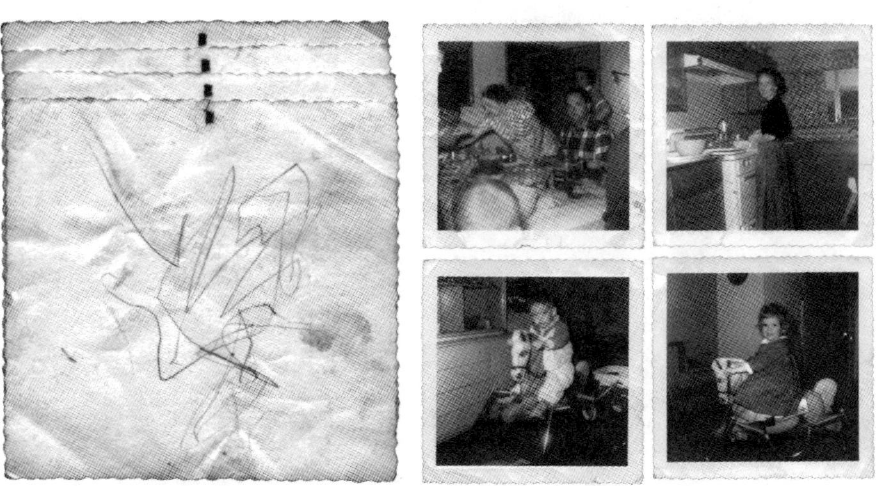

Figure 8. There are often pencil marks on the backs of prints that were made during processing.

A Ghost Image

A ghost image can appear on the back of one photograph when it has been stacked against the face of another photograph for a long time See Figure 9. (Note a ghost image is different from an image of a ghost.) Photographs that exhibit ghost images are not uncommon in antique stores where pictures have been stored in contact with each other over a long period of time. Ghost images can also appear on facing pages in albums that have remained unopened. Although a photograph might not be interesting, a ghost image on the reverse side can yield valuable information about an individual or a family. (See the following chapter, Two Short Case Studies, I. The Hodder Comparison).

Ghost images are produced by photographs with a high platinum or silver-gold-platinum content (called platinotypes). William Willis developed the platinotype process in 1873. He founded the Platinotype Company in 1879, which produced the first commercially available platinum paper in 1881. This gives an earliest date for a photograph that can cause a ghost image.

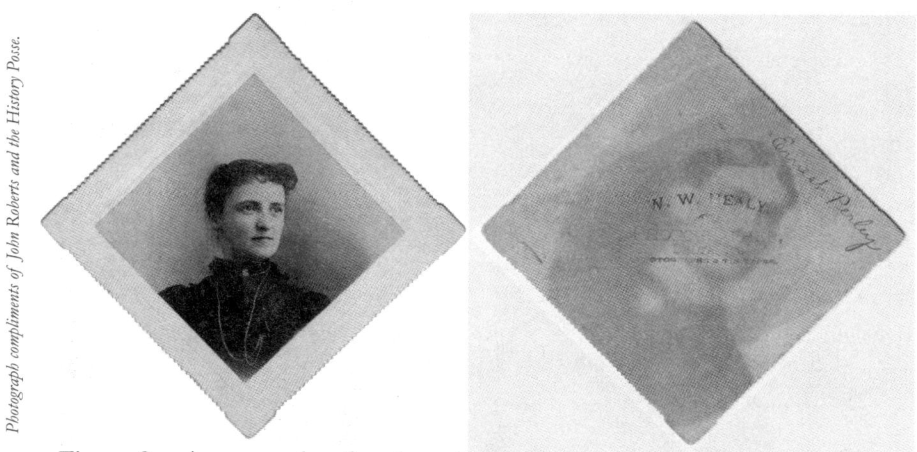

Photograph compliments of John Roberts and the History Posse.

Figure 9. An example of a ghost image formed on the back of a photograph.

Although a platinotype image itself is very stable, the platinum in the image is a powerful catalyst that can cause the deterioration of paper (particularly lower quality paper) in contact with it. This deterioration can be in the form of the transfer of a positive image to paper in contact with the print surface. Sometimes the platinum in a print also causes its mat to deteriorate[2].

The Edges

Photos with crinkly edges can sometimes be fit together like a jigsaw puzzle. For a group of photos with matching edges, it does not matter if photo #1 lies next to photo #5 or photo #100 - the edges should fit together and the logo should be in about the same position on each photo. (Figure 10.)

Photographs with matching edges were produced by the same darkroom. They were created after the development process when photographs printed on master rolls of print paper were cut apart from each other. The master rolls were large, flat rolls of print paper, the top and bottom edges of which had crinkly edges. Paper from the roll was incrementally advanced through a machine to expose it section by section to negatives that were simultaneously advanced on a facing reel. The roll of exposed paper was spooled on a take-up reel, after which it was passed through a developing tank and then dried

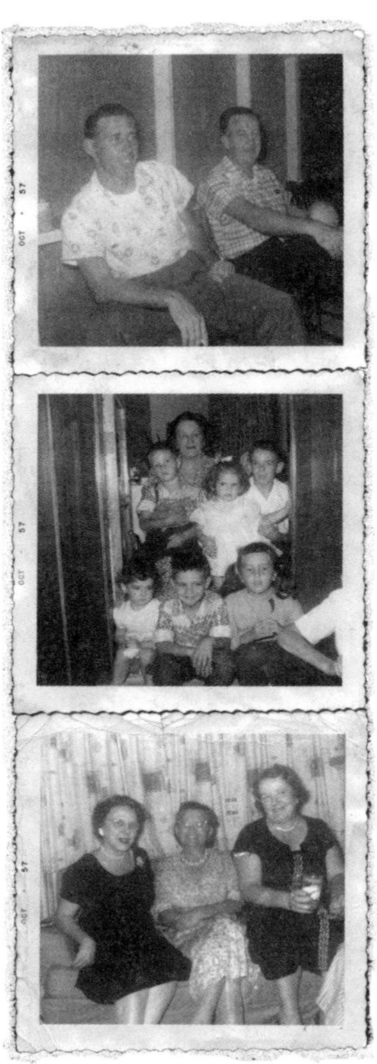

Figure 10. Crinkled edges that match.

on a hot drum. In the final step, the roll passed through a cutter where a crinkly-edged blade was used to separate individual prints[3]. The right edge of each print produced by the cutter would match the left edge of every other print produced, even if the prints were processed months apart, and came from different rolls of film.

Crinkly edges on photographs were formed in the very last step in producing a print from a negative, not beforehand during the manufacture of the print paper. Prints with crinkly edges that match were produced by the same cutting machine in the same darkroom. Although matching prints were not necessarily from the same roll of film, having information about one or more of them can yield valuable information about the others.

The pictures shown in Figure 11 were taken in at the same family get-together, judging by the people and the cars in them. Yet only three of the four prints have the same lot number on the back. The photo of the young couple standing in front of the car has a different lot number on it. A further mystery is that although the crinkly eges of all four photos fit together one of the photos sharing the lot number 023 fits into th group upside down.

The explanation for these inconsistencies is simple. During their time together, the family used three rolls of film. The ones bearing lot number 023 are prints made from the first two rolls. During the printing process, the negatives from these two rolls were loaded into the printing machine in opposite orientations. Since all the photos from both rolls were printed using the same roll of print paper, and then cut apart using the same crinkly-edged cutter, they all fit together side by side, but can be sorted into two groups according to orientation. If other matching photos were found with the same lot number, it would be possible to tell which roll they were from by checking their orientations against the present sets of pictures.

The picture with lot number 975 was developed later using a different roll of print paper. It is likely that after the family finished taking pictures that day, they did not have the chance to finish this last roll of film, so that it remained in the camera for a while before it was developed. However, since the edges of the 975 pictures match the others, they must have been developed by the same processing company. If other photos are found with lot number 975, it will be clear that they are from this last roll of film. Note that the photo with this odd lot number is a picture of the young couple standing in front of a car. Perhaps this ws the last picture taken as the couple was getting ready to leave.

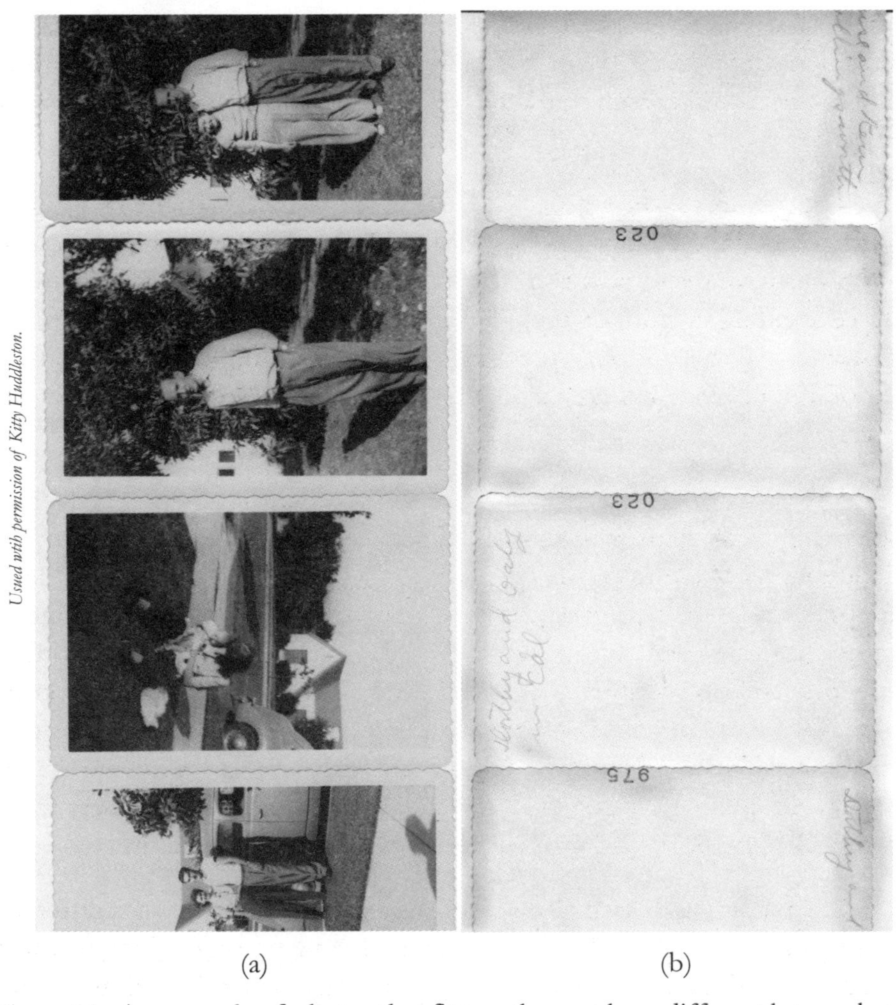

Usued wtih permission of Kitty Huddleston.

(a) (b)

Figure 11. An example of photos that fit together, yet have different lot numbers.

Even if a set of matching crinkly-edged photos has the same lot number, there is further information that you can derive from the placement of the logos on the back.

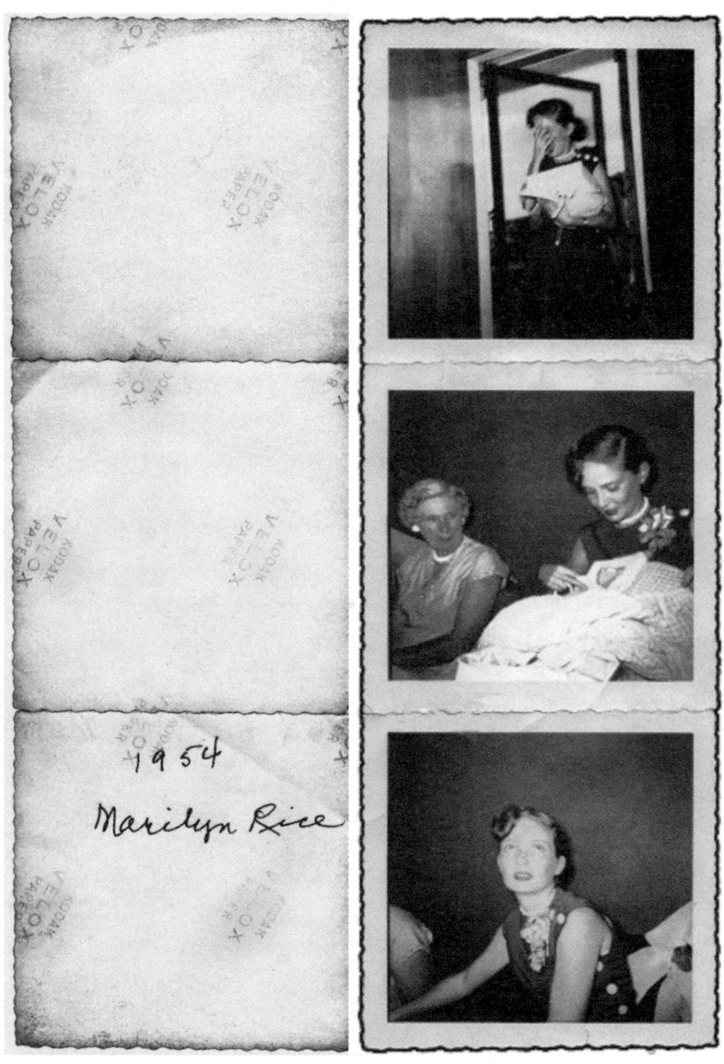

Figure 12. By arranging pictures according to the amount of creep of their logos, the pictures can be put in chronological order.

If the mechanism that advanced the roll of print paper through the darkroom cutting machine was not quite adjusted to the specified width of the prints, the spacing of the cuts will be different from that of the logos that had already been printed on the back of the roll of paper. In this case, even though the pictures will fit together as described above, the logo will not appear in the same place on the back of each photo, but will precess or 'creep' in position from one photo to the next. By organizing the photos according to the amount of 'creep', it is possible to place them in chronological order from the earliest to the latest, as in Figure 12.

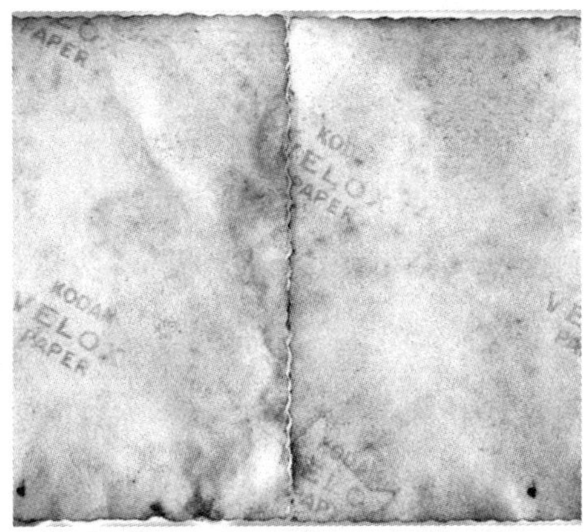

Figure 13. Sometimes the logo is divided across two photographs.

Occasionally when the cut between two photos was made in the middle of a logo, the piece of print paper on each side of the cut carries matching parts. In this case, the two photos were not only from the same roll, but they were taken one after the other. (Figure 13.)

The Paper

In the mid 1950s, some print paper manufacturers began doping the *baryta* layer of their print paper with fluorescent dye to make it look brighter. There are few references to this process before 1955, but an increasing number after[4]. The baryta layer is a thin film containing titanium oxide applied to the paper before the photosensitive emulsion is applied. It provides a flat white background, and masks irregularities of the paper surface.

Under ultraviolet light (popularly known as "black light"), print paper that has been doped with fluorescent dye will glow a cool blue color. Figure 14 shows a series of photos from 1929, 1954, 1957, 1965, 1979. When ultra-

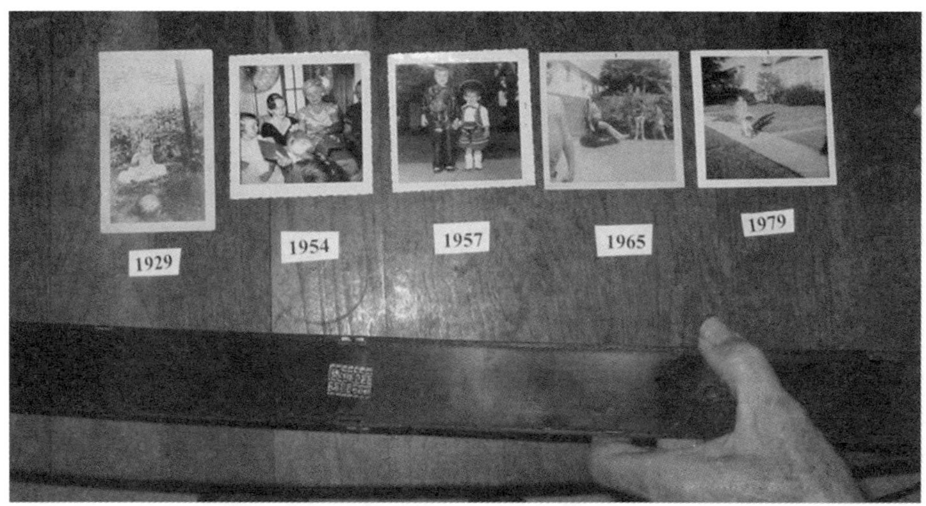

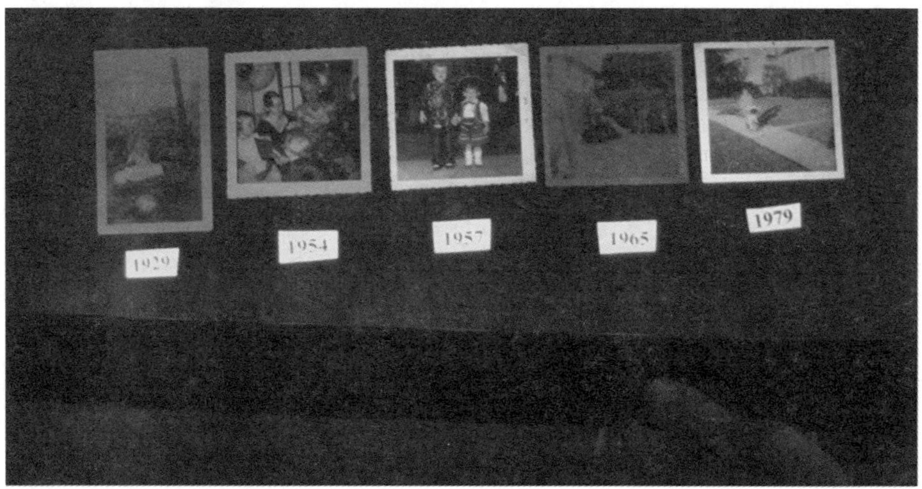

Figure 14. (Top) Five photos taken between 1929 and 1979 as seen under typical room lighting. (Bottom) When viewed under ultraviolet light, the pictures from 1957 and 1979 glow.

violet light illuminates them, the photos from 1957 and 1979 glow. The photo from 1954 might seems to glow, but the purple tint of this photo is not fluorescence. It is only reflected purple light coming from the UV source.

Note too that the picture from 1965 is very dark and is not glowing. Not all post 1955 print paper was doped with fluorescent dye. Some was left untreated. If a photo glows under a black light, it was taken after 1955. If it does not glow, it could have been taken anytime.

The Shape

After you have looked at the back and the sides of a photograph for clues to its origins, and after you have held it under a black light to see if it glows, you may think you have obtained all the information there is available from the physical appearance of a photograph. But have you ever thought about looking at its shape?

Because of the diameter of a camera lens, its focal length, and the size of the camera itself, each camera requires a certain shape recording material, whether it is a glass negative or a roll of negatives on a spool. As you will see later in the chapter *The History of Photography II*, most photographs produced through the turn of the 20th century were Cartes de Visite or cabinet cards produced by commercial studios that came in standard sizes. It is impossible to date these types of photos by their shapes. Even photographs created with studio cameras usually used a standard size glass plate. But George Eastman's innovations in the late 1800s created a huge demand for inexpensive cameras that resulted in the development of a variety of camera models, each using negatives of a characteristic shape.

A rule of thumb in dating a photograph from around the turn of the 20th century is that if it was taken at home instead of in a studio, it was probably taken after the first Kodak Brownie camera came on the market in 1900. Because the Brownie sold for only $1 (equivalent to about $20 today), after 1900 photography became an inexpensive and convenient part of everyday life[5].

The box camera had already been developed by George Eastman in 1886, and photographic film (as opposed to sensitized plates) was first produced by John Corbutt in 1888. This was followed by several more innovations: the invention of roll film by George Eastman in 1889, the introduction of the first daylight loading film by Eastman Kodak in 1894[6], and the marketing of the Kodak Pocket Folding Camera in 1898, considered to be the ancestor of all modern roll film cameras[7]. The Brownie was the first inexpensive, mass-produced camera available to the public. The Brownie made it possible for an individual to own and use his own camera conveniently at home, without advanced technical knowledge. From this time forward, photographs could be taken at home in informal settings. These early home-based Brownie photographs represent quite a few of the unidentified pictures we find in our family albums today.

The photo in Figure 15 is an interesting example of how the shape of a photograph can be the most important clue to identifying it. This picture was found in the family collection of Beth Mendel, who asked us to identify it. It is a simple photograph. Besides the man, the picture contains only a few items-a hat, a chair, a dog, and a tree.

However, there is a note written in the upper left hand corner that reads, "My grandfather, M. Noonan." Beth knew of several possible M. Noonans in her family, but did not know which one was referred to.

The possible M. Noonans supplied by Beth were:

1. Maurice/Morris Noonan, b. abt 1831, d. 1885,
2. Michael, a brother to the Maurice who was born about 1831. There is not too much known about Michael other than it is reasonably certain he died about 1900, at the age of about 60,
3. Maurice Noonan, b. 1918, d. 2004,
4. Michael, b. 1949, still living.

Although clothing usually does not lead to an exact date for a photo, it can be helpful. The top of the hat our man if wearing is high with a dip running from front to back. The narrow brim is rolled up on the sides, but not in the front. Searching Google images on the keywords "men's white hats" lead to the website www.cubanfoodmarket.com[8] where we found a picture of a Panama hat that was very similar to ours. Legend has it that a fashion craze was triggered in the early 1900s when a photo appeared in the world press of President Teddy Roosevelt sitting on a Panama Canal steam shovel in his Panama hat[9]. (Figure 16.) Although this story might be more legend than fact, it hints that the picture was taken sometime in the early 1900s.

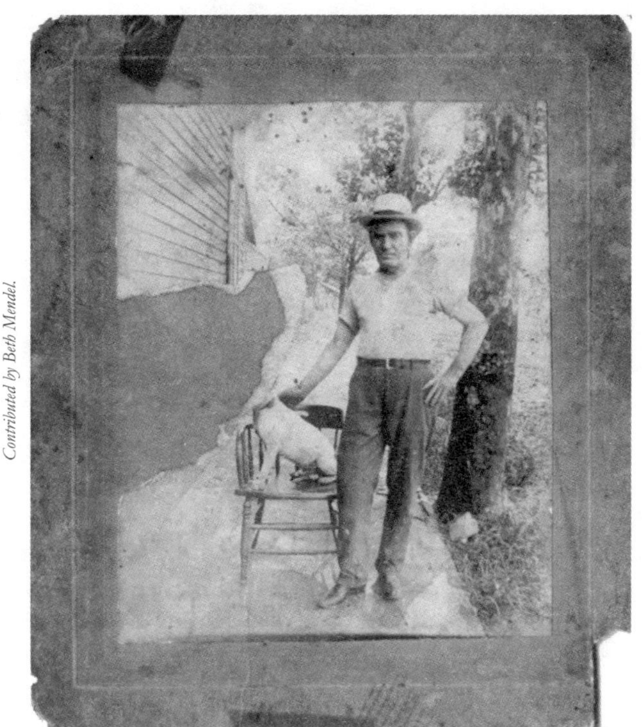

Contributed by Beth Mendel.

Figure 15.

This photograph was not taken in a photographic studio-it was probably taken outside the man's home or outside the home of the photographer. The high probability that a Brownie camera was used to take the picture pushes the earliest date forward to about 1900. Although this eliminates M. Noonans #1 and #2 from the list, it is still not enough information to narrow down which of the M. Noonans is associated with the note.

A better estimate of the photograph's date is obtained from its shape. The ratio of the length to the width of a picture, called the aspect ratio, depends on the dimensions of the negative used to print it. The aspect ratio of the print will be the same as that of the

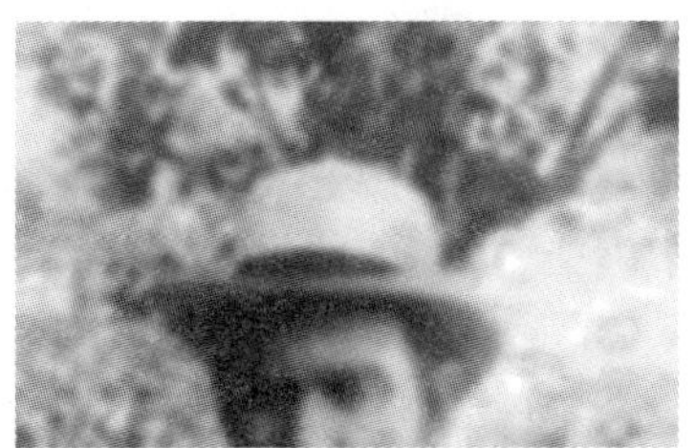

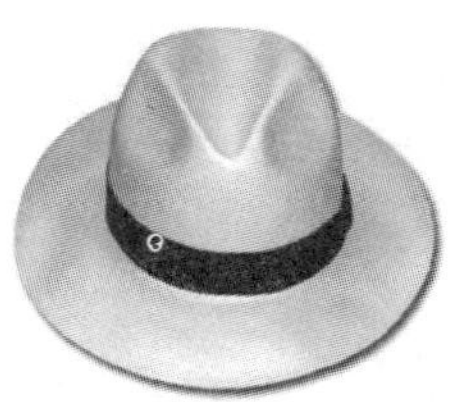

Figure 16.

negative, assuming the print is not cropped, and is characteristic of the type of camera. In this case, the photo has an aspect ratio of 1.25 to 1. A typical film size with these proportions has the dimensions 4" x 5", or 5" x 4" if the camera is held on its side.

According to the website members.aol.com/Chuck02178/brownie.htm[10], film sizes 103, 104, 109, 110, and 123 all fit this description. There were several early Kodak cameras that used this size film, starting in 1896 with the Bullet Camera[10]. The most recent of these was the No. 4 Folding Pocket Camera, which was on the market from 1907 to 1915. Assuming one of these cameras was used to take this picture, and that whoever bought it used it for several years, the range of years for the photograph is 1896 through about 1915.

Assuming that the picture was taken after the introduction of the Brownie camera slightly improves the range to 1900 through 1915.

The two remaining M. Noonans were born after 1915, so that none of the M. Noonans on this list matches the facts – at least not if the 'M. Noonan' denotes the person in the picture. However, the owner's Uncle Maurice (the M. Noonan born in 1918) swore that the man is the photograph is his father John Jeremiah Noonan (b. abt. 1868, d. May 20, 1935). If so, John Jeremiah would have been between 32 and 47 years old during 1900–1918. In 1907 when the Kodak Pocket Camera was introduced, he would have been 39. This all fits well with the appearance of the man in the picture, who seems to be in his mid 30s to late 40's.

The evidence provided by the dimensions of the photograph indicates that Uncle Maurice was right, and that the man in the picture is probably his father. Now the mystery is not which M. Noonan is in the photo. It is now to discover which one of John Jeremiah's grandchildren named M. Noonan wrote (and signed) the note.

The Mat

If the shape of Cartes de Visite (CdVs) and cabinet cards cannot be used to identify them, is there something else?

CdVs and cabinet cards are notoriously difficult to date. The features usually used to date them - the style of the photographer's logo, the size and the style of the photograph, and the size and the design of the mounting board, changed irregularly over time and location. The use of an innovation took time to spread. Photographers in urban areas were more likely to have access to the latest innovations and to accept them quickly to stay ahead of the competition. A photographer in New York City would probably be more willing to adopt a new style than his counterpart in Tickfaw, Louisiana. Figure 17 shows a typical cabinet card.

To make matters worse, each of the main elements of a CdV or a cabinet card can be considered a composite of sub-elements that changed on their own schedules. A style of mounting board or mat is usually characterized by its size, thickness, border style, the use of square or rounded corners, and so on, all of which changed at different times in different locations. It is difficult to pin down when and where a CdV was produced, although it can be helpful to compare it to one of a similar style of known origins.

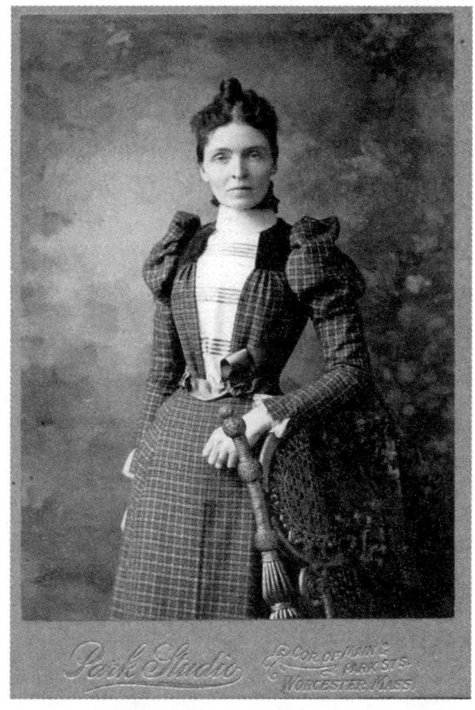

Figure 17. A typical cabinet card.

Fortunately, there is at least one characteristic of the mat that can be useful in dating a cabinet card. According to the website[11] www.city-gallery.com/?q=node/17:

"Card stock is thicker than the Carte de Visite with earlier cards being made of Bristol board, gradually giving way to various types of press board ... or cardboard (paper made from pressed layers of paper like a sandwich) ... throughout the 1880's and 1890s as technology for manufacturing cardboard advanced. Cards showing evidence of separating layers on the edges are definitely made after the introduction of pressboard and cardboard technology (after 1870) replacing the Bristol board (a single layer card stock) of the 1860s." See Figure 18.

If the mat that your photo is mounted on is cardboard made of thin layers of laminated paper, you can be certain that your cabinet card was produced after about 1870. If the mat is made of a single layer of Bristol board, it is not possible to say when it was produced, as there are photographs from the late 1890s mounted on Bristol board. We'll talk about this in more detail later in the chapter *The History of Photography-Part II.*

Summary

A good photodetective knows that every bit of a picture can be helpful in identifying it. When you are analyzing a photo, always remember to look at the *Back*, the *Edges, the Paper, the Shape, the Mat* ... You might be surprised at what you find!

References

1. Paul Messier. "A Method for Dating Photographs relative to 1950", Paul Messier, Conservator of Photographs, Boston Art Conservation, paulmessier.com/PM/PDF/AIPAD4W3.pdf

2. Stability Problems of 19th and 20th Century Photographic Materials© by James M. Reilly, Rochester Institute of Technology, SPAS, One Lomb Memorial Dr. Rochester, NY 14623, albumen.stanford.edu/library/c20/reilly-stability.html

3. John Nix, private communication.

4. Paul Messier, Notes on Dating Photographic Paper, www.paulmessier.com/pm/docs/notes_on_dating.pdf

5. www.kodak.com/US/en/corp/aboutKodak/kodakHistory/milestones78to32.shtml

6. www.rleggat.com/photohistory/

7. www.kodak.com/US/en/corp/kodakHistory/1878_1929.shtml

8. www.cubanfoodmarket.com

9. www.newyorksocialdiary.com/node/1007

10. www.brownie-camera.com

11. www.city-gallery.com/?q=node/17

Two Short Case Studies

I. A Ghost Image - The Hodder Comparison

The photo in Figure 1 was purchased at a Waterbury, Vermont antique shop by John Roberts, founding member of the History Posse for the princely sum of $6. The History Posse is a group of photo detectives dedicated to returning old photos to their rightful owners.

The photo was in very good condition and strikingly large, 14 x 19 inches. It was being sold at a discount because liquid had spilled on the upper left side, leaving light col-

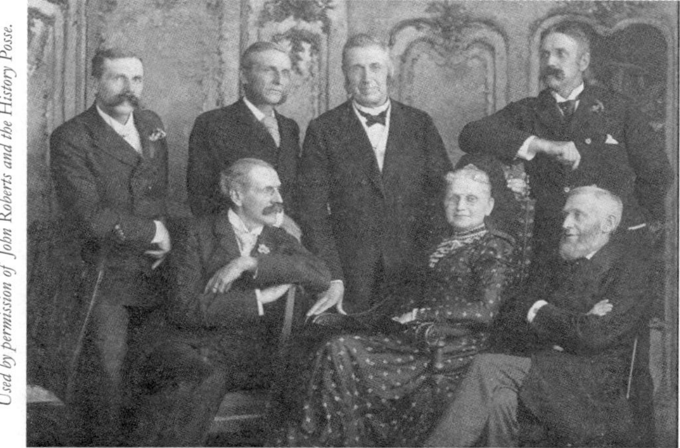

Used by permission of John Roberts and the History Posse.

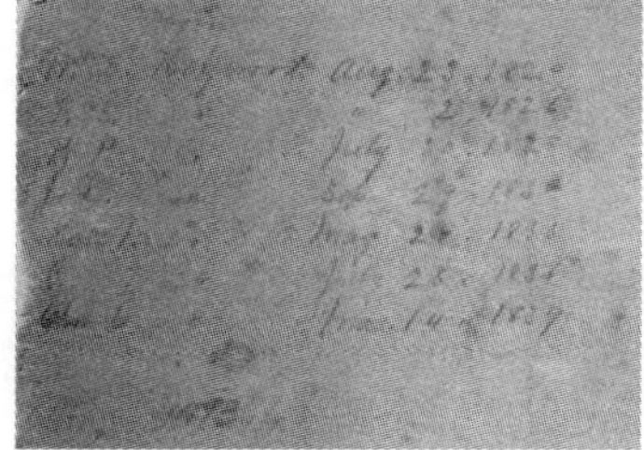

Figure 1. The children of John Heywood and Betsey Edgell of Westminster, MA, 1893. The family members were identified by an inscription on the back.

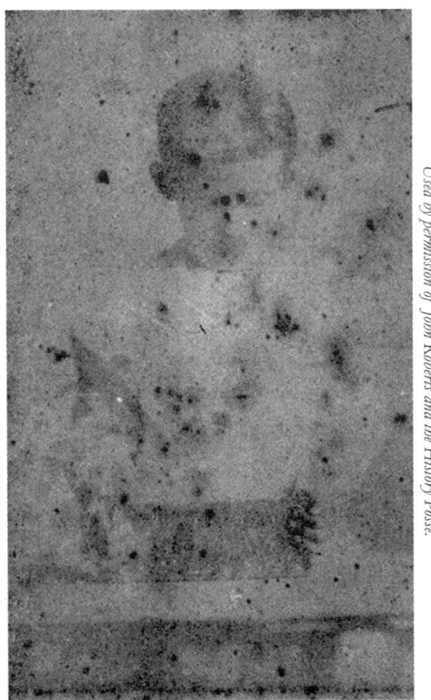

Used by permission of John Roberts and the History Posse.

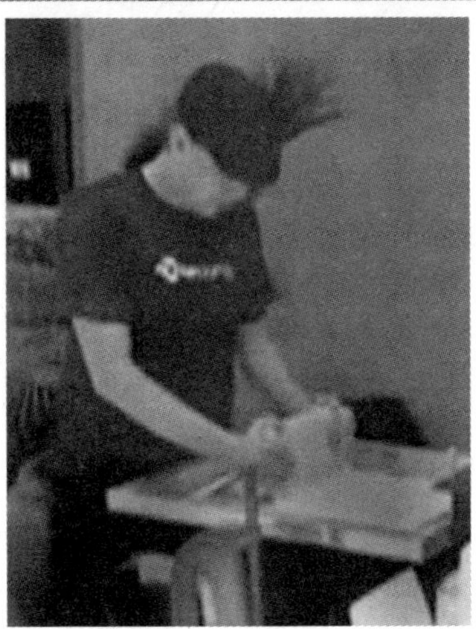

Figure 2. (Top) Residual image on the back of the Heywood family photo. (Bottom) Man engaged in same activity.

ored streaks on the three gentlemen on the left. The photograph was taken by Max Platz photography studio in Chicago in 1893.

The inscription on the back, along with census records, allowed John to identify the group as the children of John Heywood and Betsey Edgell of Westminster, MA. As per the goal of the History Posse, the photo was sent to a descendant of Porter Puffer Heywood, standing second from the left, with scans sent to a descendent of Catherine Marie Heywood Hodder, the woman seated in the front row.

However, the most rewarding part of this mystery was not identifying family members in the photo and returning it to their descendents. It was identifying the man in the residual image on the back. (See Figure 2.)

The key to the puzzle was recognizing what the man in the residual image was doing. By chance, it is the same activity John made his living at for 12 years. The bottom of Figure 2 shows someone engaged in the same activity. The camera angle of the more recent photograph is different, and about 130 years separate these two men. Before you read any further, can you identify the activity? The picture of the man on the bottom is a screen-grab from a YouTube video[1]. Unfortunately, a video of the man on the top was not available.

Give up? These men are screen printers, also known as silkscreen printers. The man on the left is printing T-shirts, but the method is the same for posters, snack trays and other items.

John's experience told him that the man in the picture from YouTube was a newcomer to his job since he doesn't appear to have the occupational side effect of a "Popeye forearm." This job builds the muscles in one's forearms because great force must be applied to squeeze the ink through the screen properly.

Since the residual image was formed through contact between two photos that had been touching for a number of years, John reasoned that there must be a connection between the people in the photo on the front and the man appearing in the residual image on the back. Researching Catherine Heywood, John learned that she married a printer, John H. Hodder. Bingo!

Through the online genealogical databases available through Heritage Quest, John found a portrait of John Hodder on page 433 of the book *Commemorative biographical and historical record of Kane County, Illinois : containing full page portraits and biographical sketches of prominent and representative citizens of the county, together with portraits and biographies of the governors of Illinois and of the presidents of the United States : also containing a history of the county from its earliest settlement up to the present time.* Chicago: Beers, Leggett & Co., 1888.

Figure 3 shows a comparison between John Hodder and the mystery man in the residual image. The almost cartoonish oversized mustache on Hodder seems to be present in the mystery man. When John sent the two images to the Hodder descendant he had located, he received the following reply from his wife:

Dear John,

Even more than the mustache is the part of the hair which is the same as the photo of John Hodder in The Biographical Index, his son Frank's hair part, and my husband's hair part. And the noses are uncannily the same for all of them. (And to boot, our grandson has the nose. I tell him "It is the nose of greatness.") Many thanks for this "extra photo." And having done some screen printing in the past, I think you are right about what is in his hands.

Louise

While an identification of John Hodder would have been impossible based on the moustache, hair part, and nose alone, combined with the fact that John was a printer, and the residual image was found on the back of a photograph of the family of his wife, it's highly likely that the man in the residual image is John H. Hodder.

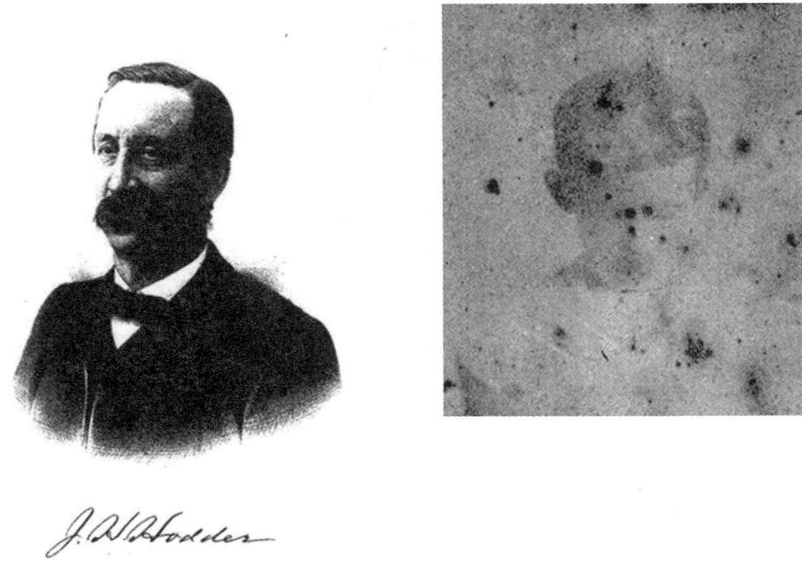

Figure 3. John H. Hodder compared to the man in the residual image.

II. The Mat - Father and Son

The CdVs shown in Figure 4 were sent to me by Judy Pfaff, one of our regulars to our Forensic Genealogy site. Judy wanted to determine the identities of the men in the pictures. They were included in a family album she obtained from distant cousins in England. From information about the family provided by the cousins, she knew that the men were either Isaac Dawson Sr. (1782-1859) or his son Isaac Dawson Jr. (1816-1888). She did not know, however, if the same man appeared in both photographs or if she had one picture of each.

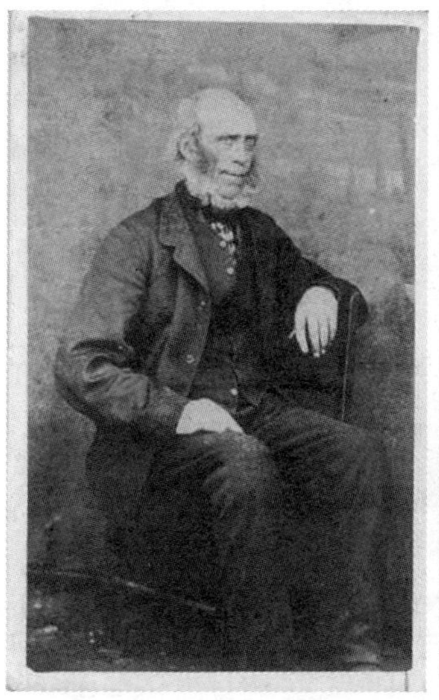

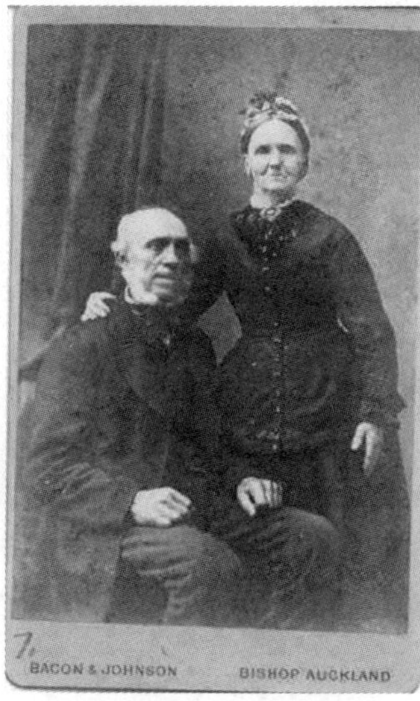

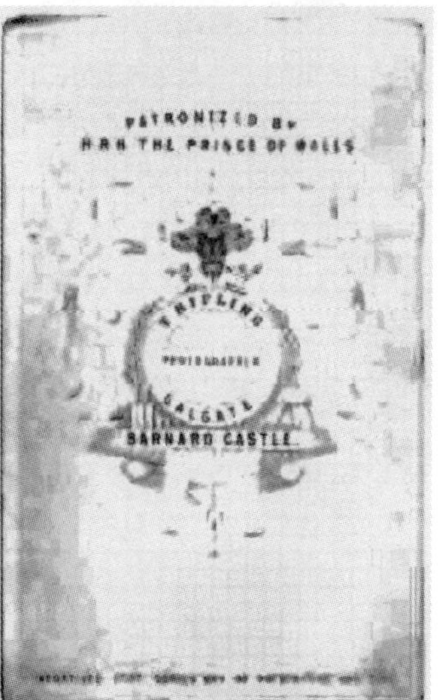

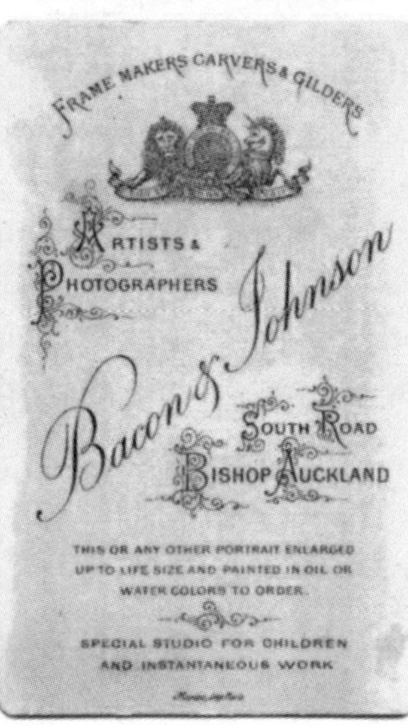

Used with permission of Judy Pfaff.

Figure 4. Assuming that the men in these photos could be either a father or his son, how can you tell if they are both the father, both the son, or one the father and one the son?

The back of the photo on the top left of Figure 1 indicated that it was taken by T. Kipling, photographer, Galgate, Barnard Castle. The back of the photo on the top right shows the logo for Bacon & Johnson, photographers, South Road, Bishop Auckland (northern UK not Australia). The studios and the photographers were known in the area for the appropriate time period 1850-1870 and the subjects lived in the area where the cards were produced. The cards are 2 1/2" x 4", typical of CdVs. Judy was wondering if she could be missing some obvious clues that would help answer her question.

The website www.city-gallery.com/?q=node/17 provided two clues that solved the mystery. The first relates to the first date that cabinet card were produced. According to this website:

"Examples of Cartes de Visite before 1858 are extremely rare and are unlikely to be encountered outside of museums. The Carte de Visite began appearing in the United States late in the summer of 1859. By the end of 1860 the Carte de Visite had become the fashion throughout the country."

Judy provided the additional information that the father died Jan. 5, 1859 after suffering from influenza for two months. To be the healthy-looking man in the photos, the card had to have been produced before November 1858. While the website does not give specific information about when cabinet cards first appeared in England, it is likely that it was sometime in late 1858 to 1859, about the same time as they first appeared in the United States. While an argument can be made that the man in the picture is the father Issac Dawson Sr., and that he happened to be the subject of one of the earliest cabinet cards produced in England, it is unlikely.

The second clue provided by the website is more useful in identifying the man in the photo. To requote a passage in the chapter, *Remember to Look at the Back.....*

"Card stock is thicker than the Carte de Visite with earlier cards being made of Bristol Board, gradually giving way to various types of press board...or cardboard (paper made from pressed layers of paper like a sandwich)...throughout the 1880's and 1890s as technology for manufacturing cardboard advanced. Cards showing evidence of separating layers on the edges are definitely made after the introduction of pressboard and cardboard technology (after 1870) replacing the Bristol Board (a single layer card stock) of the 1860s."

By examining the photos edge-on, and by noticing that the corners of the CdV were frayed and separating, we were able to determine that the two photographs are mounted on cardboard. Dawson Jr. is the man in both pictures. Since the wife of Dawson Jr. died in 1873, we can date the photo to between 1870-1873, assuming she is the woman in the second picture.

References

1. www.youtube.com/watch?v=PqHE4Iuyja0

Details, Details

The devil is in the details.

Sherlock Holmes could not have said it better. It's so important when analyzing a photograph to pay attention to details. No matter how simple a photograph may be, it can still hold important clues to where, when, or why it was taken, or perhaps who is in it. Even a typical 19th century cabinet card of a portrait showing little more than someone's head and shoulders can yield important clues. The size of the picture, the thickness of the paper it is matted on, the style of the photographer's logo, the type of borders around the edge of the mat, and other physical aspects of the photograph itself can lead you to an approximate date for it. The importance of many of these features was discussed in the chapter *Remember to Look at the Back......*

Just Plain Details

Sometimes important details are obvious, sometimes careful examination is needed to find them. A detail can be something that is missing from the picture or something that is there, but should not be. Sometimes a single detail will be the key to identifying a photo, and sometimes there will be a collection of details that are important. It all depends on the photo.

Consider the family photograph in Figure 1. How can you tell that the couple in the picture probably had at least five children? (No, it's not because they look so tired!) Have a close look at the picture before you read further.

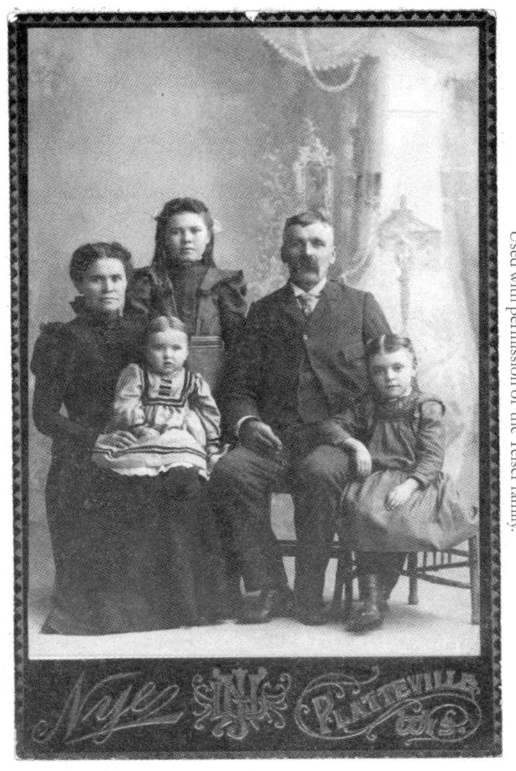

Used with permission of the Yeiser family.

Figure 1.

Here is a hint. There is something important missing from the picture.

You can tell the couple probably had at least five children by the gaps in the ages of the children.

The style of this cabinet card, along with the style of dress of the family, tell you that it was produced in the late 1800s or early 1900s. During this time period, it was typical for a couple to have children every two to two and a half years. Yet the age differences between the oldest and the middle child, and between the middle child and the baby are significantly larger than this.

The couple almost certainly had at least one child in each of these gaps that they lost, either to miscarriage or to disease in early childhood. Counting the two children that were lost and the three shown in the picture, the couple probably had at least five children. Because of the large age difference between the two oldest girls, it is likely the couple had six children. The parents could have had children before the oldest daughter, or after the picture was taken. However, the photograph cannot give you any information about them.

The possibility of children missing from the photo is a useful clue in matching the picture against the families in your tree. You are not looking for a family with three children, you are looking for a family with at least five, with the two oldest living children widely spaced in age. If you can identify the family, you can then search the birth and death records for the missing children.

There are alternate explanations to account for the age gaps among the children. The father could have been away in the military for an extended period of time, or in jail. Each of these presents an interesting possibility for further research. But no matter what the explanation, the moral of the story is that sometimes what is *missing* from a picture is the best clue to identifying who is in it.

What about the picture is Figure 2? One of the members of this family has a severe medical condition. Can you figure out who it is, and what condition he or she has? What details give this away? And how can knowl-

Used with permission of the Fitzpatrick family.

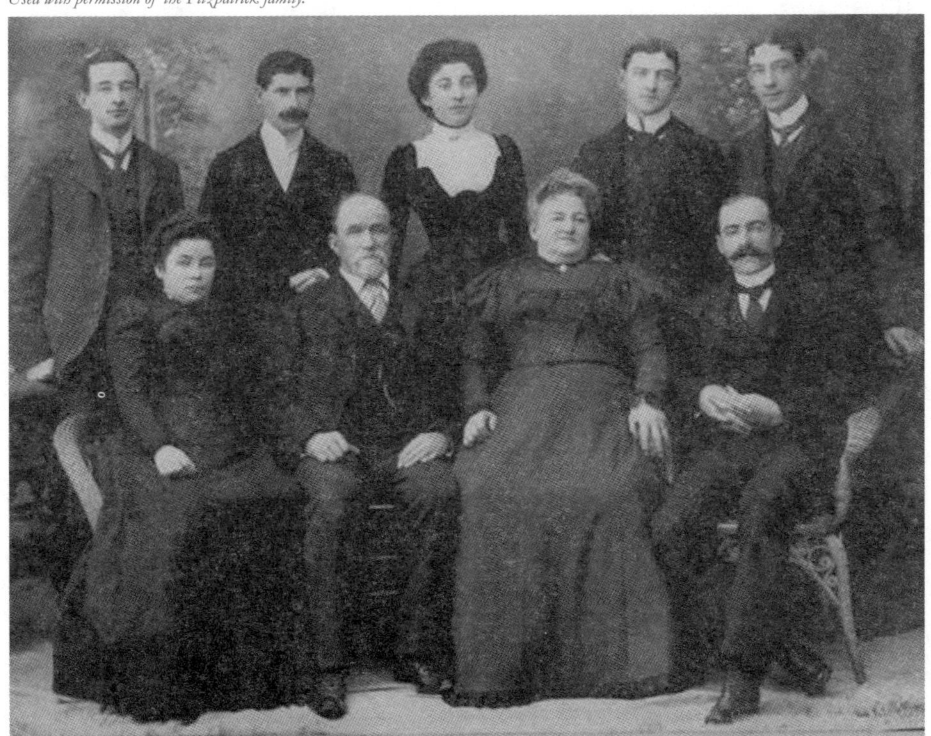

Figure 2. Peter Fitzpatrick and family, c. 1900.

edge of the condition help you determine which members of the family are present?

At first glance there is nothing unusual about this family portrait of Peter Fitzpatrick (b. 1826, Co. Louth, Ireland; d. 1909 New Orleans, LA), his wife Mary Hanlon (b. 1832, Co. Wexford, Ireland; d. 1918 New Orleans, LA), and seven of their eight children. It was taken in New Orleans, LA.

Judging by the ages of the parents and their children, the style of the photograph, and the way the family members are dressed, the photograph dates to the late 1890s or early 1900s. The couple had six sons and two daughters who survived into adulthood. One of the sons is absent from the picture, making it hard to assign names to the other five. One son moved to Pensacola, FL in the mid 1890s. Another son died in 1901. Because the old man died in 1909, we know the photo could not have been taken later that this. We have not been able to determine which daughter is which, although they were born seven years apart.

While this seems to be a typical family portrait, appearances can be deceiving. The picture holds several clues that give away the fact that one of the family members is not in the best of health. Can you figure out who is sick and what his or her medical condition is? (No, the woman in the back row is not near asphyxiation because her corset is too tight.)

The family member with the medical condition is the elderly woman in the front row, Mary Hanlon. She has had a stroke. The telltale signs of her condition are her lopsided face and the curled fingers of her right hand. Her waistline is also noticeably higher than the others who are seated in the front row, indicating she is probably propped up in a wheelchair.

If we could determine when Mary Hanlon Fitzpatrick had the stroke, we would have an earliest date for the photo. This could be the key to identifying the missing son.

The lesson here is that the most important detail in a picture is often something that not obvious. Even when a photograph looks like it has no details that can help identify it, careful observation may prove otherwise.

What Can I Tell about the Picture from the Clothing?

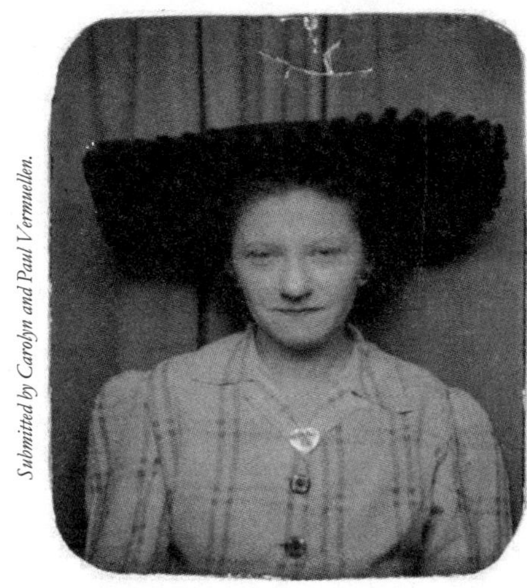
Submitted by Carolyn and Paul Vermuellen.

Figure 3.

One of the first questions I am often asked by someone about a photograph is, "What can you tell from the clothing the people are wearing in the picture?" The answer is maybe a lot, and maybe nothing. The clothing in a picture can be a critical clue to dating a picture, but it is only one out of many possible clues that can give it away.

For example, what is the most important clue for finding the earliest date the photo in Figure 3 could have been taken?

If you answered "the hat", you are wrong. Guess again. No, it's not the style of the woman's dress, her buttons, nor her hair style.

Give up? The most important clue for finding when this picture was taken is the curtain behind the woman, along with the shape of the picture. This picture was taken in a photobooth. According to the website www.photobooth.org:

In 1925 Anatol Josepho, a Socialist from Siberia, patented his 'Photomaton.' An automatic photography machine, the Photomaton produced a strip of 8 photographs of good quality in 8 minutes. The inventor had drawn up his plans for the machine while traveling across China as an itinerant photographer, refined his technical prowess in Hollywood, built the prototype in a Harlem loft and set up his first photobooth studio at Broadway and 51st Street in New York City.

In 1927, the enterprising Josepho, 33 years old, achieved the Great American Dream by selling the rights to his invention for the considerable sum of $1,000,000 [$10M in today's currency]. The buyers were a group of businessmen planning to establish 70 of these mechanical studios at Coney Island, Atlantic City and strategic points *throughout the United States by the end of the first year, hoping to "do in the photographic field what Woolworth has accomplished in novelties", reported the Edison Monthly (October, 1926).*

The earliest date the photo could have been taken was 1925. If it was known that the woman never traveled to New York City, the earliest date would be 1927.

Even though the hat the woman was wearing is one of the most prominent features of the picture, it is a distraction that diverts attention away from clues that are much less noticeable, yet much more valuable in dating it.

Figure 4 is another example of the role clothing might play in dating a photograph.

We featured this picture of a group of elderly gentlemen in a weekly photoquiz on our Forensic Genealogy website www.forensicgenealogy.info in April 2005. The men are evidently assembled for a reunion. Mary Miller, the owner of the photograph, told us that her great grandfather George Washington Jackson was the man with the long white beard seated in the middle of the front row. Mary's mother had researched the photograph for many years before she died, hoping to identify the other members of the association so she could share the picture with their families. Since she was never successful, Mary asked us to post the picture with the hope of finding out more about it.

The most obvious clue to a date for the photo is the American flag in the background, with six rows of stars, including a bottom row with at least eight. According to www.ushistory.org/betsy/flagpics.html, the only flag carrying 46 stars was used starting in 1908 when Oklahoma became a state, through 1912 when New Mexico and Arizona joined the Union. The picture must have been taken between 1908 and 1912. (Figure 5.)

Another clue leading to the identity of the group is the banner in the background next to the American flag. It reads "Survivors of the Battle of Shiloh Association". (Figure 6.) According to Deborah Barker, Director of

Used with permission of Mary Miller.

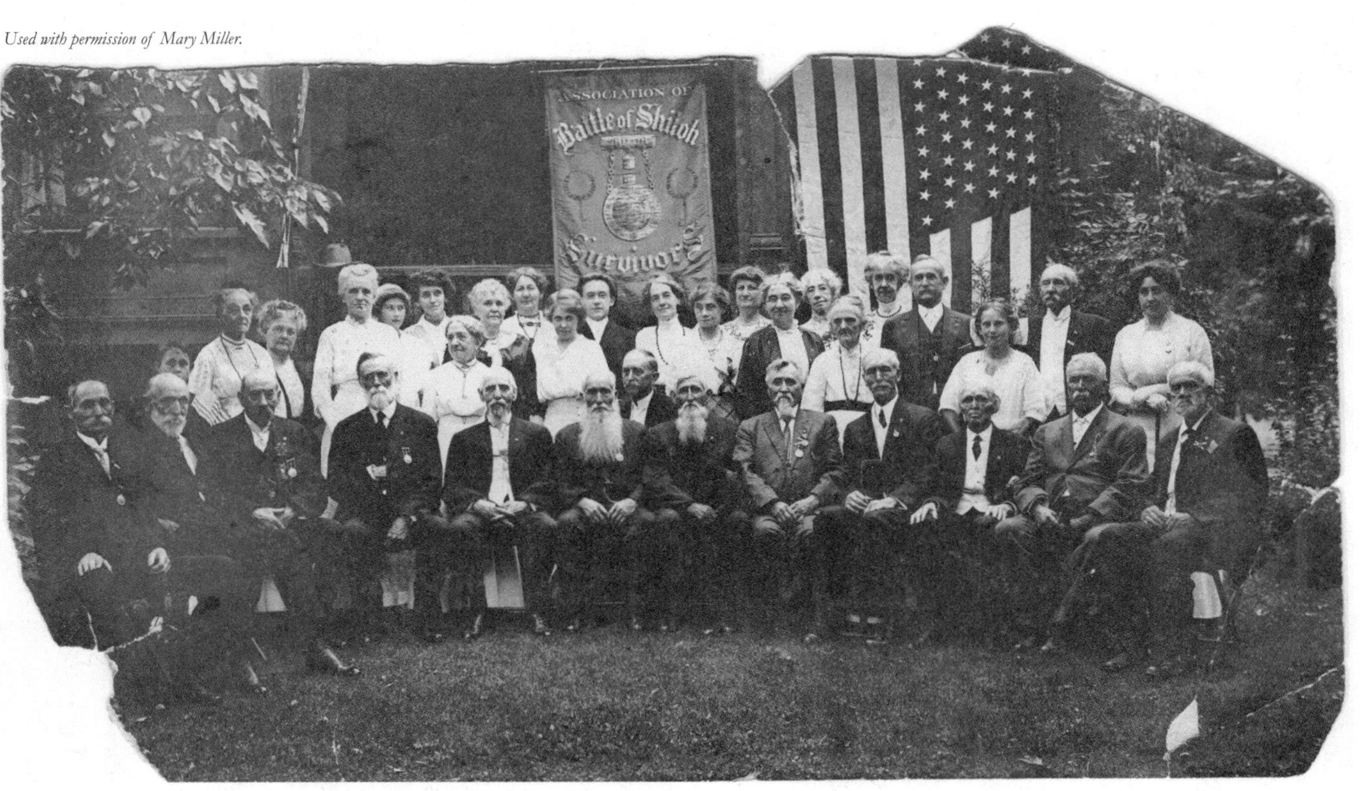

Figure 4. Survivors of the Battle of Shiloh Association.

the Franklin County Historical Society in Ottawa, KS, this association was founded in 1906 by George P. Washburn, an architect who had fought for the Union Army next to his father at the battle near Shiloh Church and Pittsburgh Landing, April 6-7, 1862. (Top of Figure 7.) The early headquarters of the association were located in Ottawa, KS, Washburn's hometown. The association held annual reunions on the anniversary of the battle from 1907 until as late as 1925. (Bottom of Figure 7.) The men in the pictures were veterans of the Civil War who had survived the Battle of Shiloh.

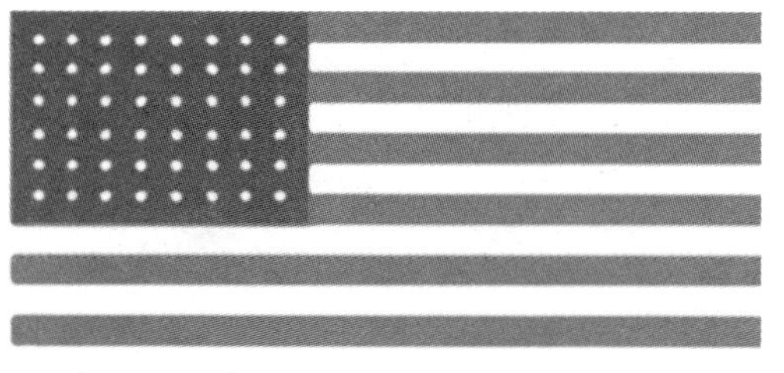

Figure 5. American flag 1908-1912.

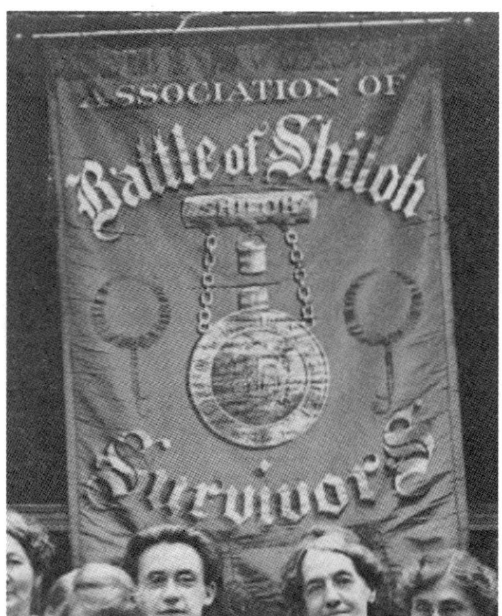

Figure 6. Survivors of the Battle of Shiloh Association banner.

Since the reunion would probably be held on the anniversary of the battle, the picture was likely taken on April 6 or 7th, between 1908 and 1912. This is consistent with the advanced age of the men, who appear to be in their 70s and 80s. For obvious reasons, this association no longer exists, so it is not possible to contact any of its members for further information.

However, there is another source of information. What about contacting The Shiloh National Military Park? The Park was established by Congress in 1894[1], so that is was in existence over the time period when the reunion took place. The Park would be the logical place for the Association to meet, and might have a record in its archives of the group's visits.

The Chief Park Ranger Stacy Allen's replied to our inquiry as follows:

We have examined the website photo and cannot confirm the image location as being made on Shiloh battlefield. The structure located behind the group does not match any of the buildings present on the battlefield park during the period in question, which appears to be 1908-1912 given the number of stars present in the United States flag.

The first annual meeting of the "National Association of Battle of Shiloh Survivors" was held offsite on August 14, 1906. Park records cite the Association made its first excursion to the Shiloh battlefield in April 1907. These records cite the group present on the field routinely each April 1907-1911.

We...found published documentation placing the Survivors Association reunion on the battlefield 6 April 1912[3]. The day was spent touring the battlefield. The weather turned cold and inclement on April 7th and most members stayed aboard their steamboat throughout the day. The party departed by boat the next morning.

While Ranger Allen does not believe the photo was taken at the Park, she does agree with the time period of 1908-1912, and confirms

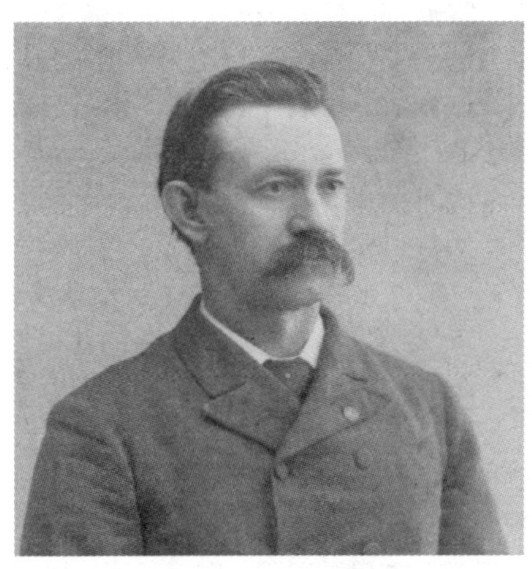

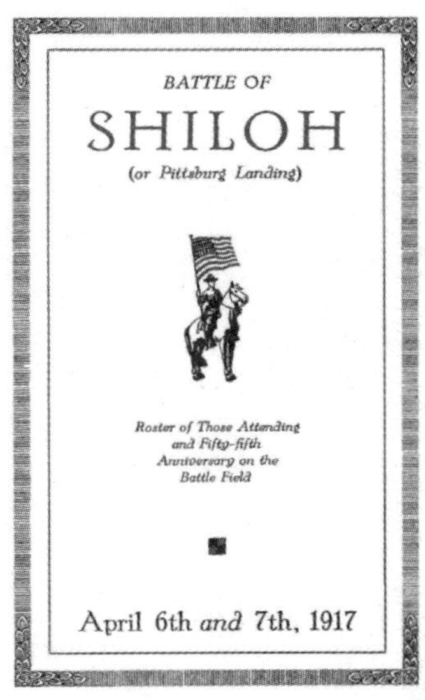

BATTLE OF

SHILOH

(or Pittsburg Landing)

Roster of Those Attending and Fifty-fifth Anniversary on the Battle Field

April 6th and 7th, 1917

Figure 7. George P. Washburn and the program from the 1917 reunion of the Survivors of the Battle of Shiloh Association.

that presence of the Survivors' Association at the Park during April of each of these years. Without any further information, it would be impossible to pin down a more exact date for the photograph.

There is one more clue that we have not discussed yet. April 7, 1912 was not only the 50th anniversary of the battle, it was also Easter Sunday.

This section is on clothing isn't it? There was a fashion rule in the "old days" that you never wore white before Easter. The women in the picture are dressed elegantly in white dresses with high lace collars. Their hair is neatly pulled back from their faces and several are wearing long necklaces.

Without doubt, the picture was taken Easter Sunday, April 6, 1912, the Fiftieth Anniversary of the Battle of Shiloh. In this case, the most important clue to the date the photo was taken was the clothing the people were wearing in the picture.

If you are interesting in more information on the use of clothing for analyzing old photographs, you might check Maureen Taylor's website at www.photodetective.com, and the books *Dating Old Photos* and *More Dating Old Photos* by Halvor Moorshead, available through www.amazon.com.

The "Occasional" Photograph

A photo might contain details associated with a particular occasion and date. A good example would be a child smiling over a birthday cake with three candles.

The photograph in Figure 8 was taken at an event. From the details of the picture, you should be able to tell not only what kind of event it was, but also the person being honored, where the event occurred, and the date it took place to within three days.

There are several good clues that give away the fact that the picture in Figure 8 was taken at a wake or a funeral. These include the draped coffin to the left of the photo, and the sprays of flowers arranged around the room. Another clue is the picture on the far wall, known as *The Entombment*, that

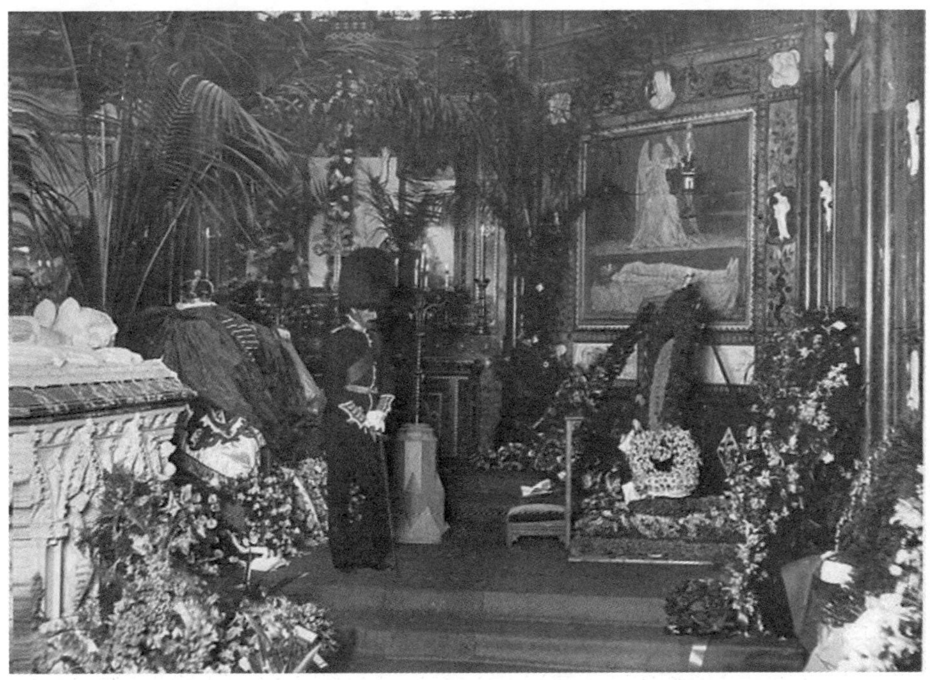

Figure 8.

shows an angel above a reclining figure (probably a corpse). There is also part of a sarcophagus in the left foreground showing the feet of the effigy on the lid.

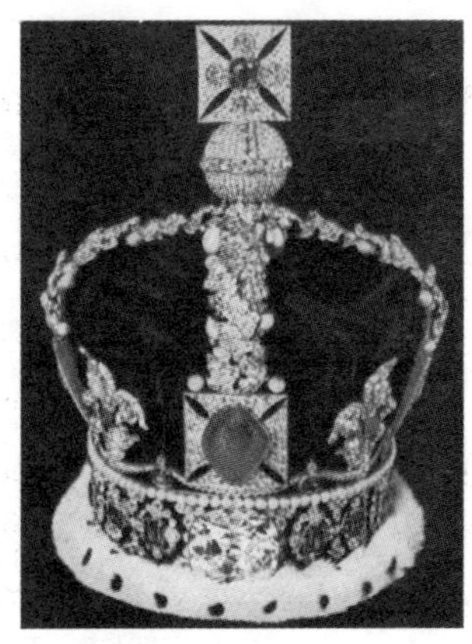

Figure 9.
The Imperial State Crown[2].

The soldier guarding the coffin is an indication that this is not the funeral of just anyone. The person who died was highly placed, perhaps military or royalty. The most important clue of all is the crown resting on top of the coffin that gives away the fact that the deceased was a king or queen. (Figure 9.) It can be identified as The Imperial State Crown, the crown worn by a British monarch as he leaves Westminster Abbey after his coronation.[2]. The style of the guard's uniform, that of the British King's (or Queen's) Guard, indicates that this picture relates to the death of a British sovereign.

There have been only five British Monarchs who have died since the invention of photography[3]:

Queen Victoria (1901)
Edward VII (1910)
George V (1936)
George VI (1952)
Queen Mother (2002)

There are many photographs of each of these royal funerals that can be easily found by searching on Google. Comparing them to our mystery photo shows that this is a picture of the coffin of Queen Victoria as she lay in state in the Albert Memorial Chapel, February 2-4, 1901. The effigy to the far left is that of her husband, Prince Albert, who died December 14, 1861. Albert is buried in the Royal Mausoleum at Frogmore House, the royal retreat near Winson Castle, and not in the Albrt Memorial Chapel. His effigy is atop a centotaph, a memorial that is similar to a tomb but which does not contain the body of the deceased.

Where?

A photograph is always taken *somewhere*. There can be many indications in it where that *somewhere* is located. Knowing where the picture was taken can often lead you to discover when it was taken and who is in it. For example, you might find a photographer's logo printed on the mat that indicates the studio an the city where it was located. By researching the city directories, you might be able to find out when the photographer was in business to obtain a range of dates for the picture.

The photograph in Figure 10 was included in a collection of about 90 photos that our friend Sue Ramsey received from her cousin. The time period of the collection stretched back several generations. She had researched her family genealogy for many years so she was able to identify most of the people in the pictures, but this photo was a complete mystery

Used with permission of Sue Ramsey.

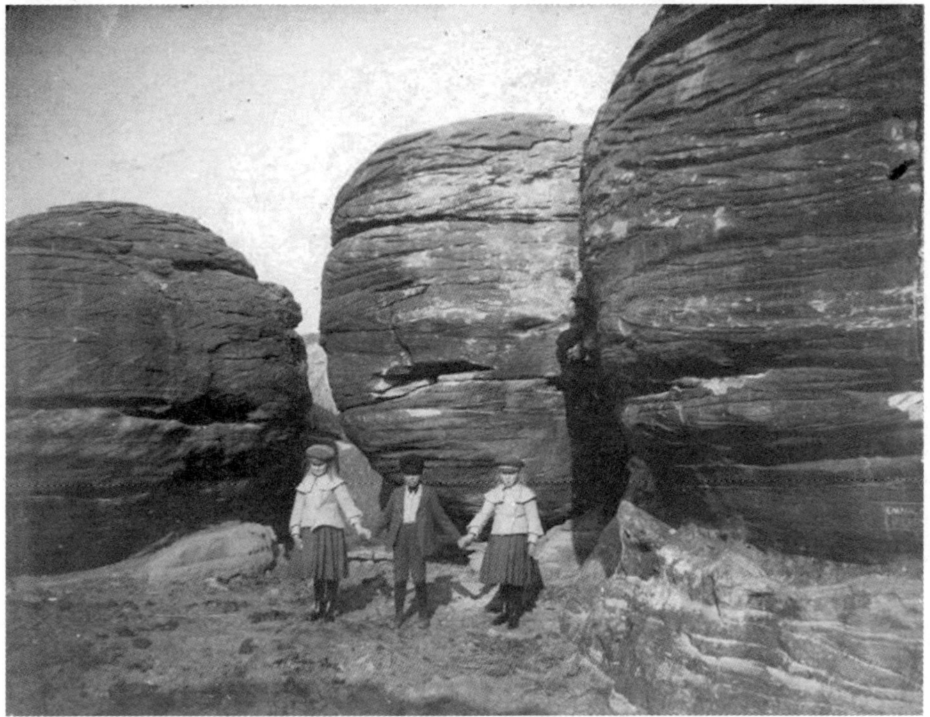

Figure 10. Picture of children in front of an unusual rock formation.

to her. Sue had a hunch that it was taken at Castle Rock, Grant Co., WI, since it is the site of an interesting old rock formation near where her great grandfather settled when he immigrated to the U.S. in 1884.

The unique terrain led us to search Google Images using the keywords 'unusual rock formations'. After looking through several pages of thumbnails, we found photographs of the same rock formation in Rock City, a small park about 3 1/2 miles southeast of Minneapolis, KS[4]. See Figure 11.

Sue had not considered Kansas as a possible location. She had not noticed that, other than the rock formation, the landscape was flat. After further research, she found that her great great grandfather George Elliott (along another line of her family) was living in Kansas when he married the widow Sarah Babcock, who had four small boys from her first marriage. George's son, Sue's great grandfather Melvin Elliott, grew up in Minneapo-

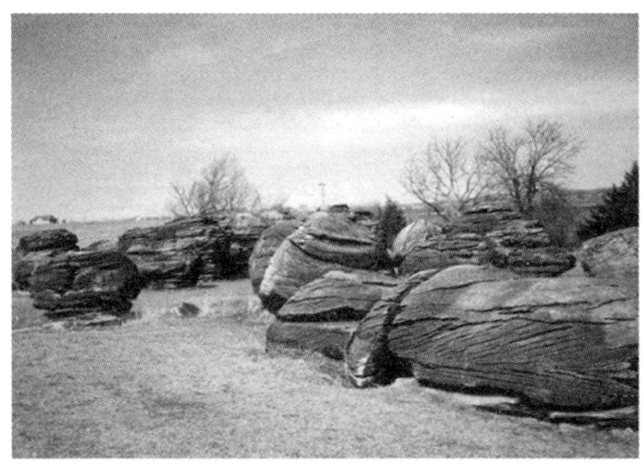

Figure 11. Unusual rock formations near Minneapolis, KS.

lis, KS with his four half-brothers. Melvin's son Elmer, Sue's grandfather, graduated from high school there.

Sue contacted her Babcock half-cousins and found that one of them had a photo that was similar to hers. It was included in a small collection of family pictures that were apparently taken on the same occasion. The collection included the photo in Figure 12.

The half-cousin also had the journal of her great grandfather, Friend Babcock (one of Melvin's half-brothers) with an entry for February 1900 that mentioned that two of the other half-brothers, Thomas and Ep(enetus) Elliott, came for a visit "to see the country." Sue believes that the picture was taken during this February visit, considering the men in the second

Used with permission of Sue Ramsey.

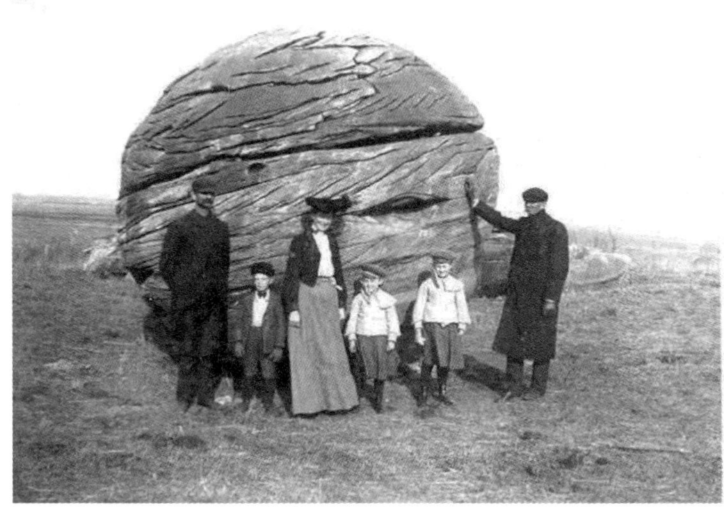

Figure 12. Photo probably taken at the same outing as the one in Figure 10.

picture are wearing coats and gloves appropriate for cold weather. Thanks to Google Images and Sue's hard work, she now knows the location where the photo was taken along with an approximate date. She has a lot more information to go on for researching who the people are in the picture.

As Time Goes By

Another reason scenery can be useful in dating a picture is that a landscape usually changes over time. Trees grow taller, a house might be repainted a different color, more modern furniture might appear on a porch. The roof of the next door neighbor's house might be missing because it was recently torn off by a storm. If you know the location of a picture, you might be able to find an approximate time period for it by comparing it to pictures of the same location with known dates.

Figure 13 shows two views of the Robinson House Hotel in Bucksport, ME. They were given to us by Sharon Sergeant of Ancestral Manor who was researching one of the oldest surviving Concord Light stagecoaches, built in 1848 by Lewis Downing & Sons in Concord, NH. The coach traveled the Bangor-Bucksport-Castine route and used the hotel as a base station. We were able to enhance the photo on the right enough to read the name of the route across the top of the coach's window, thus confirming that it was the coach that ran the Bangor route. Sharon wanted any informa-

Used by permission of Sharon Sergeant.

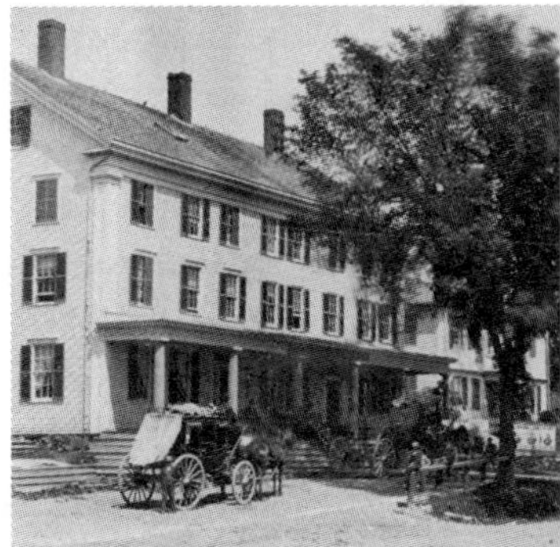

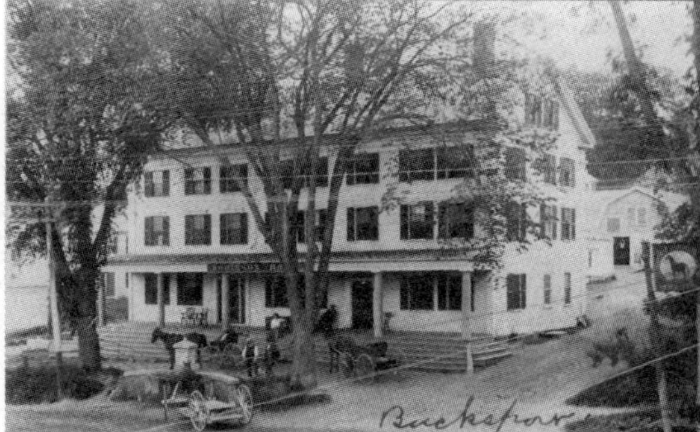

Figure 13. The photo on the left was taken earlier than the photo on the right.

tion we could obtain about the two photos, with the ultimate goal of determining whether the coach in the picture on the left was the same one she was researching.

There are many indications that the picture on the left was taken earlier than the one on the right. The trees are shorter and the trunk of the tree in front of the house is not as thick. The wire that is visible in the earlier picture was probably a telegraph wire, or possibly a 'parade wire' used to hang banners during parades. There does not appear to be any electrical wires in this earlier photo, although there are a few visible in the later photo.

This information is interesting, but we still do not have an earliest or latest date for either photo. However, through additional research on the construction of the hotel, we found that the horse watering trough shown in the front in the picture to the right was built and dedicated in 1910[5]. This change in the front of the hotel gives us the earliest date for the photo on the right. It also gives us a latest date for the photo on the left, since it does not show the trough.

We could go further with this if we had a series of pictures of the Inn with known dates. By comparing the heights of the trees in the series to their heights in the unknown photo, we could bracket the date of the unknown photo. Better yet, based on the height of the trees in the photos with known dates, we could estimate the growth rate of the trees (assuming they were never topped). This would lead to an approximate date for the unknown picture by calculating how much time it took for the trees to grow the additional height relative to the height of the trees in the next earliest photo in the chronological lineup.

The photograph in Figure 14 is a better example of how a small change in scenery can be critical in dating a picture. This photo of the Bunker Hill Monument in Boston was taken by one of our top Quizmasters, Dale Niesen. Although it is a well known landmark, if you did not recognize it you could still find out where the photo was taken by noticing the writing on the brick building to the left of the church, "Boys and Girls Clubs of Boston." See Figure 15.

Used with permission of Dale Niesen.

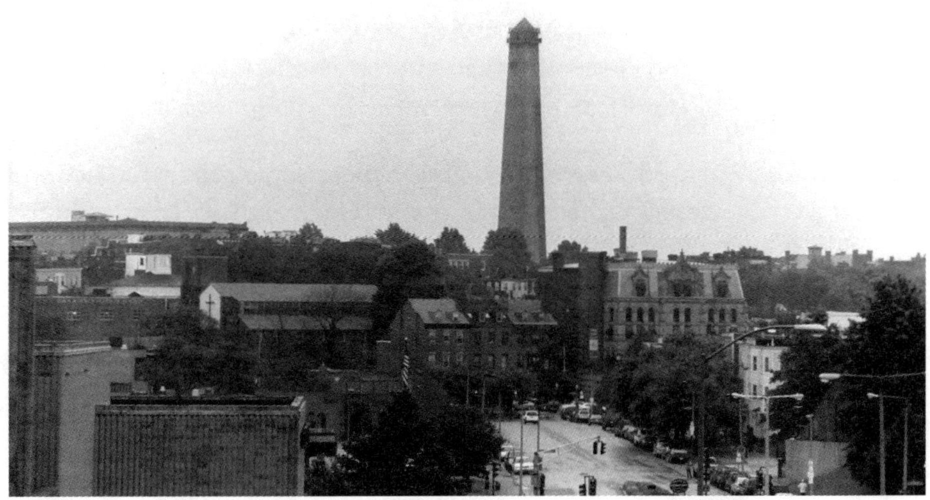

Figure 14. The Bunker Monument, Boston, MA.

Figure 15.

Quizmaster Evan Hindman was able to date the picture by noticing the scaffolding that was present around the top of the monument. The picture was taken while it was being cleaned or repaired. Searching www.Flicker.com, a website that allows people to post and share their photographs, Evan found a picture taken in the summer of 2006 that showed the same scaffolding! We also looked at the live Bunker Hill webcam at www.mtanew.ashtonservices.com/traffic_cameras/trafficcams.html and noticed that the scaffolding was no longer present as of Labor Day 2006. This allowed us to narrow the date from about late May until about late August, 2006.

Wanna Date?

Sometimes the earliest or the latest date for a photograph can be obtained from something that appeared for only a limited period of time. Ads for products that were only on the market for a short time, a photo of a relative wearing his high school uniform, a company sign hanging on the front of a building where it was located only briefly, are all examples of things that can tip you off to when a picture was taken.

It's usually a good idea when dating a picture to cross reference the dates of several items with each other or with characteristics of the photograph itself. It's possible that an antique car might appear on the street long after that model has vanished from the showroom, or that an old magazine might be seen lying on a contemporary coffee table. There are some modern photographs that are produced in vintage styles. If you can find more than one item associated with the same time period, you can be more certain that your date is correct.

The photograph in Figure 16 is the front of a postcard of Rushville, NE sent to us by Gwen Upton, an avid collector of vintage photographs. It is a good example of how even a small detail can be very important in dating a picture. The reverse side of the card shows that it was mailed by someone with the initials C. E. to Miss Bess Anthony in Gordon, NE, just ten miles to the east of Rushville. We included the back of the card in the quiz as it is shown in Figure 17 without the postmark, so that we could challenge our readers to discover the earliest date it could have been mailed. We'll talk about this later.

The picture depicts a beautifully detailed scene of the main street of Rushville. It appears as if a moment in the life of the town were frozen in time by the camera. The street is crowded. A small audience of men under a tent seems to be listening to a speech while a group of women chats on the sidewalk in the background. (Figure 18.) A couple of Indians sit crouched between two buildings. Far in the distance, over the tops of the roofs, a man stands in his field with his cow. (Figure 19.)

Used with permission of Gwen Upton.

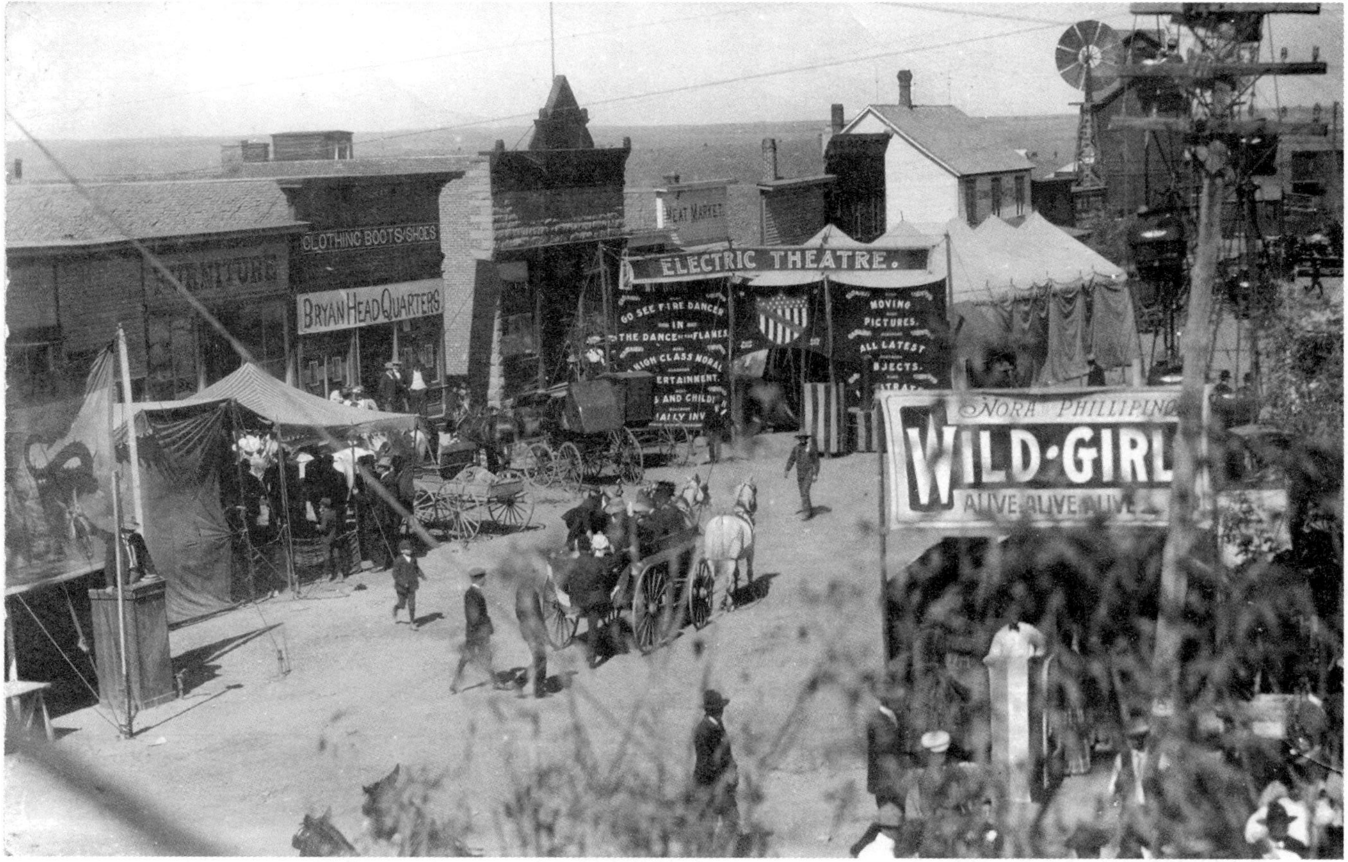

Figure 16. Rushville, NE.

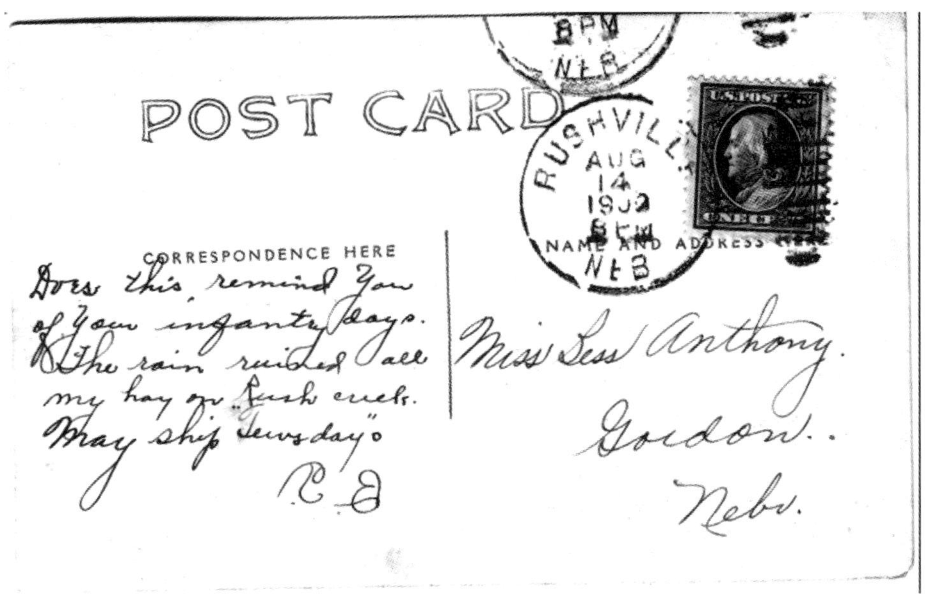
POST CARD

CORRESPONDENCE HERE

Does this remind You
of Your infanty days.
The rain ruined all
my hay on Rush creek.
May ship Tewsday.
R. E.

NAME AND ADDRESS HERE

Miss Sess Anthony.
Gordon..
Nebr.

RUSHVILLE
AUG
14
NEB

Figure 17. The back of the Rushville postcard. The date of the postmark has been blocked. Can you determine when it was mailed?

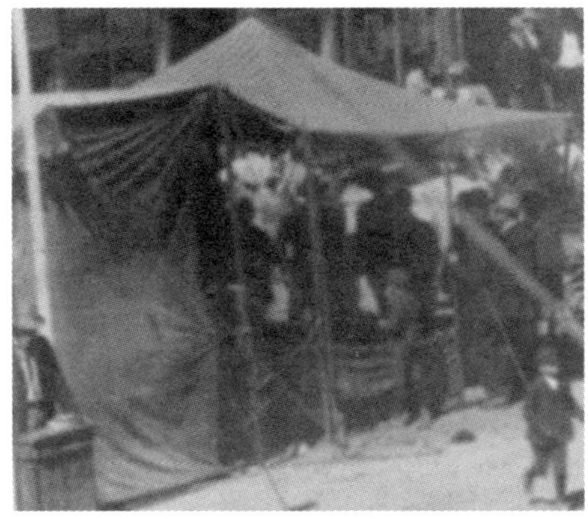
Figure 18. Men listening to a speech.

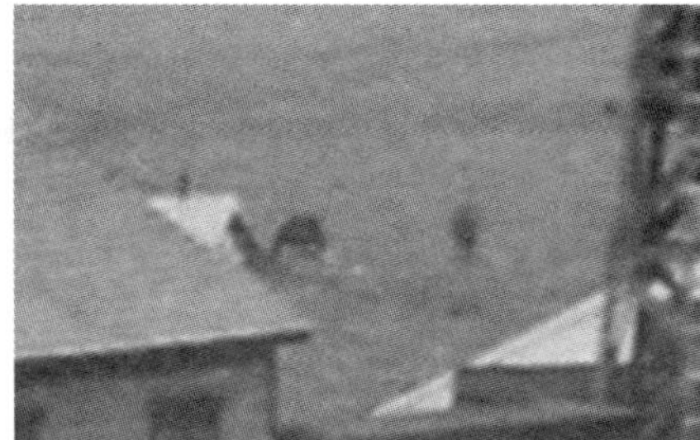
Figure 19. A man in a field with his cow.

The picture was probably taken around the beginning of the 20th century because of the size of the town, the lack of cars on the street, and because of the general way the people in the picture are dressed.

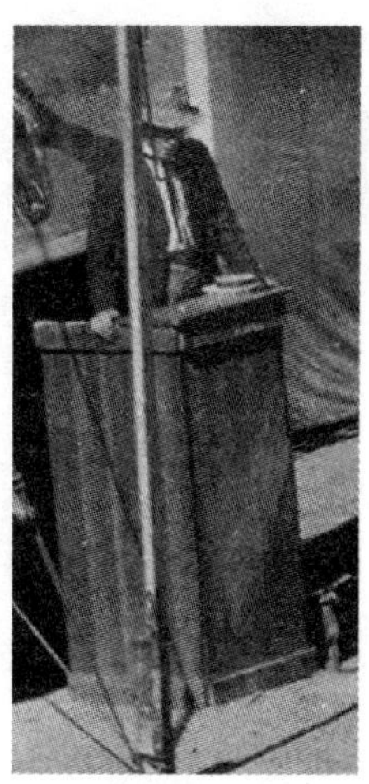

Figure 20.

There are so many items in the picture that can be explored for clues about when it was taken. Several of these relate to the carnival that was in town at the time. For example, there is a man standing at a podium to the far left selling tickets to a show. (Figure 20.) When it is enlarged, the photograph is so detailed that you can even distinguish the individual tickets on his roll.

In the center of the picture appears the Electric Theatre, a traveling movie house, advertising "Go See Fire Dancer in the Dance of the Flames, High Class Moral Entertainment, _____s and Children, _ally Inv___" and "Moving Pictures, All Latest Objects, ___strat___." In those days, movies were not always regarded as a decent form of entertainment, hence the reference to "High Class Moral Entertainment," with the next words presumably "Ladies and Children, Cordially Invited."

A second barker wearing a bow tie stands at a podium to the far right, advertising "Wild Girl, Nora Phillipino, Alive Alive Alive." (Figure 21.) Many of the passengers on the Ferris wheel behind him can be seen riding in one of its seven cars, including two men wearing hats who are visible just above and to the right of the word "Phillipino." (Figure 22.)

A search on Google using the term "Electric Theatre" yielded too many unrelated hits. We were not able to find further information on this type of portable entertainment that could help us date the picture.

A Google search on Nora Phillipino did not produce any useful information either. The only links we came up with led to Nora Fillipino, a current porn star. Searching for information on the Ferris wheel was not helpful. Although the first Ferris wheel was introduced by George Washington Ferris in 1893 at the Chicago World's Fair, the patent, (#1262687)

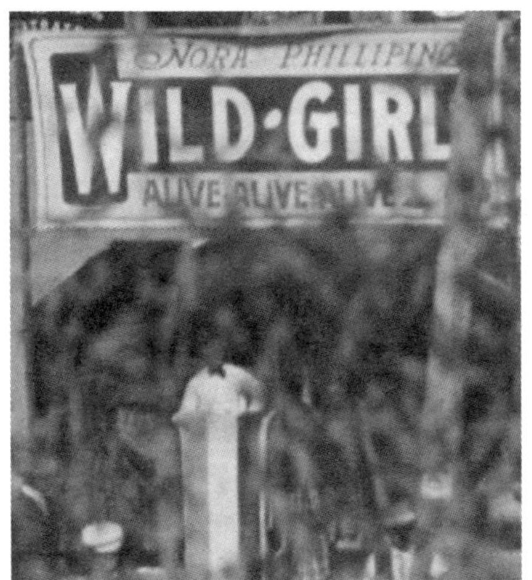

Figure 21.

was not issued until April 16, 1918[6]. Portable Ferris wheels toured the Midwest during the early 1900s[7].

Continuing our search on Google using the word "Rushville" led us to the site www.1.cedar-rapids.com/hindman where several vintage photographs of Rushville have been posted by Evan Hindman. The picture that resembles our mystery picture most closely is shown in Figure 23. The time period of this picture seems to be about the same as that of our mystery photo-it features the same buildings on an unpaved street. There are horses and carts but no cars. A comparison of our picture with those on the website tells us that the date could be as early as 1908, based on the electrical pole in the left foreground. This gives us 1908 as a starting point for further research.

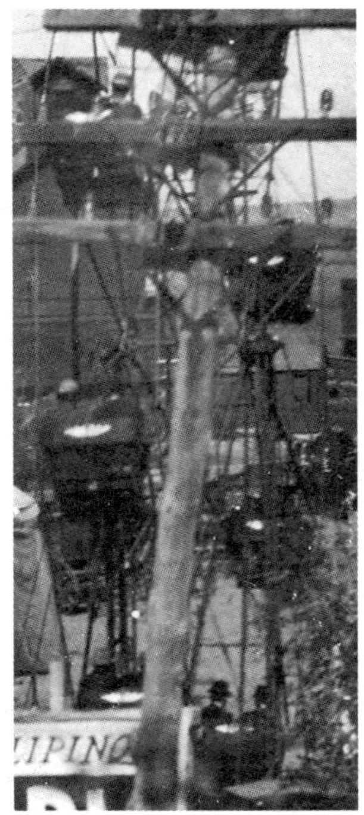

Figure 22. Ferris Wheel passengers.

Fortunately there is one item in the photograph that can be used to pin down the earliest date of the picture to within a few days. It is something that could only have been photographed for a limited time. Before reading further, can you identify it?

Here is a hint: The banner reading "Bryan's Head Quarters" that hangs on the front of the clothing store (Figure 24) indicates that the store was being used as the headquarters for a political campaign for someone name Bryan.

An investigation of Nebraska history produced two possibilities for the identity of the candidate. The banner could refer to Charles Waylan Bryan, who served as mayor of Lincoln, NE from 1915 to 1917 and from 1935 to 1937. Charles also ran (both successfully and unsuccessfully) for Governor of Nebraska several times during the 1920s and 1930s.

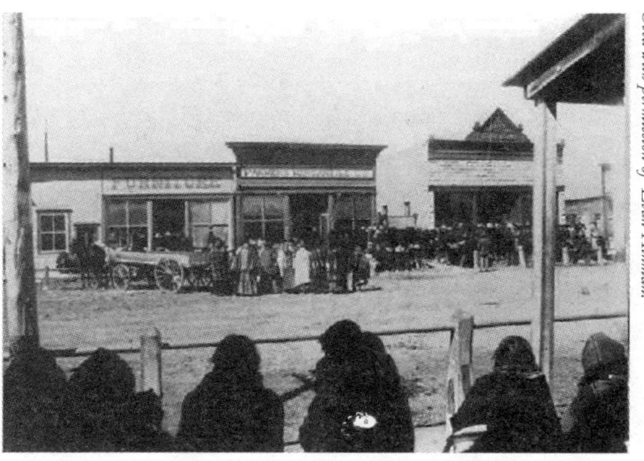

Used with permission of Evan Himman.

Figure 23. Rushville c. 1908.

A second possibility is that the banner refers to Charles' more famous older brother, American statesman and politician William Jennings Bryan, who is most widely known as Clarence Darrow's opponent in the Scopes Monkey Trial of 1925. William Jennings Bryan ran three times unsuccessfully for President of the United States in 1896, 1900, and 1908. Perhaps the shoe store was the Rushville headquarters for one of William Jennings Bryan's runs for the presidency.

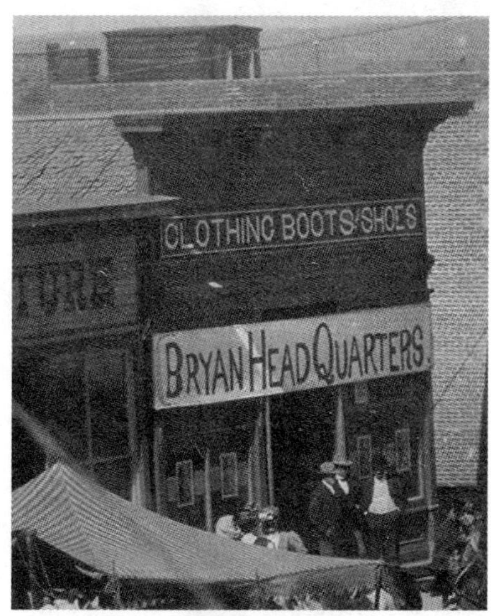

Figure 24. Bryan Headquarters.

Wikipedia (www.wikipedia.org) is an online encyclopedia that is constantly updated by its readers. Although anyone can add a new article or can edit an already-existing article, recent comparisons between Wikipedia and the Encyclopedia Britannica indicate that they are nearly comparable in accuracy[8].

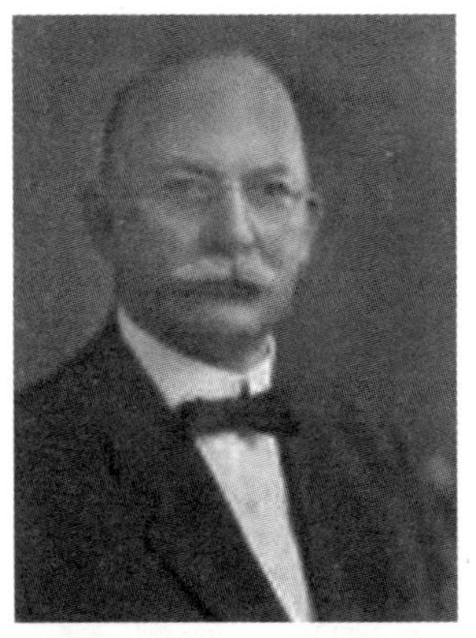

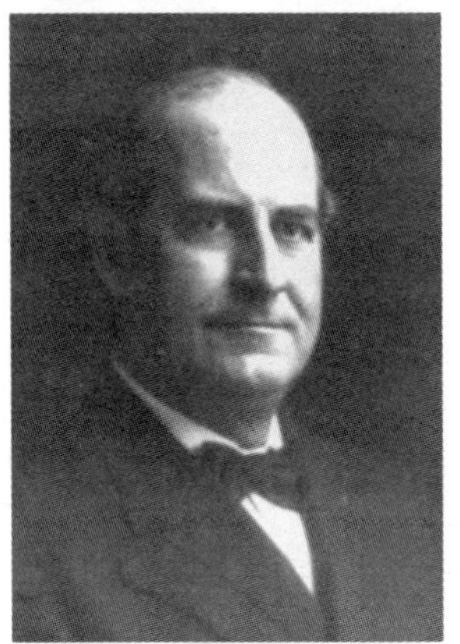

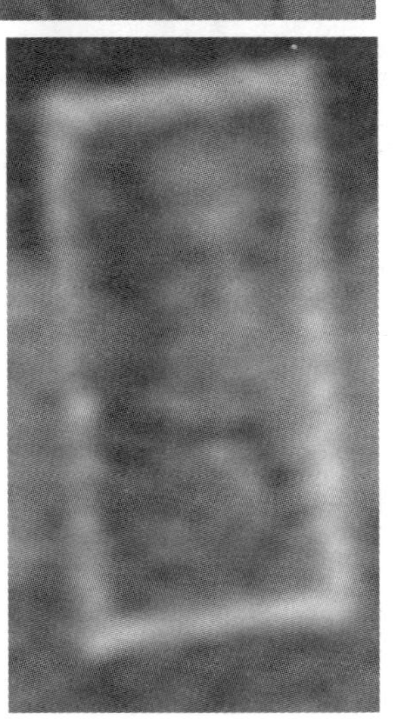

The Wikipedia article about Charles Waylan is rather brief and includes the photograph at the top of Figure 25[9]. The article about William Jennings offers a more detailed biography, accompanied by several pictures of him taken at different times in his career. The Wikipedia photo of William Jennings taken in 1907 during his last bid for the presidency is shown on the center of Figure 25[10].

Is there a way we can determine which, if either of the Bryan brothers had his headquarters in the shoe store?

Yes there is!

The front of the store reveals several copies of a campaign poster that feature a photograph of the candidate (bottom of Figure 25). Let's have a closer look to see if we can distinguish which one of the Jennings brothers it depicts.

There are not many similarities between Charles Waylan Bryan and the candidate in the poster. Charles is somewhat thinner, for one thing.

A comparison of Williams Jennings Bryan with the candidate is more promising. Like the man in the poster, William was a chubby, balding man with a high forehead. Both are wearing a white shirt with a black bow tie. William is facing in the same direction as the candidate. The photograph

Figure 25. Top to bottom: Charles Waylan Bryan, c. 1915, William Jennings Bryan, c. 1907, poster in store window.

used in the poster is same one from 1907 appearing in the Wikipedia article. The shoe store must have been the local headquarters for William Jennings Bryan's third and last unsuccessful run for the Presidency in 1908 when he was defeated by William Howard Taft.

The latest date the picture on the card could have been taken is shortly after Election Day, November 3, 1908. Presumably the headquarters was dismantled within a few days after Bryan lost the election, after which the building reverted to a shoe store. Note that we now have an earliest date for the photo of 1907, when the campaign picture of William Jennings Bryan was produced.

And what about the earliest date the card could have been mailed?

There are three clues that point to the date of the postmark. Have another look at the back of the card in Figure 17 to see if you can spot them before reading any further.

The first clue to the earliest date the card could have been mailed is the divided back style of the card, first produced on March 1, 1907[11]. On a divided back postcard, the right was reserved for the address, and the left was meant for writing the message. Note that the photo itself could have been taken earlier in 1907, depending on when the campaign picture of William Jennings Bryan was taken. The photo could have been applied to the front of the card later.

The second clue to the earliest date of the postcard is the stamp, a Franklin Head One Cent Stamp, Series of 1908, Scott #331 or Scott #331a[12]. (Figure 26.) The stamp can be identified as either of these kinds by its various shades of green, and by the 12 perforations that appear on each side. The Scott #331a stamp was sold in booklet form, so that a #331a would be perforated differently along its edges depending on its position in the book. Another way of telling the #331 from the #331a would be to examine its watermark, but this is impossible to do without physically

Figure 26. Franklin one-cent stamp, series 1908.

CORRESPONDENCE HERE
Does this remind You
of Your infanty days.
The rain ruined all
my hay on Rush creek.
May ship "Tewsday"
C E

Figure 27. The message.

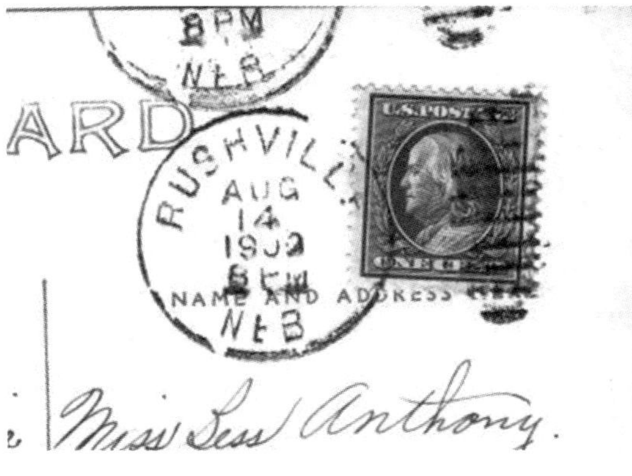

Figure 28. The postmark.

examining the stamp. The #331 was first printed on December 1, 1908; the #331a was first printed December 2, 1908. The latter date is the earliest the postcard could have been mailed.

The final clue is the message on the card (Figure 27): *Does this remind you of your infantry days? The rain ruined all my hay on Rush Creek. May ship "Tewsday". C. E.*

Based on the writer's comment about his hay being destroyed, the earliest date the card could have been mailed is pushed back to late spring or early summer 1909 after the next hay harvest.

Figure 28 shows the card was postmarked on August 14, 1909.

When we featured this postcard in one of our weekly photoquizzes on our website at www.forensicgenealogy.info, an interesting detail about Rushville emerged that does not directly relate to the answer, but that nevertheless contributes to the historic backdrop of the picture. Mary Fraser, a top Quizmasters, provided extra insight into the history of Rushville with her comment:

Buffalo Bill Cody headquartered in Rushville when he was hiring talent on the reservation for his wild west shows. Cody paid the Indians in script that was redeemable only at the Asay Store while the performers were in Rushville. Cody always stayed with the Asay family when in Rushville. (It has been said that Cody entertained Mrs. Asay on picnics on the Niobrara River while Mr. Asay tended the store.) In later years, Cody returned to Rushville to film a re-enactment of the "Battle of Wounded Knee". The Pine Ridge Indian Reservation continues to be a major part of the Rushville economy.

Don't Miss a Thing!

Sometimes a picture is rich in details that provide background information on its setting, or a general idea of when it was taken. Yet "the" clue that could give it away appears to be insignificant, and can be overlooked. Without that key detail, however, the story the picture tells is like a jigsaw puzzle that can only be completed by finding its missing piece.

Christine Gregg, the owner of the picture in Figure 29, told us that she had found it among her mother-in-law's collection of papers. She was not sure, but she assumed that it was taken in Arenac Co., MI, because her mother-in-law was from that area.

A few other items point to the shop being that of a blacksmith. There are chimneys on the roof that could have been used to vent a blacksmith forge. There is an anvil for shaping parts, a trough for quenching hot metal, and a shovel to smother a fire with dirt. (Figure 30.)

The photograph in Figure 31 of a blacksmith shop in Enderby, British Columbia, Canada[13], taken around 1895, shows many of the same implements that appear in our mystery photo. Both the man in our picture and the Enderby blacksmiths are wearing the same type of apron. The two shops look similar, with the horseshoes hanging upside down and the wagon wheels leaning against the walls. (Figure 32.) We conclude from this that the man was probably a blacksmith.

However, the most significant detail is not nearly as obvious as these others. In fact, we dismissed it at first as irrelevant. The pile of lumber to the far right background of the picture is not just a pile of lumber. Dale Niesen, a reader from Michigan, recognized it as the heavy wooden frame of a logging sled in disrepair, with the front runner stacked on top of the

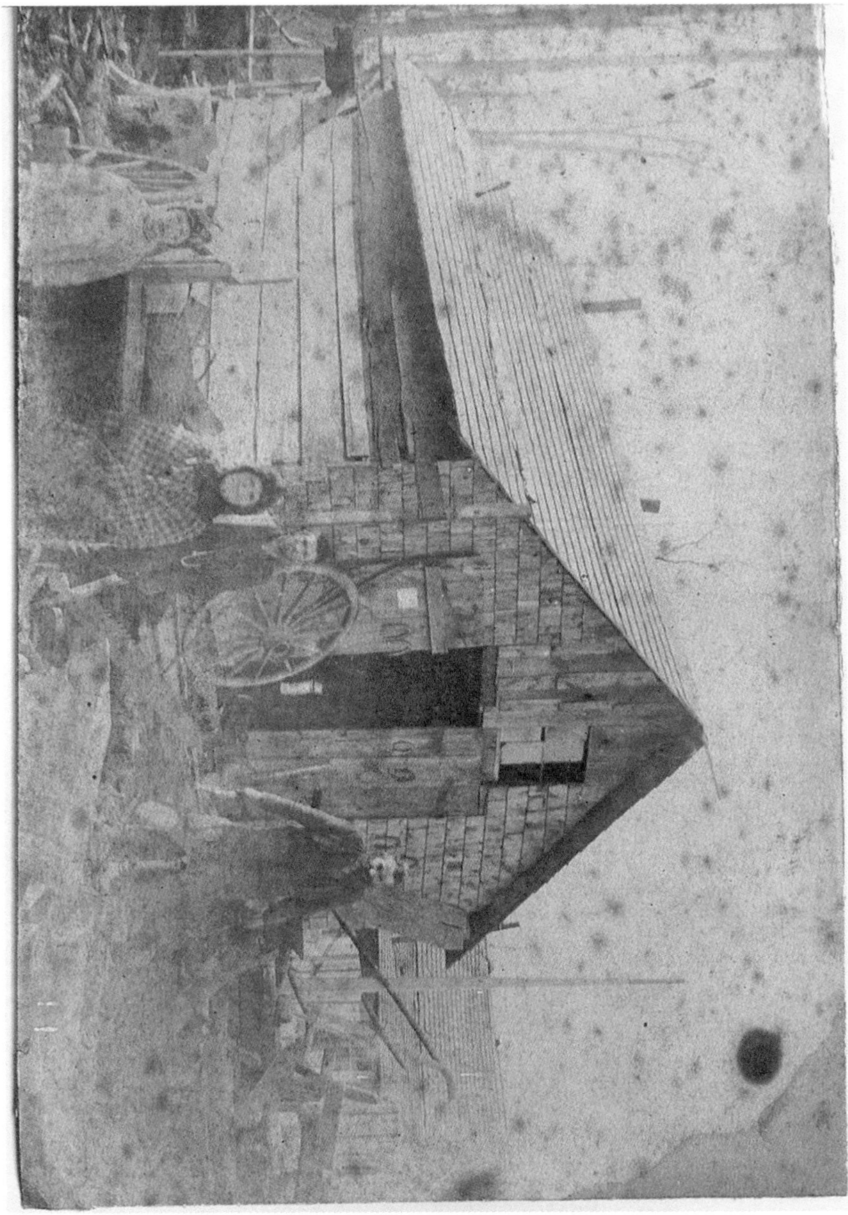

Used with permission of Christina Gregg.

Figure 29.

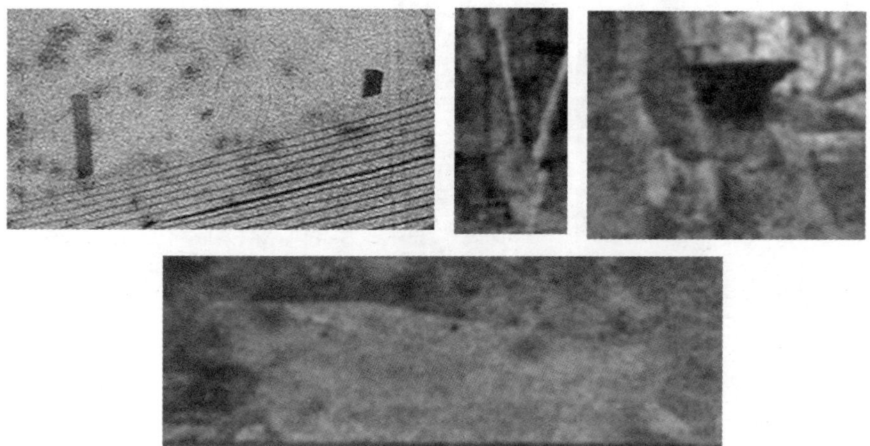

Figure 30. (Top left to right) Chimneys on roof of shack, shovel, anvil and (bottom) trough.

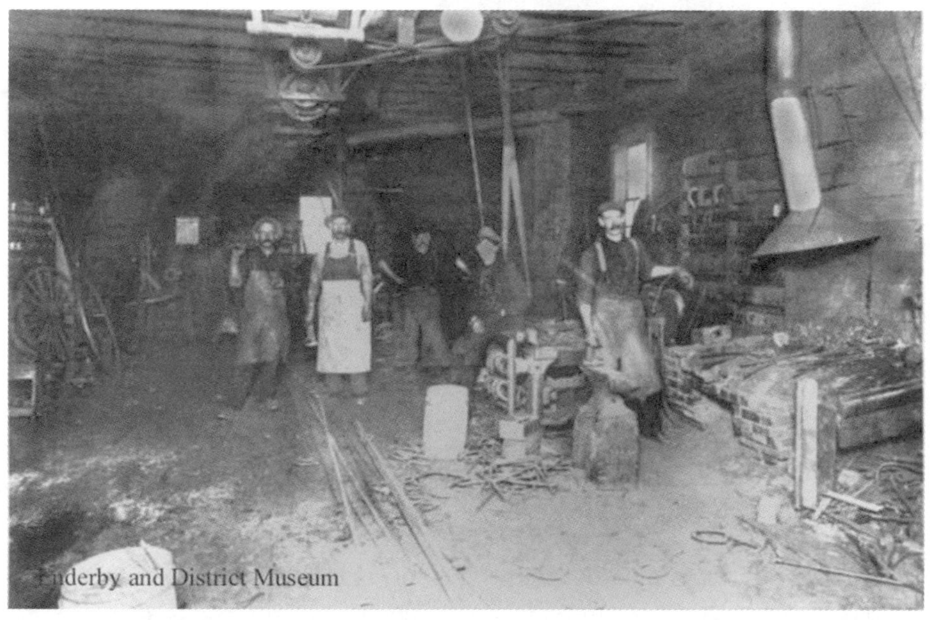

Figure 31. Blacksmith shop, Enderby, British Columbia, Canada, c. 1895.

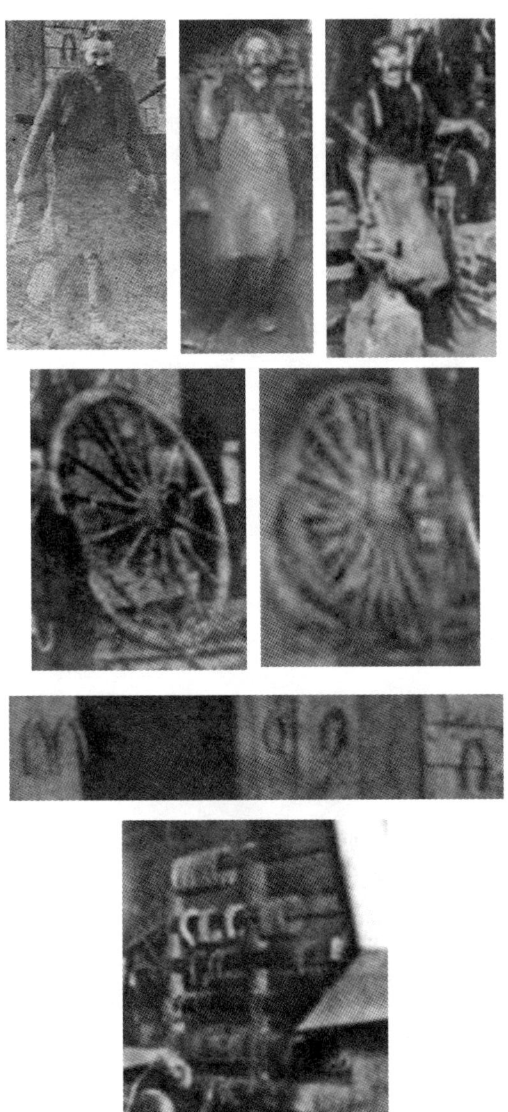

Figure 32. Top: Apron worn by man in mystery photo (far left) compared to aprons worn by blacksmiths in Enderby photo (center and far right). Center: Wagon wheel in mystery photo (left) compared to wagonwheel in Enderby photo (right). Bottom: Horseshoes hanging on door of shack (upper) compared to those in Enderby photo (lower).

main body. The tongue of the sled is leaning against the runner. The sled is the type used in logging camps in north Michigan even today. (Figures 33 and 34.)

This provided an interesting direction for researching other items in the photo that otherwise would have seemed insignificant. We discovered that both the shack and the open cart behind the woman closely resemble those used by Scandinavian immigrants in the late 1800s through the turn of the 20th century. (Figures 35 and 36.) We also found an example of the kind of two-man crosscut rip saw that is still used in lumber camps. A similar saw is seen in our picture leaning on the trough to the immediate right of the woman. (Figure 37.)

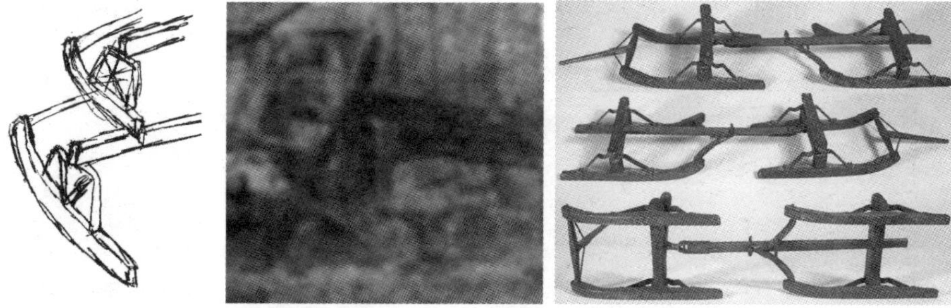

Figure 33. (Left) A sketch of (center) the 'pile of lumber'. Right: a set of miniature logging sleds[14].

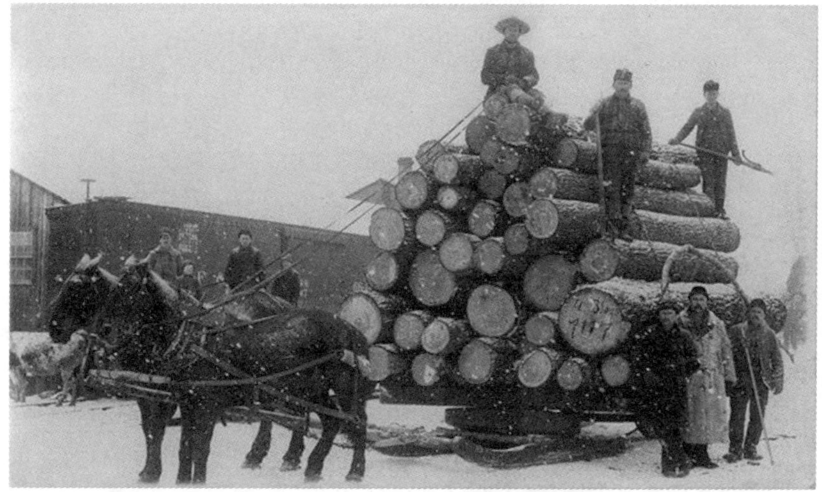

Figure 34. A typical logging sled[15].

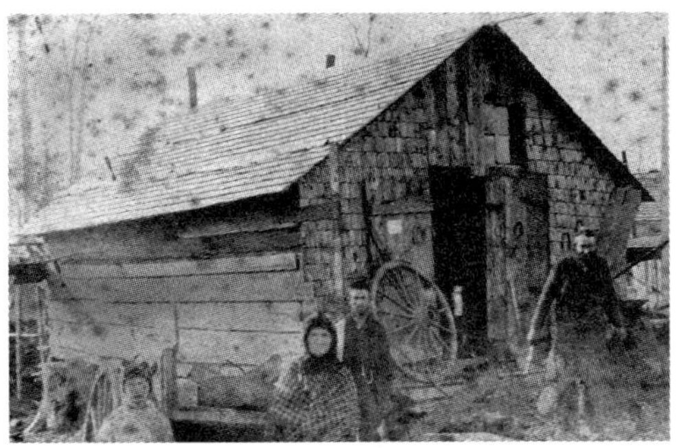
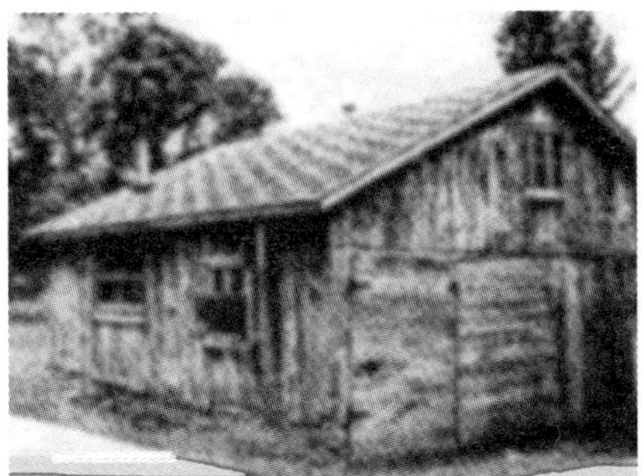

Figure 35. The shack in the mystery photograph compared to a typical shack of Scandinavian immigrants[16].

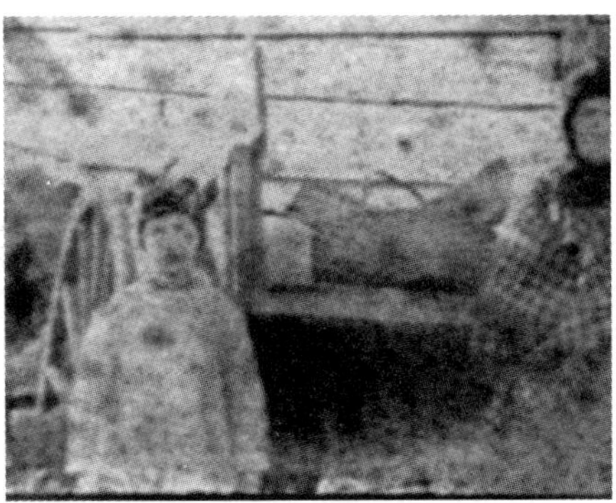
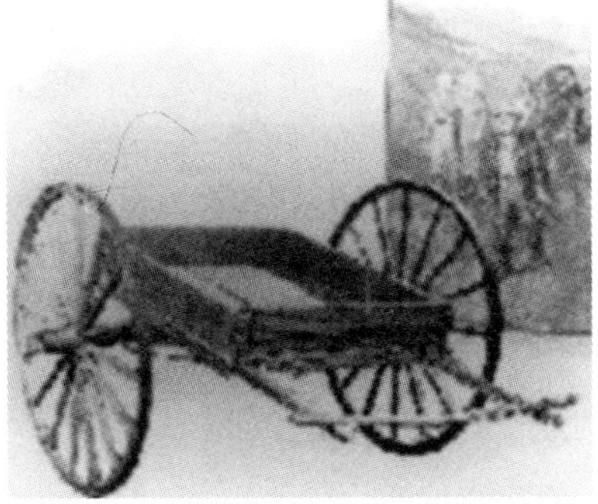

Figure 36. The handcart in the picture compared to the style of open cart used by Scandinavian immigrants[17].

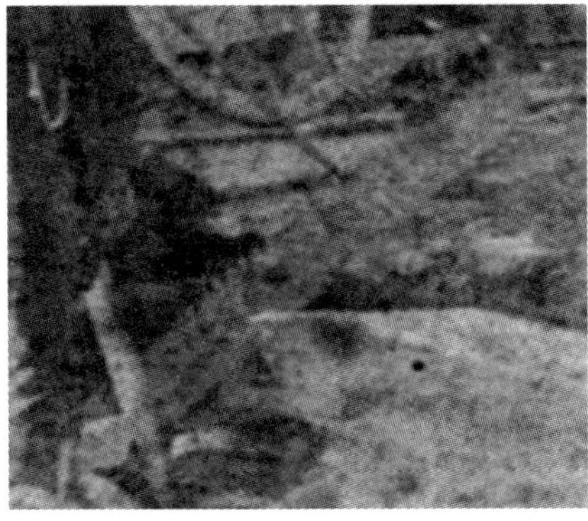
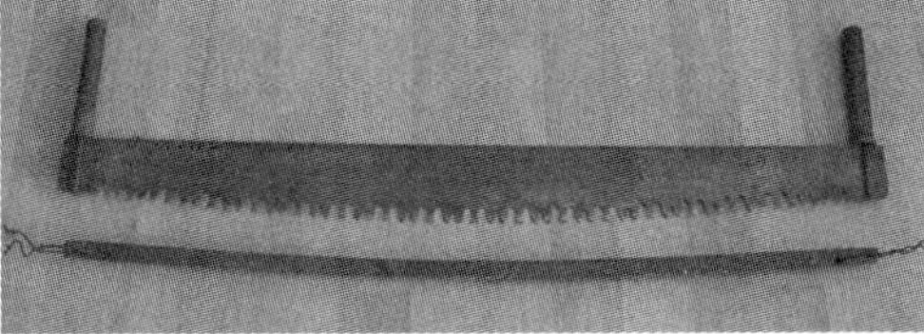

Figure 37. Typical two-man cross cut rip saw used in lumber camps.

Our original purpose was not only to identify the photograph, but also to find out if any of the people were members of Christine's family. All the clues point to the picture being a photograph taken in a lumber camp in northern Michigan around the turn of the 20th century. The man in the center is probably the camp blacksmith. Christine was puzzled by this at first because she did not immediately know of any member of her mother-in-law's family who fit this description. It took her as much time to research how the blacksmith fit into her family as it did to research the photo in the first place.

In Christine's own words:

[In researching my family] I have found a Christopher Rulason who was listed as a blacksmith in the 1880 and 1900 censuses of Arenac County, MI where my mother-in-law was born in 1908. [Arenac Co. is prime logging territory.] Christopher would have been a great uncle to my mother-in-law, so it is reasonable that she might have a picture of him. Christopher never had children of his own but in Feb 1896 he married a woman who was much older. According to the 1900 census she did have several children (although I have not been able to find them yet).

Christopher was born in Allegheny County NY in October of 1848 and his wife was born in Feb 1829 in Canada... I found a woman of the same name and the right age living near...Christopher...in the 1880 census. If she is the old woman in the picture the other two younger people could be her children. This woman lived until 1913 which gives a time period they would have been together as a couple.

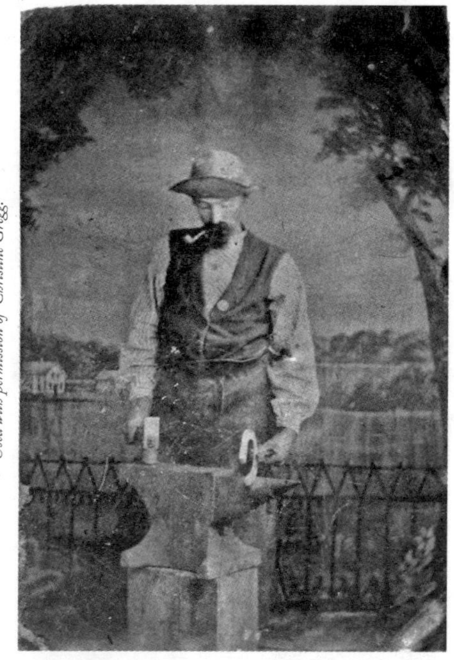

Used with permission of Christine Gregg.

Figure 38. This young blacksmith is probably Christopher Rulason at a young age.

At least one of the Rulason nephews worked for a time in the logging camps but in general the family were farmers or laborers — except for this one blacksmith. Rulason was very probably originally Scandinavian but the family had been in this country for a couple hundred years. His elderly wife (if it is indeed Christopher Rulason) was Canadian born of Irish parents. I am looking though my pictures of Irish immigrants to see what types of clothing they wore and continuing to look for her children to see if any of them fit the people in the picture.

Christine

Christine later added:

Among my sister-in-law's family pictures I found a tintype of a bearded young man with blacksmith tools. (See Figure 38.) *Because there was also a tintype of his mother in the same collection and because he was the only known blacksmith in the family, I think this is a young Christopher Rulason. You may recall that my operating hypothesis was that the man in the blacksmith shop was Christopher taken several years later.*

Love your stuff,
Christine

One final item of interest that we researched is the occasion for the photograph.

This picture is not a posed studio portrait, but rather a candid photo taken on the spur of the moment. The blacksmith has tools in his hand and was apparently interrupted from his work by the arrival of the photographer.

Some areas of the country had intinerant travelling photographers who travelled the side roads with portable camera equipment taking pictures of the locals. The photographer who took this picture probably just happened by near the logging camp and the Rulason family took him up on his offer to take their picture.

References

1. Deborah Barker, Director, Franklin Co. Historical Society, Ottawa, KS, private communication.

2. en.wikipedia.org/wiki/Imperial_State_Crown

3. www.thamesweb.co.uk/windsor/windsorhistory/royalfunerals/index.html

4. www.kansastravel.org/rockcity.htm

5. Sharon Sergeant, info@ancestralmanor.com, private communication

6. patft.uspto.gov

7. www.xroads.virginia.edu/~CAP/PALACE/early.html

8. networks.silicon.com/webwatch/0,39024667,39155109,00.htm

9. en.wikipedia.org/wiki/Charles_Waylan_Bryan

10. en.wikipedia.org/wiki/William_Jennings_Bryan#1900-1912:_on_the_Chautauqua_circuit

11. overanalysis.org/postcards/faqsec1.htm

12. www.1847usa.com/washfrank/1cFranklinQuickChart.htm

13. www.enderbymuseum.ca/images/0422.jpg

14. www.aagal.com/Toysgen.html

15. www.lumberheritage.org/pioneers_of_logging_photo_gallery.htm

16. www.rootsweb.com/~mnrenvil/mus-rchs.htm; LERUD CABIN

17. www.americanwest.com/trails/pages/mormtrl.htm

CASE STUDY

The Belgian Orphans

= Putting All the Details Together =

A picture may hold a clue that will tell you something about it, but not everything. Yet this clue may lead to other clues that together will lead you to the time and place a photo was taken.

Hard and Soft Clues

The photograph of a group of girls posed under a tree in Figure 1, is a good example. Several "soft" clues in it lead us to research in a certain direction, but do not themselves tell us the where, when, who, and why of the picture. Based on these clues alone, our analysis of the picture would remain in the realm of conjecture.

The picture's style and the way the girls are dressed are soft clues. From them, we can guess that the photo probably dates from the late 1800s or early 1900s. The presence of several adult women in the picture imply that the girls probably belong to a school group. We can also guess, because of the location in the forest, that the group may be stopped to pose for the picture during a field trip.

Used with permission of Joe Bott, www.deadfred.com.

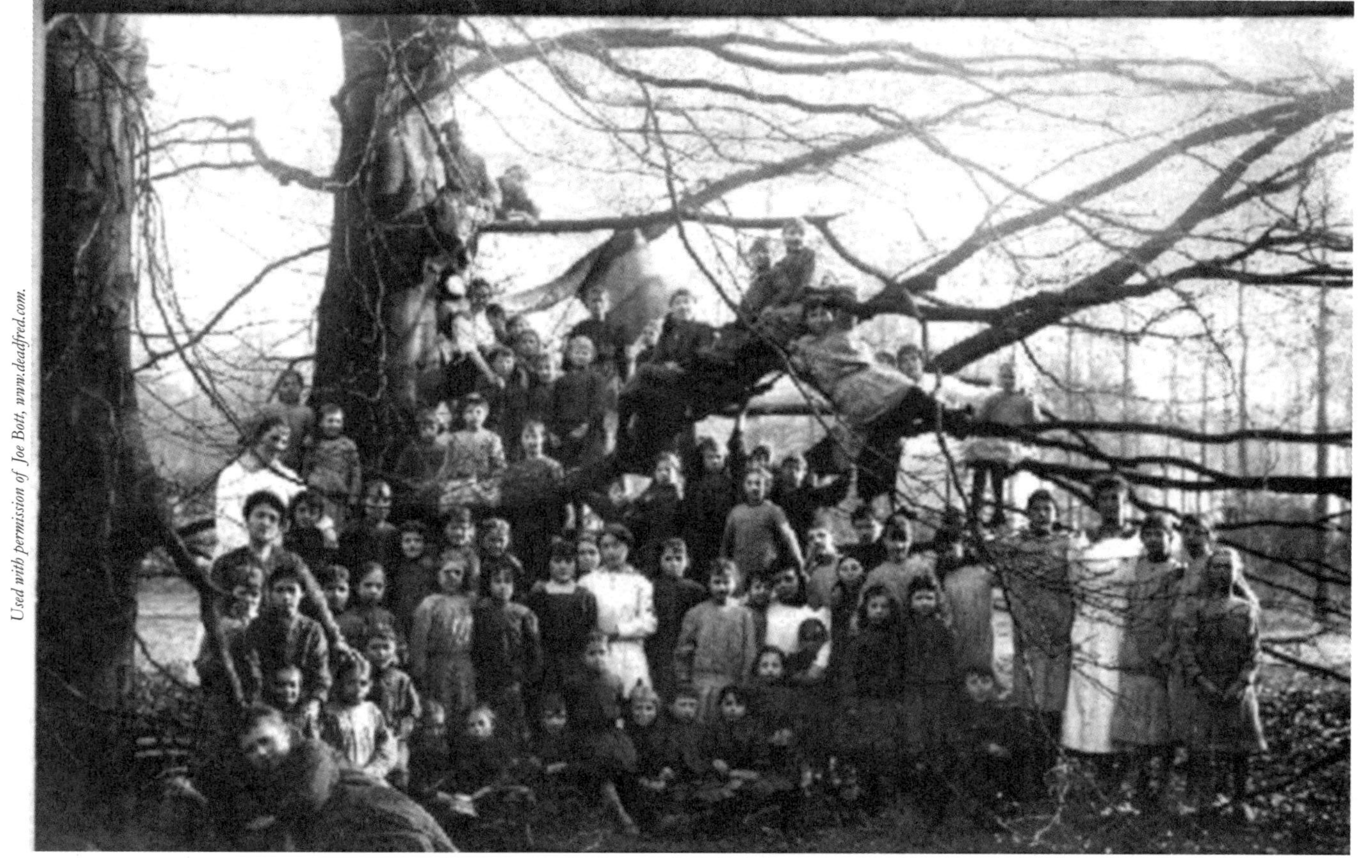

Figure 1. Girls in a forest.

"The" Clue

Fortunately, there is one "hard" clue in the picture that reveals specific information. Can you find it?

Did you notice the flag the children are holding? If we identify the flag, we will likely identify the origin of the girls and their teachers. Because the photo is black and white, it is hard to tell the color of the stripes, but we can say that the flag has a light colored center stripe with a darker stripe on either side. This design is characteristic of European flags, so let's assume that the picture was taken in Europe. We can always backtrack and change if this assumption doesn't work.

According to en.wikipedia.org/wiki/Flags_of_Europe, there are ten tricolor European flags that fit this description. They are shown in Figure 2. How can we narrow the possibilities?

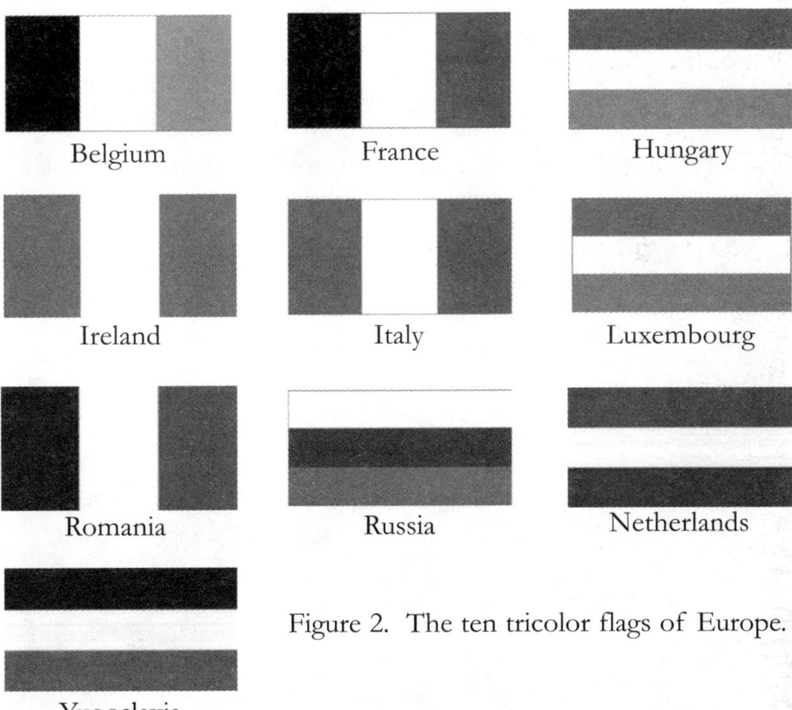

Figure 2. The ten tricolor flags of Europe.

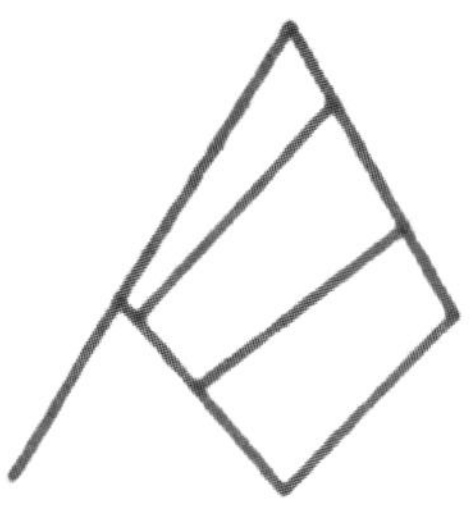

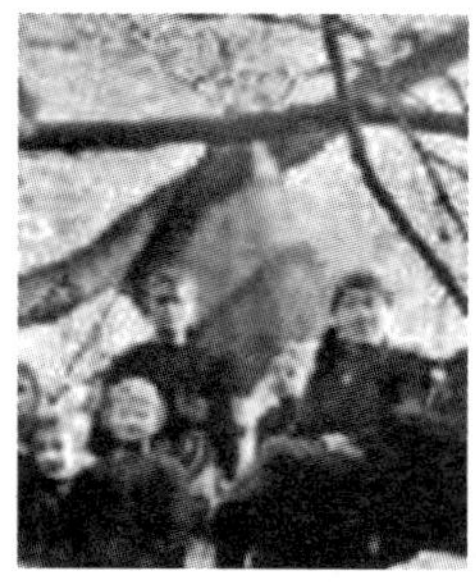

Figure 3. Which way does the flag hang?

Which Way Does the Flag Hang?

Are the stripes are horizontal or vertical? A sketch of just the flag is shown in Figure 3. The flag is hanging from a pole on its left telling us that the stripes must be vertical. This eliminates Hungary, Luxembourg, Russia, the Nether-lands, and Yugoslavia from our list of possibilities. The remaining countries are Belgium, France, Ireland, Italy, and Romania. The flags of these five countries have vertical stripes with either a white or a yellow stripe in the center. If we can determine the color of the center stripe, we will narrow the possibilities even further. How can we do this?

White or Yellow Stripe?

Several of the older women in the picture are wearing white dresses. (Figure 4.) How about comparing them to the center stripe of the flag? It

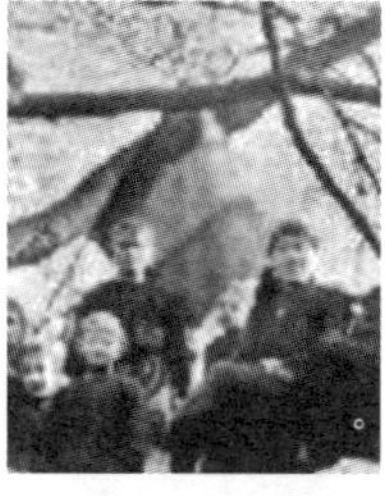

Figure 4. The flag and the white dresses.

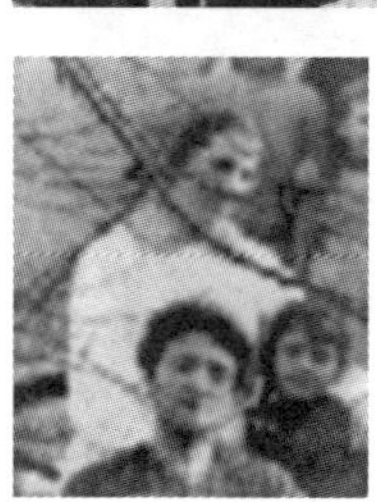

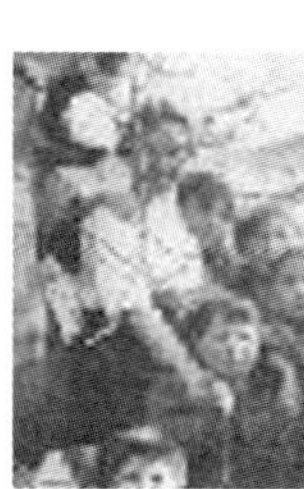

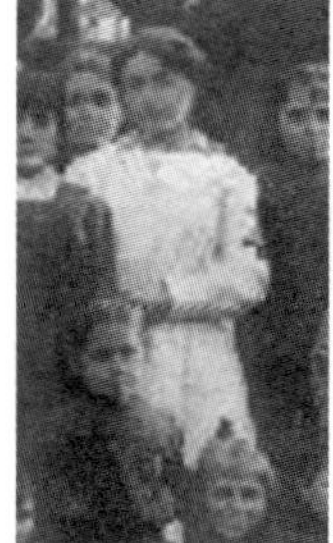

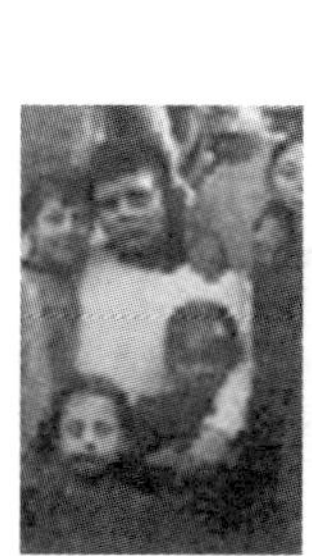

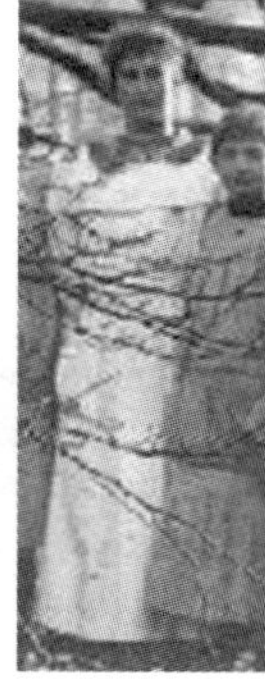

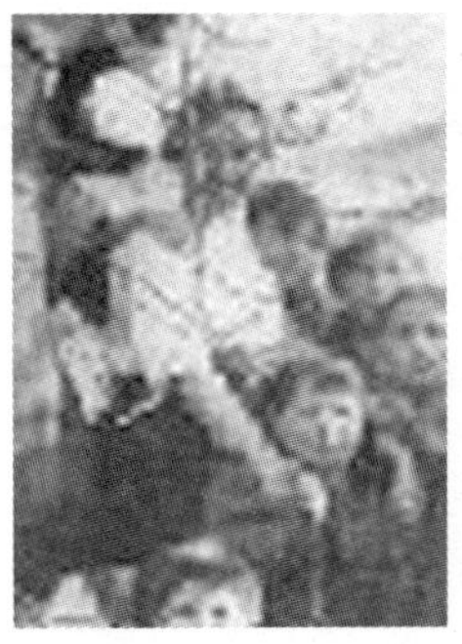
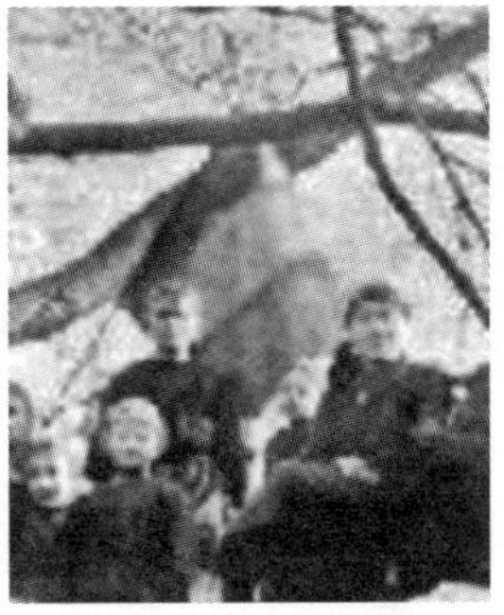
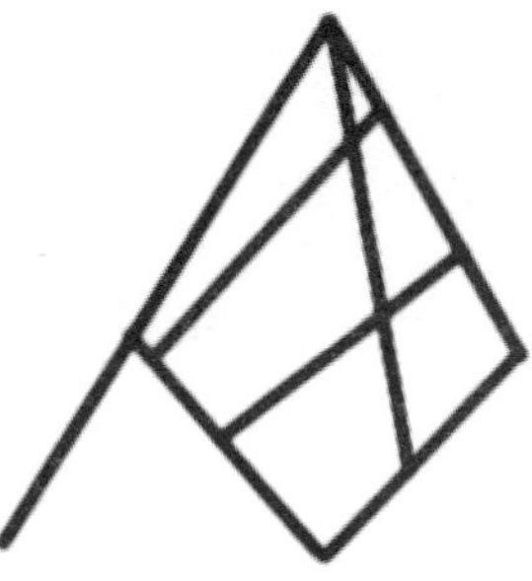

Figure 5.

might be argued that the because the flag is in the shade of the tree that the stripe is white it appears to have a different tint than the dresses. However, there is a small triangle-shaped area on the right side of the flag that is exposed to the sun. Since the tints of both the shadowed and illuminated parts of the flag are darker than the blouse of the teacher sitting in the tree a few feet to its left, we have reason to believe the middle stripe is not white. It must be yellow. See Figure 5. The only countries that have flags having three vertical stripes with a yellow center stripe are Belgium and Romania.

Where?

The flags for Belgium and Romania are very similar. The Belgian flag has a black stripe to the left, while the Romania flag has a dark blue stripe to the left. It would be difficult to distinguish dark blue from black in this picture. (In fact I have a hard time distinguishing dark blue from black clothes when I get dressed in the morning!) The three stripes in each flag have the same relative sizes. Based only on the flag, the nationality represented by the flag is still ambiguous.

Since the girls are in a forest, one way to choose between the two possible locations is to find pictures of forests in Belgium and Romania that look similar. We start by using our "soft" clue that the picture was taken around the turn of the 20th century. We'd search Google Images for photographs taken in forests in these countries about this time, and we'd also ask older friends if they recognized the landscape.

Our research produced the photo in Figure 6 that was sent in by Dale Niesen, one of our long-time Quizmasters. The photograph shows the mobile kitchen of the 107th Field Signal Battalion, 32nd "Red Arrow" Division, taken in the Argonne Forest during WWI. The man standing eighth from the left, with only his face showing between the shoulders of the men in the front, is Dale's great uncle Private Charles Livernois. The landscape is very similar to that shown of the children sitting in the tree, suggesting that the children in our photograph probably stopped to get their picture taken in the Argonne Forest. Another possible location is the Ardennes Forest on the border between France and Belgium. It was similarly decimated during World War I. The children could still be either Belgian or Romanian, but considering the logistics of travel for a school group that size during that time period, the children are likely Belgian.

When?

There are a few clues in the picture that were not of much use earlier in the investigation, but which now are quite important in dating it. The forest is still in bad shape. It has not had time to recover from the devastation evident in Dale's photo. Because the forest has not had time to grow back after it had been denuded of foliage during the war, the photo was probably taken shortly after Armistice Day, November 11, 1918. Also note also that the children and their teachers are not dressed for cold weather, nor for the summer months when it can get very hot and humid. The photo was likely taken in the spring of 1918.

We originally obtained this photo of the Belgian children from *Dead Fred*, a popular website for posting unidentified photos. (See www.deadfred.com.) After our analysis, we found a second photo on the Dead Fred website, very similar to ours, that apparently shows the same group of children. See Figure 7. The writing above the door is in Dutch (top line) and French (bottom line). Translated, it says "National Committee for Assistance and Food". This was a relief organization formed by Herbert Hoover and Emile Franqui in 1914 to deliver supplies to Belgium during World War I. (Figure 8 shows an enlarged version of the writing above door.)

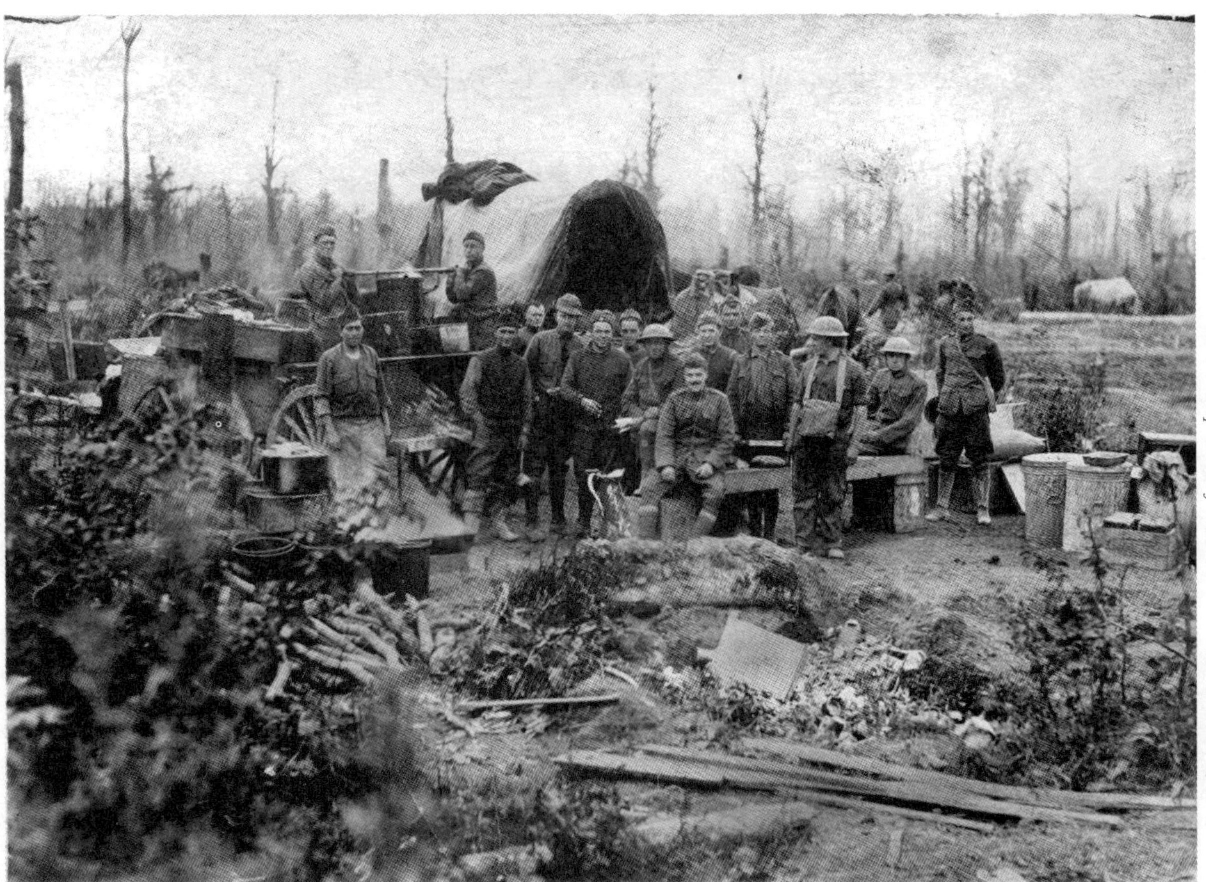

Used with permission of Dale Niesen.

Figure 6. Mobile kitchen of the 107th Field Signal Battalion, 32nd "Red Arrow" Division, Argonne Forest WWI.

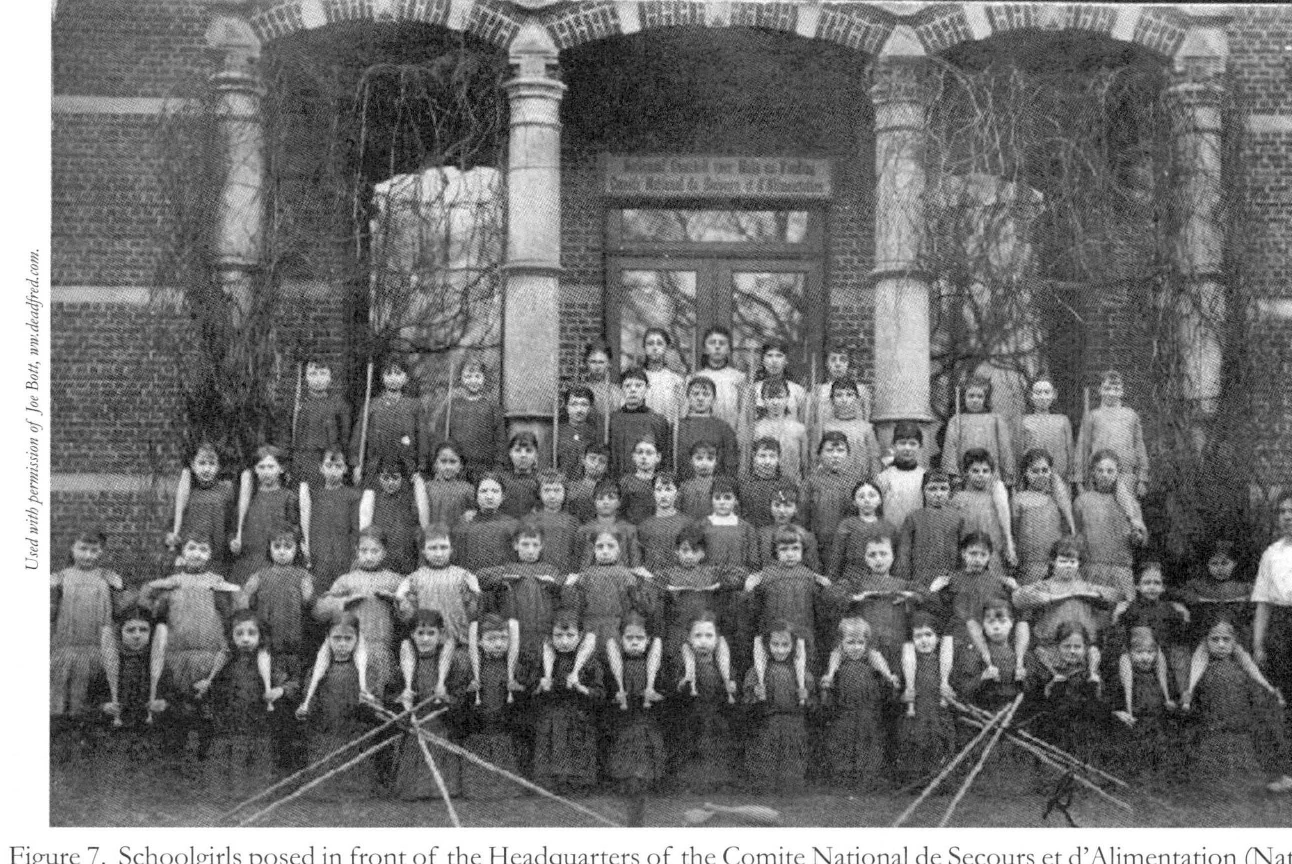

Figure 7. Schoolgirls posed in front of the Headquarters of the Comite National de Secours et d'Alimentation (National Committee of Aid and Food), Brussells, Belgium, c. 1918.

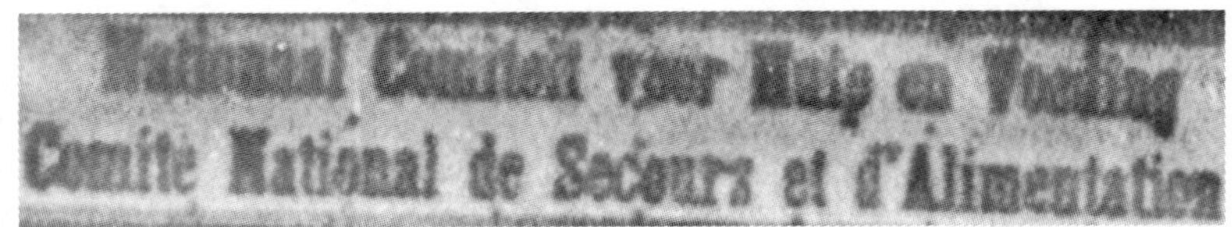

Figure 8. Enlargement of the writing over the door in Figure 7.

Comité National de Secours et d'Alimentation

From www.francquifoundation.be/ang/emile_en.htm:

With the German army occupying most of the country [at the beginning of WWI], the population of Belgium was threatened with starvation. American public opinion decided that America should do something about the fate of our people and a large-scale demonstration of generosity was launched under the name "C.R.B.- Commission for the Relief of Belgium". Its chairman was Herbert Hoover. Funds collected in Belgium and other countries, mostly the United States, were used to organize a supply of food to Belgium via the Netherlands, which remained neutral during this war.

Looking for a reliable partner in Belgium, Herbert Hoover remembered Emile Francqui who had been a formidable opponent during [business] negotiations in China. This led to the two working closely together to organize the 'Comité National de Secours et d'Alimentation' (in French) or 'Nationaal Hulp en Voedingscomité' (in Dutch)- the National Relief and Food Committee. The Committee was to take delivery of food that arrived from the United States and to distribute it among the Belgian population. The Committee continued its work until the end of the war.

Further Investigation

The fact that the writing over the door of the headquarters is in both French and Dutch is a good indication that the second photo was taken in Brussels, and not in front on one of the satellite offices of the Committee. To investigate this a little further, we wrote to Dirk Ruyver, webmaster of South-East-Flanders website at www.geocities.com/dideru/. South East Flanders is a region in the west of Belgium lying between Brussels and the Belgian border with France. His response:

Dear Dr. Fitzpatrick,

Thank you for your e-mail. The picture with the school girls in front of a large building was definitely taken in Belgium, maybe in Brussels. The reason is that the name of the building is both written in French and Dutch. Nowadays, only in Brussels both French and Dutch are used on official buildings. But, during the first quarter of the 20th century (and before), also in Flanders both languages were written on buildings.

So, there is a very good chance that this picture was taken in Flanders or in Brussels.

Best regards,
Dirk De Ruyver
webmaster of South-East-Flanders
www.geocities.com/dideru/

A Few Notes

Sometimes it's hard to stop checking out clues even after you've figured out when, where and why a photo has been taken. Even after we were satisfied that our original picture was of a group of Belgian schoolchildren on a field trip through the Argonne or Ardennes Forest, Spring 1918, we found interesting items in the second photo that merited further investigation.

As Quizmaster Stan Read noted:

Colleen,

The girls in the calisthenics class are holding Indian Clubs and outdoor size Pick-Up Sticks. The girls in the second row are posing with arm exercise positions. Thank you for pointing out the fact that the tricolor was the Belgian with yellow as the center stripe.

Cheers,
Stan Read

Misconceptions about Indian clubs abound. Indian clubs are not bowling pins as some shops continue to mislabel them, nor are Indian clubs of Native American origin. In fact, Indian clubs can be traced to one of the

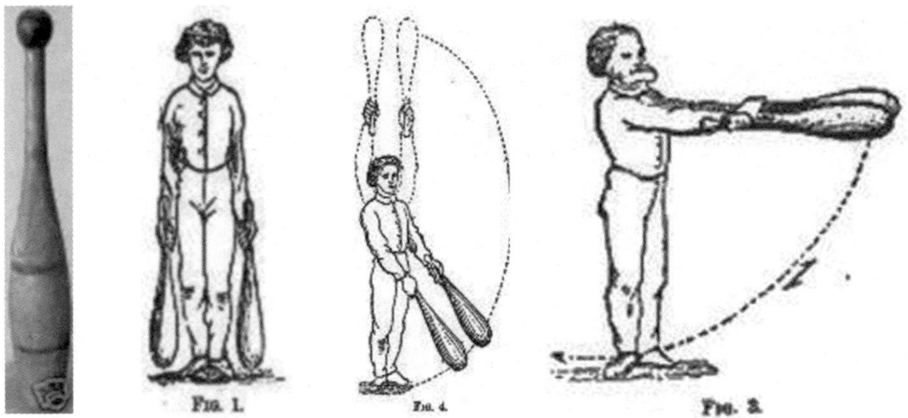

Figure 9. (Left) An Indian club; (Right) Three Indian club exercise positions from ejmas.com/pt/ptart_dick_0101.htm.

most ancient weapons in India, the war club, or *gada*, a symbol of invincible physical prowess and worldly power.

Almost every god and goddess of Hindu belief is depicted holding a war club. Through the ages, the war club changed in both name and form. Eventually, its use evolved in India as a means of physical exercise.

Figure 9 shows a picture of an Indian club, with sketches showing several positions for Indian club exercises. You can read more about Indian clubs at: www.antiquesjournal.com/Pages04/archives/indianclubs.html.

Summary

The children in the picture are probably a group of Belgian students who are members of a sports club. They were likely on a field trip around Belgium and western France in the spring of 1918, shortly after the end of WWI when our photo was taken during a stop in the Argonne or Ardennes Forest. The second group photo was probably taken about the same time in Brussels, Belgium in front of the head-quarters of the Comite National de Secours et d'Alimentation, an organization founded in 1914 by Herbert Hoover and Emile Franqui to deliver assistance to Belgium during the First World War.

The Photographer

Sometimes the subject matter of a photograph is not the key to discovering its story. You might be able to get more information by researching the photographer.

From the earliest days, photographers have marked their product with their company logos. The name and location of a studio that produced a Daguerreotype or an ambrotype can sometimes be found inside its Union case, under the photograph. In the case of a tintype, if the name of the photographer appears at all, it is usually on the envelope or cover slip the tintype might be enclosed in, and not on the tintype itself. Cartes de Visite and cabinet cards are more often than not marked on the bottom or back of the mat with the studio that produced them. On occasion, a photographer who was active during the U.S. Civil War can be identified by his initials on a canceled tax stamp. Incidently, the presence of the tax stamp dates the photo to between August 1, 1864 and August 1, 1866. See Figure 1. We'll talk more about these types of photographs, about Union cases, and about tax stamps in the chapters *The History of Photography I and The History of Photograph II.*

Knowing when and where the studio was in business is valuable information in dating a photo.

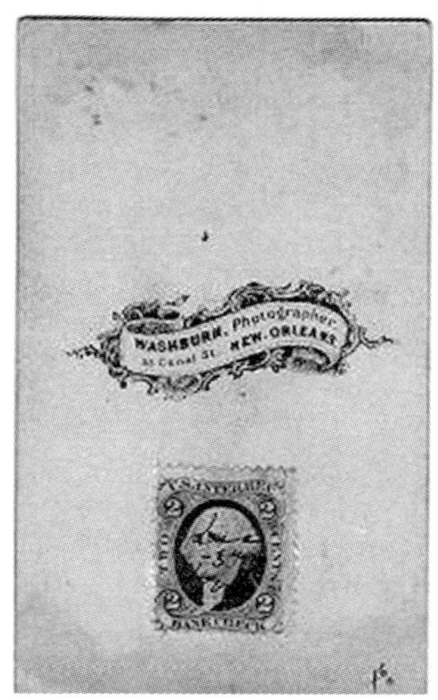

Figure 1. Washburn Photographer, 86 Canal St., New Orleans. Includes a 2-cent Civil War tax stamp canceled with the photographer's initials.

You may be able to refine the date of a photograph by studying the style of the photographer's logo, and the name and address of the studio that produced it, as these items sometimes changed during the time period the studio existed. For example, a photographer might have taken on a partner, or brought his son into the business, changing the name of his company from Smith Photography to Smith & Son Photography. As the studio grew, the photographer might have moved to a new location, changing his address. Comparing the studio's name and address to its listings in the city directories can be useful in narrowing down the time period of a photograph.

Figure 2 shows two photographs by the Lilienthal photography studio in New Orleans. They have the same style logo, and show the

Photo used courtesy of Audrey K. Borde.

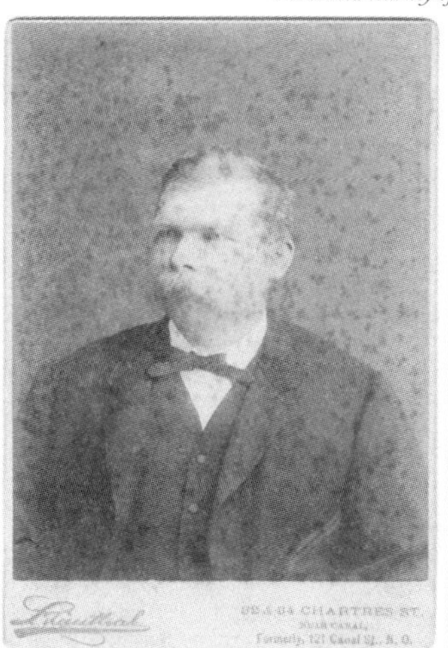

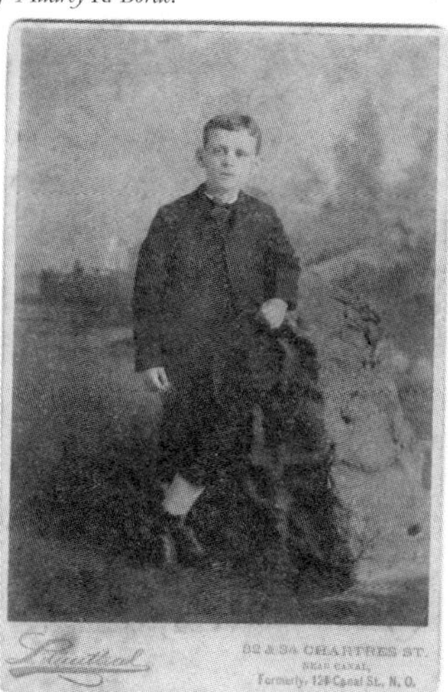

Figure 2. These photos can be dated by the address shown for the Lilienthal photography studio in New Orleans in the 1890s.

same address. By consulting the New Orleans city directories, the photos can be dated to between 1881 and 1882 when Lilienthal relocated from 121 Canal St. to 32 Chartres St. after which he moved back again to the previous address.

Sometimes, however, the photographer might be have been well-known in his time, so that you can find the information you are looking for by simply doing a Google search on his name. Even if he was not famous, you may run across other people who have posted pictures by the same photographer, and who might have more information about him.

The picture in Figure 3 was obtained from the Dead Fred website www.deadfred.com, dedicated to unidentified photos. It is a good example of how researching the photographer can lead you to more information about a picture than you can ever imagine.

Photo used courtesy of Joe Bott, www.deadfred.com.

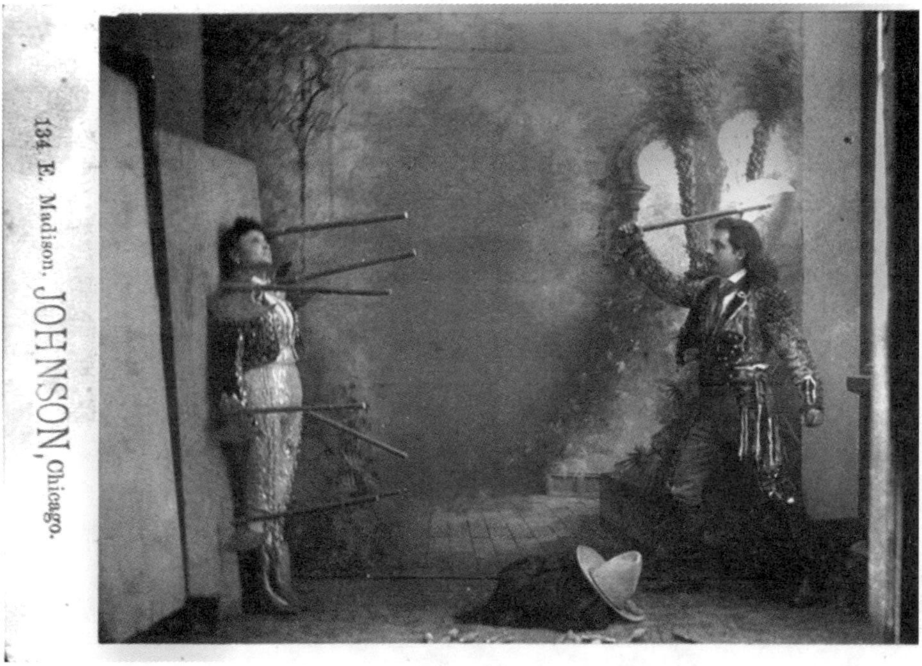

Figure 3. Unidentified knife thrower and his target girl, c. 1890-1900.

The picture is a type of cabinet card from the late 19th century that was commonly used by a performer to advertize his act. Because the photo has few hints to the identity of the knifethrower and his target girl, we first tried researching the photographer on Google.

Unfortunately, the name "Johnson" was too common to produce any specific results, even when combined with the address "134 E. Madison St., Chicago". While we could have located a historical society that would be willing to look up the photographer in old Chicago city directories, we decided it would be easier to continue our Internet search using other keywords.

When we searched on Google using the term 'Knife Thrower' we were put in touch with The Great Throwdini, a.k.a. ".he Rev. Dr. David Adamovich, an ordained minister and the Guiness-recognized fastest knife thrower in the world. (Figure 4). David identified the thrower as his idol, The Great Arcaris, Father of Modern Knife Throwing.

David had several photographs of Arcaris posted on his website www.knifethrower.com, including the two shown in Figure 5. One was similar to the picture we found on Dead Fred. The other was a cabinet card of Arcaris at about the same age, taken by a photographer identified by his logo as Eisenmann, New York. Additional photos from David's website are shown in Figure 6.

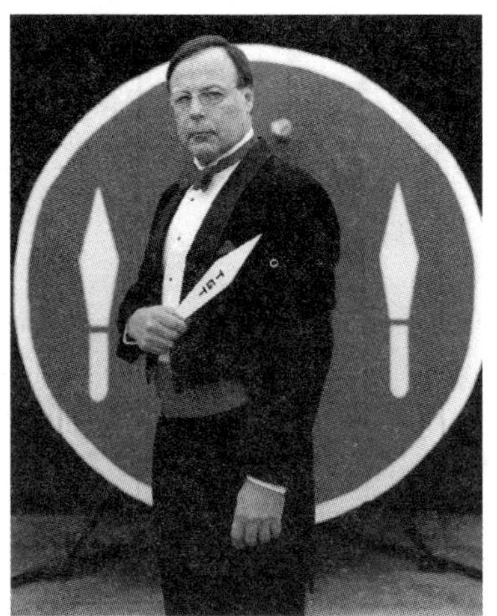

Figure 4. Rev. Dr. David Adamovich, a.k.a The Great Throwdini.

While it was promising to know the identity of the knife thrower, a Google search using the word 'Arcaris' produced too many hits that were unrelated to the picture.

However, Googling the photographer's name 'Eisenmann' produced much more useful information.

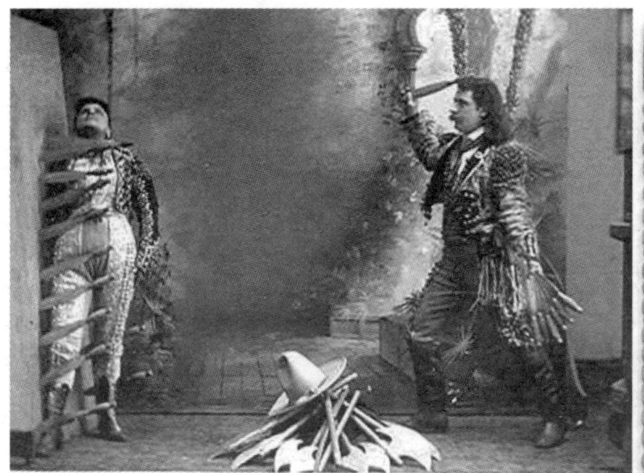

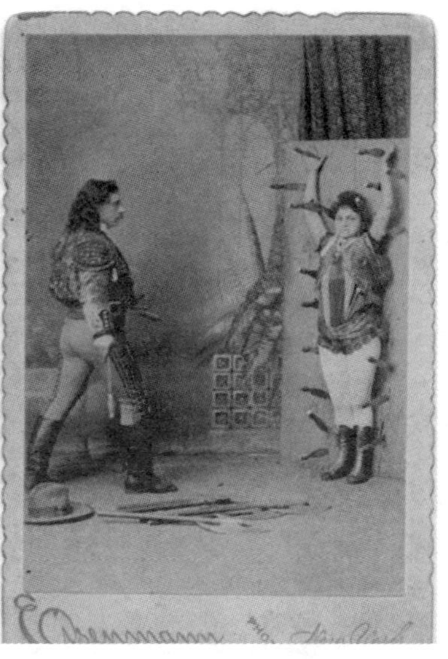

Figure 5. Cabinet cards of The Great Arcaris found on www.knifethrower.com. Photographer logo on the photo to the left reads *Eisenmann, New York.*

Charles Eisenmann was a well-known photographer in the Bowery of New York in the 1890s. He was famous for photographing circus performers and sideshow performers, including many who worked for the well known Barnum & Bailey and Ringling Brothers circuses. Google led us to the Ronald G. Becker collection of Charles Eisenmann photographs housed at Syracuse University in New York. According to library.syr.edu/information/spcollections/digital/eisenmann/:

The Ronald G. Becker Collection of Charles Eisenmann Photographs includes more than one thousand photographs of 19th century sideshows and circuses, 403 by photographer Charles Eisenmann and 155 by his successor Frank Wendt, the remainder by unknown photographers. Most of the photographs depict the physical abnormalities of humans and animals featured at these shows. Subjects include P.T. Barnum, the P. T. Barnum Firm (Barnum and Bailey Circus), and Tom Thumb.

The collection included several cabinet cards of The Great One dating from the 1890s, including the photo shown in Figure 7 of Arcaris with the same target girl appearing in our Dead Fred photo. She is identified by

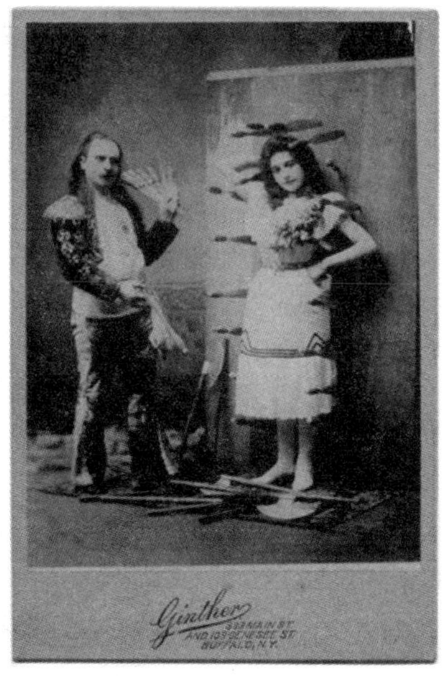

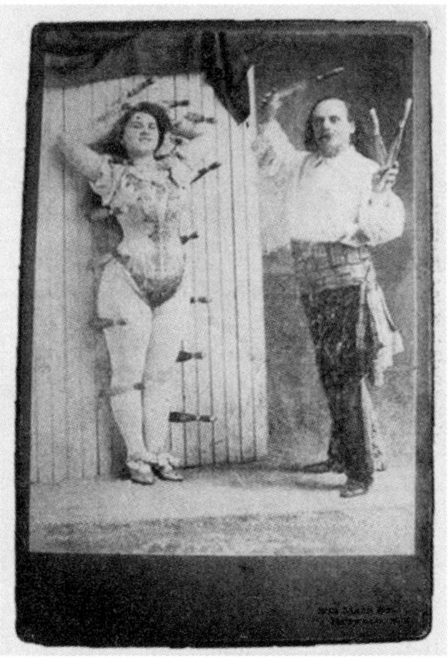

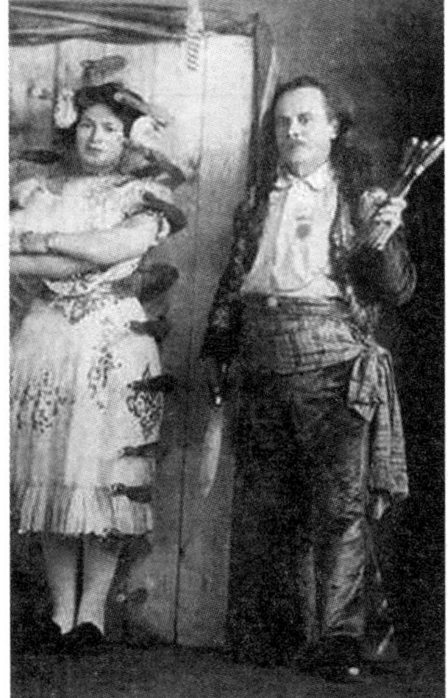

Figure 6. Additional photos from www.knifethrower.com.

the autograph as his sister Kate. It reads:

To Bert Cole
Sig. G. Arcaris and Sister Kate
Walter L. Main and Von Amberg Show
1890

Figure 8 shows additional cabinet cards from the Beckman collection taken by Eisenmann in New York City, by Ginther in Buffalo, NY, and by an unknown photographer.

We now had useful information about our knife thrower: (1) his first name started with a G, (2) the woman in the picture was his sister Kate, (3) he lived around 1890, (4) he performed for the circus, and (5) he was probably Italian as *Sig.* is the abbreviation for *Signore*, Italian for *Mister.*

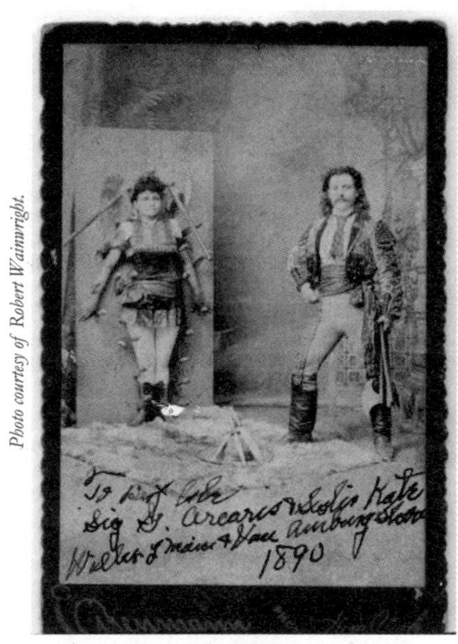

Photo courtesy of Robert Wainwright.

Figure 7.

These leads allowed us to quickly unearth the Arcaris family history through census records. In 1920, we found him living in Detroit with his wife Mary and their four children The census told us that Gustavo Arcaris (67) and his wife May (66) were both born in Italy. They immigrated to the U.S. in 1887, where they were naturalized in 1897. Gustavo's occupation was listed as actor in the theatre and the circus. The couple is listed with their three sons Salvatore (24), Louis (22), and George (18) and one daughter Virginia (23).

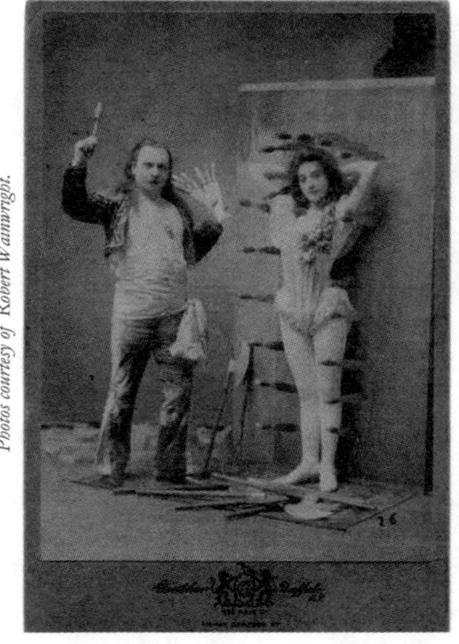

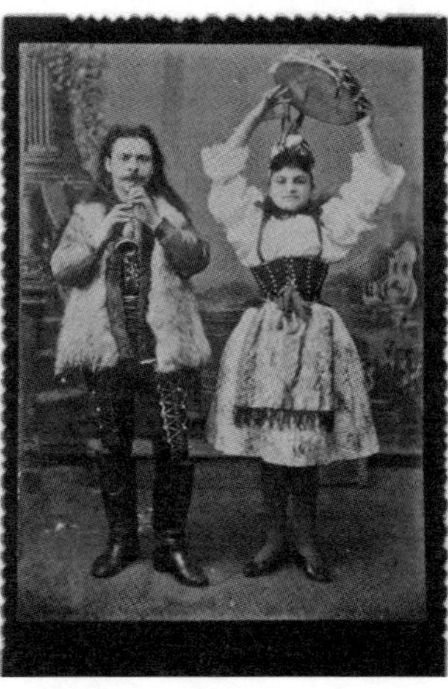

Photos courtesy of Robert Wainwright.

Figure 8. Photographs of Sig. G. Arcaris included in the Ronald G. Becker of Charles Eisenmann photographs at Syracuse University. Sig. Arcaris with his niece Rosena (left), and with his sister Kate (right).

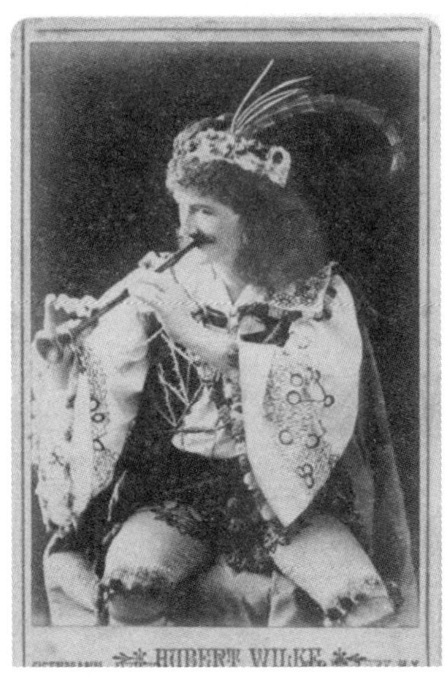

Figure 9. Hubert Wilke

The daughter was still with the circus, but the three sons had gone into the adding machine repair business. All their children had been born in Illinois. Also listed was Clara (24), Louis' wife.

By 1930, Gustavo and May Arcaris were living in Detroit with their youngest son George and his new wife Joy. Salvatore is listed next door with his wife Margarett and their three daughters Olive Mae (8), Esther Jane (4) and Bernie Catherine (2).

Knowing the names of the Arcaris children, we were also able to find the two oldest sons in the 1900 census living without their parents in a boarding house in Chicago. It is likely that Gustavo and May were on tour at the time, and left the boys to be cared for by friends and family. Their daughter Virginia was not listed with her brothers, so perhaps her parents had taken her with them on tour, not wanting to leave her at the boarding house.

We were temporarily thrown off the track by a comment on the back on one of the photo from the Becker collection that referenced Hubert Wilke. The collection had a cabinet card of Wilke, produced by Eisenmann, that closely resembled the picture of Arcaris playing his flute. (Compare the photo of Arcaris on the right of Figure 8 with the photo of Wilke in Figure 9.) We quickly discovered that this was a case of mistaken identity. Wilke was a contemporary of John Barrymore who performed on the state and screen during the 1920s. Wilke had no connection to Arcaris other than a passing resemblance.

In the meantime, 'Throw' (we had come to be on a first name basis with him) unearthed a playbill of an Arcaris performance for Winstanley and West. (Figure 10). We weren't able to find any info on this theatre group

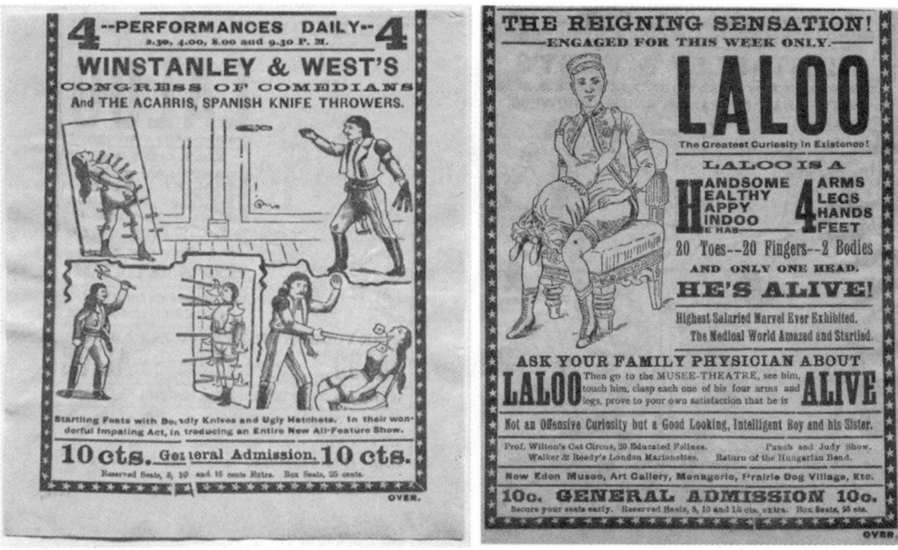

Figure 10. Winstanley and West's Circus Playbill featuring The Great Acaris' on the front (top), and Laloo the Happy Hindoo on the back (bottom).

or circus, but judging from Arcaris' appearance on the flyer, it probably dates to the late 1890s or early 1900s.

The other side of the playbill featured *Laloo, The Handsome, Healthy, Happy Hindoo; Not an Offensive Curiosity, but a Good Looking, Intelligent Boy and His Sister*. Laloo, an Indian Muslim, was born in Oovonin, Oudh, India in 1869 (some say 1874). His parasitic twin was nearly a perfect miniature man attached to his chest, although it lacked a head[1]. Laloo became a sensation, touring with the major circuses, including Barnum & Bailey and the Ringling Bros. in the late 1800s. In 1905 Laloo embarked on a tour with the Norris & Rowe Circus with the intent to tour Mexico, but the train crashed soon after leaving New York and Laloo died in the accident. (This tells us the playbill was printed before 1905). The cabinet card in Figure 11 of Laloo was taken by Charles Eisenmann.

Throwdini was determined to find the Arcaris family. "Where should I look?" he asked me. "I found over a hundred *Arcari* (plural of Arcaris) in the US phone books online." "Throw," I replied, "take *a stab* at it."

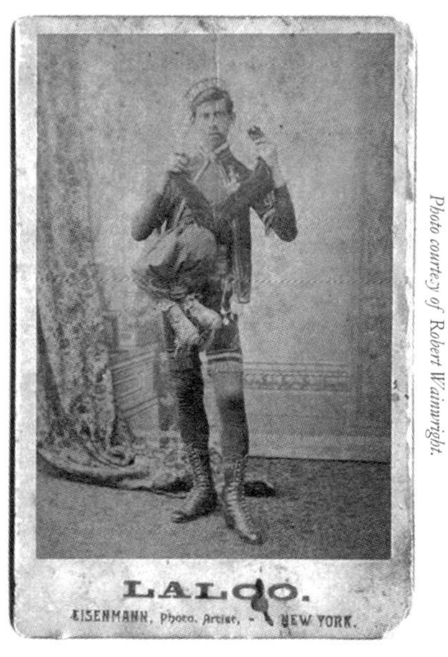

Photo courtesy of Robert Wainwright.

Figure 11. Laloo with his parasitic twin.

David is not called the best knife thrower in the world for nothing. He picked the name David Arcaris from the online records because David is his own first name. Bingo! David Arcaris was The Great One's great grandson, and he still had his great grandfather's old knives and his flute. He also had a poster advertising his act. (Figure 12). But he and the rest of the Arcari had no photographs of their famous ancestor. That was all about to change.

The Arcaris clan were amazed at the amount of information we had unearthed about their famous ancestor,

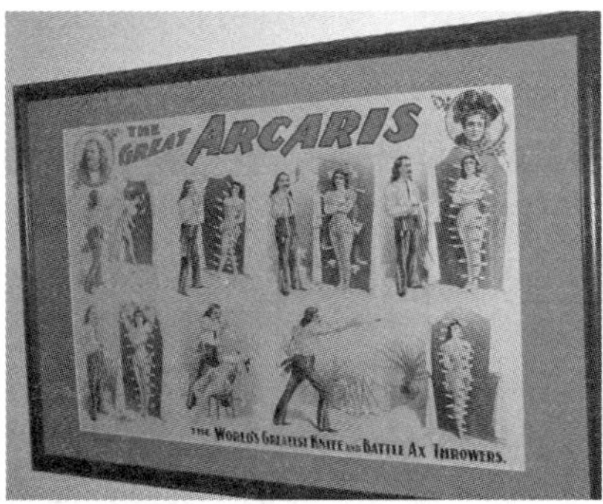

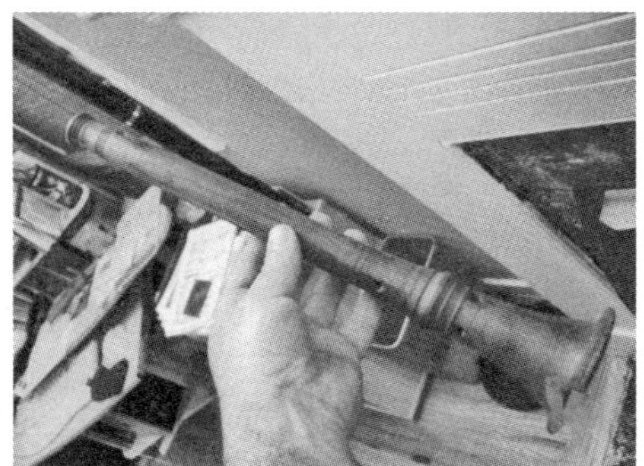

Photos courtesy of the Acaris family.

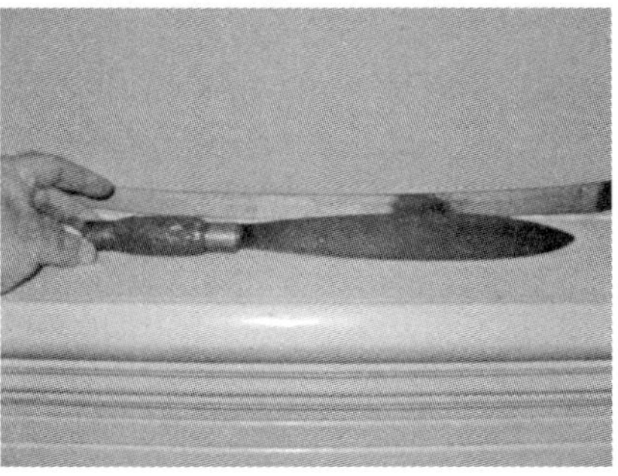

Figure 12. Arcaris' poster, his flute and his original knives.

starting with our search for information about the photographer who took his picture. As Jacqueline Arcaris expressed to Throw:

David,

I think this is amazing. How wonderful of you and Dr. Fitzpatrick to work so hard on our family's history. I can't tell you how many times I admired Gustavo's clarinets, knives, and battle axes as a child. My mother (Susan Lio Arcaris) has them still. I have always thought that Gustavo was discovered in Italy by Barnum and Bailey Circus. B & B liked him so much that they brought him to the US as part of their act. I also thought that his last name in Italy was really Arcari, and that the "s" was added on when he came to the US. My Godmother, Bernie (Arcaris) Rustemeyer also knows a lot of the history too.

Thank you for sharing yours and Dr. Fitzpatrick's hard work on the web. It is truly fascinating to see. I love all the old photographs.

Jacqueline (Jax) Arcaris

Charles Eisenmann

There is a postscript to this story. Since we featured the original picture of the then-unknown knife thrower we found on Dead Fred as one of our weekly quiz photos, we were contacted by Bob Wainwright, the great grandson of Charles Eisenmann. Bob has shared nearly 500 Eisenmann photographs with us, including pictures of Eisenmann's family and friends. In return we have helped Bob research Eisenmann's genealogy. A photo of Charles Eisenmann is shown in Figure 13.

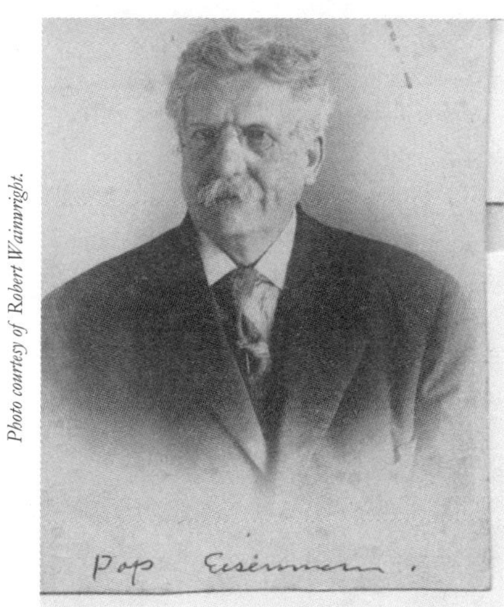

Photo courtesy of Robert Wainwright.

Figure 13. Charles Eisenmann 1845-1927.

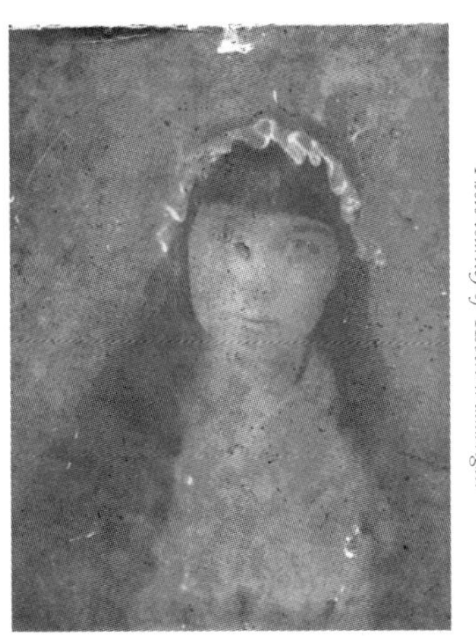

Photo courtesy of Robert Wainwright.

Figure 14. Possibly Amelia Gastauer, Charles Eisenmann's first wife who died in childbirth.

Charles Eisenmann was born in Germany in 1848s. According to census records, he came to the US in 1868 when he was 20 years old. As a young man he was apprenticed to the W. W. Washburn photography in New Orleans as a photograph printer. There, he married Amelia Gastauer on March 18, 1875, against her father's wishes. The couple moved to New York City immediately, where Amelia tragically died in childbirth along with their newborn son, Charles Jr. on November 28, 1875. The faded photograph in Figure 14 was discovered by Eisenmann's descendents on the back of a photograph of Eisenmann and his second wife. It is assumed to be of Amelia Gastauer, but it has never been conclusively identified.

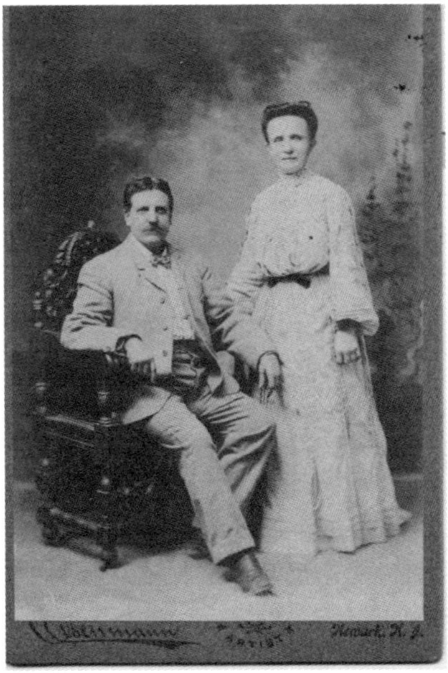

Photo courtesy of Robert Wainwright.

Figure 15. Charles and Dora Eisenmann, c. 1903.

Eisenmann married his second wife Dora Reicher on June 29, 1879 in Manhattan. See Figure 15. He was 31, she was 16. Dora's parents owned the boarding house where Eisenmann lived. At the time Eisenmann and Dora married, her parents had just died leaving Dora as the oldest of seven children. Eisenmann supported Dora and her siblings while they raised eight children of their own, seven daughters and one son.

Eisenmann continued in the photography business, photographing many stage actors, circus performers, and other notables of his day. He pho-

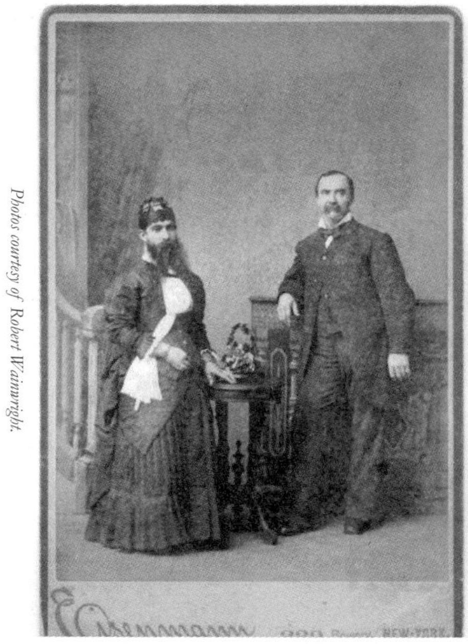

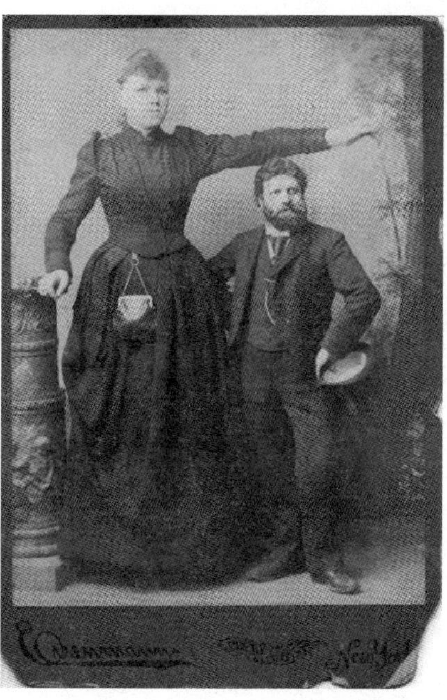

Photos courtesy of Robert Wainwright.

Figure 16. Top: Madame Jane Devere, possibly with her manager and husband J. W. Devere. Bottom: Eisenmann photographed with a giantess in the 1890s.

tographed the famous as well as obscure. His subjects included Mark Twain, P. T. Barnum, and circus performers like General Tom Thumb, Jo Jo the Dog-faced Boy, the Wild Men of Borneo, Madame Devere the Bearded Lady, and the Skeleton Man. He also photographed Siamese twins, giants, dwarfs, the obese, skeleton men and women, armless and legless "wonders," albinos, and tattoo artists. (Figure 16.) While many of these "freaks" were genuine, many were not, having been created out of the imagination and costuming talents of sideshow managers[2].

In the late 1890s Eisenmann sold an interest in his studio to George Wendt, his business partner who later became his son-in-law. By this time, the albumen print was losing popularity in favor of the silver gelatin print. (See the Chapter The History of Photography, Part II, The Birth of Paper Photography). After financial reversals put the company out of business in

1901, Eisenmann became the head photographer for the Dupont Corporation. Charles Eisenmann died in December 8, 1927 at the age of 78.

References

1. phreeque.tripod.com/laloo.html

2. Syracuse University Digital Projects Library, The Ronald G. Becker Collection of Charles Eisenmann Photographs, library.syr.edu/information/spcollections/digital/eisenmann/

Reach Out and Touch Someone

After you've thoroughly researched a photo on the Internet, you may still have unanswered questions. How can you get more information? How about obtaining it the old fashioned way over the telephone?

While it is more convenient to email historical societies and genealogical organizations with your questions, email has its limitations. When you send someone an email, it is not usually possible to know whether he has received or read your message. You cannot be sure when you will get a reply, if at all. The emails you send are limited in length and complexity, and do not allow a real-time flow of information. Nuances are lost in the transmission.

Phoning is better for people who are into immediate gratification. If you call someone, you know if he answers, you can be redirected if you are talking to the wrong person, and you can ask new questions that come to mind as you get answers to the old ones. You can exchange more information in a shorter period of time. In my experience, the people I talk to on the phone are more likely to get personally interested in my search and help me if they can hear the interest in my own voice.

The postcard in Figure 1 features an appealing picture of a young woman dressed as a cowgirl seated on an outcrop of rock. It was submitted to us by Gwen Upton for use as a photo quiz on our Forensic Genealogy

Used by permission of Gwen Upton.

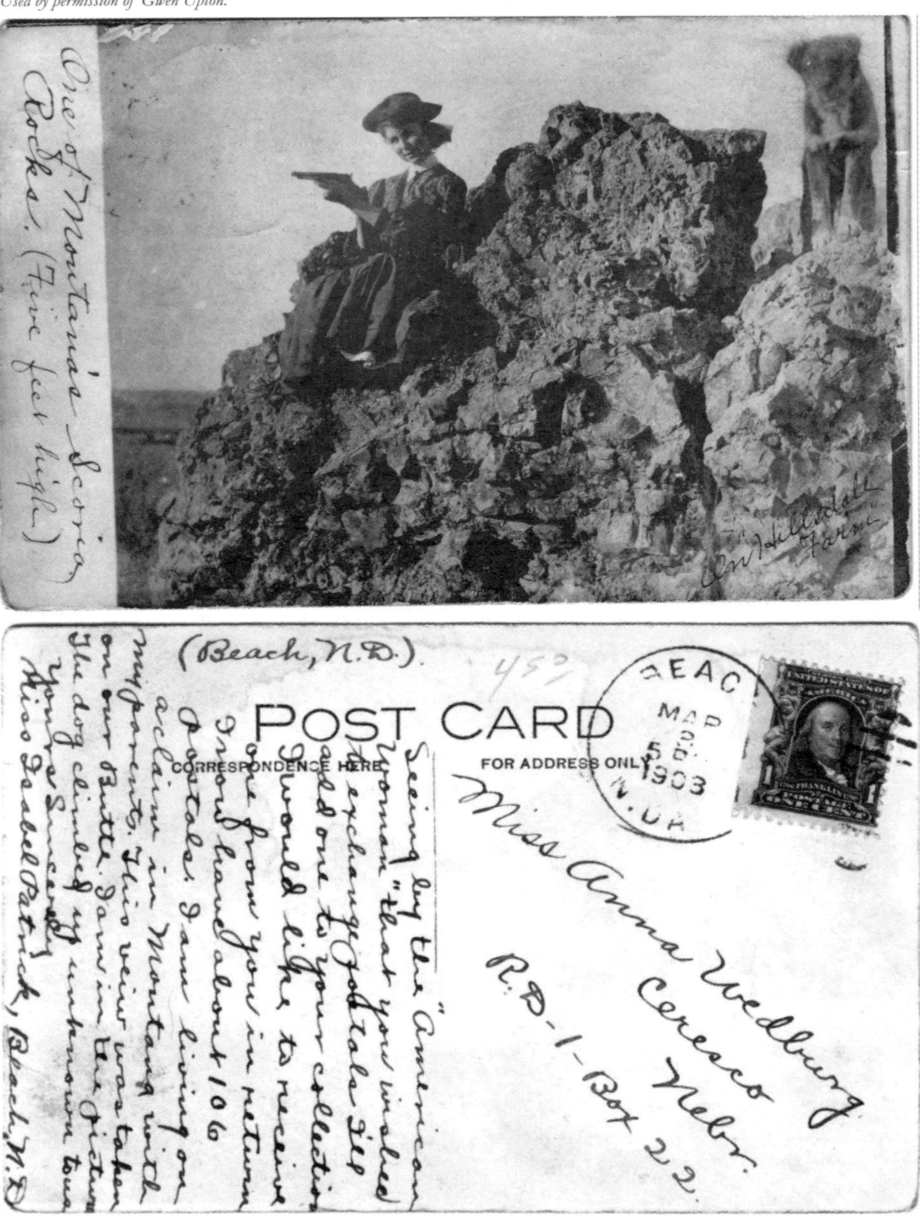

Figure 1. The front and back of the postcard.

website. The card, postmarked Beach, ND, March 8, 1903 is addressed to Miss Anna Wedburg, Ceresco, Nebr., RD-1-Box-22.

The message reads:

Seeing by the "American Woman" that you wished to exchange postals, I'll add one to your collection. I would like to receive one from you in return. I now have about 106 postals. I am living on a claim in Montana with my parents. This view was taken on our butte. I am in the picture. The dog climbed up unknown to us.

Yours sincerely,

Miss Isabel Patrick
Beach, N.D.

The town was not named Beach because it is located on a body of water. According to the official Beach, ND website www.beach.nd.com, "Beach is named for Captain Warren Beach of the Eleventh Infantry who accompanied the Stanley railroad survey expedition ... in 1873. It is the county seat of Golden Valley County. Beach showed little growth in early years. It was just a small mark in the landscape, and until the Land Survey settled the question, no one was sure if it was in North Dakota or Montana." As of 2000, Beach had a population of about 1,100 people. The nearest city with a population of over 50,000 is Rapid City, SD, 200 miles away. (Figure 2.)

We were able to find quite a bit of information about the Patrick family through conventional sources. The Patrick family was listed in both the 1900 and 1910 census records, available on the Internet through several websites, including www.Ancestry.com. The censuses indicated that Sarah Isabel Patrick was born in October 1891 in Dakota, oldest child of William Patrick (b. January 1862, Wisconsin) and Maggie (b. November 1865, Ireland). Isabel had three siblings: Cynthia E. (b. September 1894), W. Hunter (b. September 1896) and Wayne W. (b. April 1898). She was named after her grandmother Isabel Patrick, b. March 1821 in Ireland, who also appeared in the 1900 census living next door.

By 1910, the older Isabel is no longer listed. Isabel Jr. at 19 years old is listed as living next door to her family and married to Freeman Whittaker, a

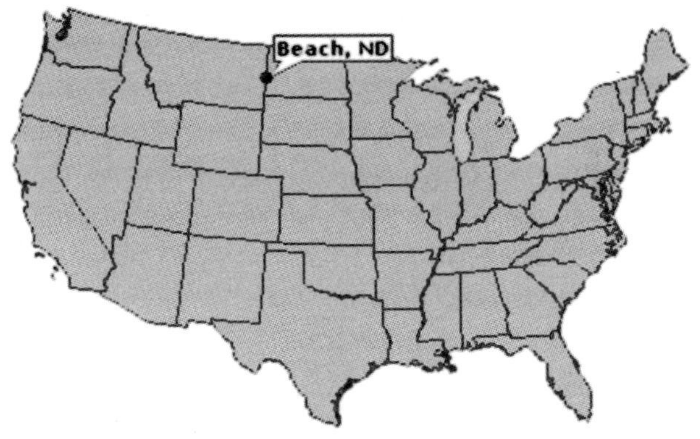

Figure 2. Beach is on the North Dakota/Montana border.

21-year-old drayman. The census indicates that he served in WWI, as did Isabel's two brothers.

Isabel's great grandchildren would probably be alive today and we could return the picture to them - if only we could find out where they lived. But by the 1920 census, the Patrick family had disappeared from Beach. Because the family name Patrick is so common, without further information, it would be difficult to locate them elsewhere.

I decided that the quickest way to find out what happened to the Patrick family would be to telephone the public library at the number listed on the Beach city website. The librarian JoAnn Tesher would undoubtedly know everyone in town, including the Patrick family - if they still lived in the area. It was 10 am on a Wednesday morning, and I let the phone ring 100 times. No one answered.

Resorting to email, I spent a half hour composing a message on the "Request More Information" page on the Beach site. But to my horror I found the page had no Submit button. Against my better judgment, I clicked on the only alternative, the Reset button, and *poof* my work of art was gone!

I tried again, recomposing the email from memory, but this did not have the magical effect of making a Submit button appear at the bottom of the page.

I was now on a mission from god. Next stop was the Beach, ND county agent's office. Someone in Beach finally answered the phone (the telephonic equivalent to a Submit button). I was directed to call Sandy at the Golden Valley Historical Society.

The clerk reassured me that someone was there because she could see the Open sign in the window., directly across the street.

Sandy was very pleasant and knowledgable about Beach history. But no, she didn't know of any Patrick family in the area. Since the claims were archived by claim number and not by name of claimant, it would be difficult for her to look up the info about the Patrick family. Thanking her for her help, I offered to scan the photo and send it to her for the Historical Society but she refused. "Thanks", she said, "but we don't have email."

Before my astonishment had subsided at finding a place in the civilized world without email, the phone was abruptly grabbed by another woman who introduced herself as Joan Tescher. "Oh," I exclaimed, "you're the librarian! I bet that's why you didn't answer the phone at the library - you were on your way over to have lunch with Sandy, right?"

"No," Joan responded. "You must mean *JoAnn* Tescher. She's the wife of my nephew and married into the family. I'm a *real* Tescher." We chatted briefly about the weather and the fact that there were only 1,500 people in the entire Golden Valley County. *(Gosh I thought, there are more people than that living in my housing complex.)* No, Joan didn't know of any Patrick family in the area.

But Joan did have a book *The Golden Valley Pioneers* that contained information on the Patricks, with pictures of Isabel, her parents, her sister Cynthia, and her two brothers, Hunter and Wayne. (Figure 3.) Joan read to me from the book:

William and Margaret Patrick settled on Section 8-13-60 in Wibaux County in about 1906. They lived in a five-room cottage with their four children: Isabel, Cynthia, Hunter, and Wayne.

Patrick bought a half interest in a flour mill in Beach, commuting daily in a horse drawn buggy. As soon as the homestead was proved up, the family moved to Beach to live.

WILLIAM J. PATRICK

William and Margaret Patrick settled on Sec. 8-13-60 in Wibaux County in about 1906. They lived in a five-room cottage with their four children: Isabelle, Cynthia, Hunter and Wayne.

Patrick bought half interest in a flour mill in Beach, commuting daily in a horse drawn buggy. As soon as the homestead was proved up, the family moved to Beach to live.

Patrick also clerked in Heath's Grocery Store in 1911, then held office as sheriff. His wife was an invalid in a wheelchair.

Their sons, Hunter and Wayne, both served in France during the war, while their father worked in Seattle. He leased the farm to Ben Simonson,

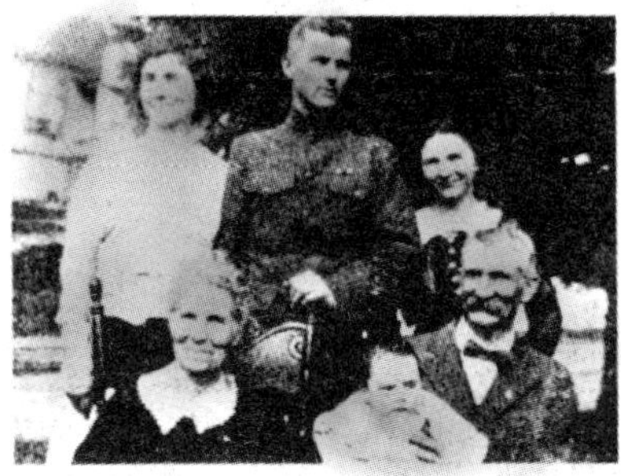

The W. J. Patrick Family, Less Hunter. *Front Row, L. to R.:* Mrs. Patrick, Mr. Patrick (holding Wallace Preston). *Back:* Isabelle, Wayne and Cynthia.

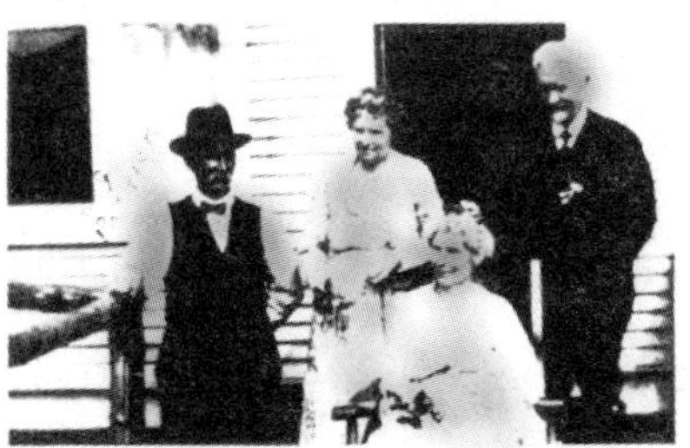

W. J. Patrick, Minnie Volin, Margaret Patrick and Robert Patrick. 1933

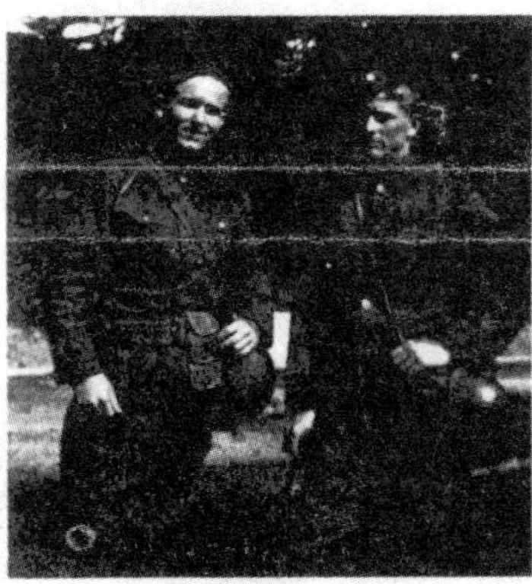

William H. Patrick and Wayne W. Patrick. A Job Well Done. Returning Home from France after World War II. March 1919.

whose son Erwin now holds the lease on the land.

Mrs. Patrick died in 1929, after not being able to walk for over 30 years. Patrick died in 1941 at age 79.

Figure 3. The story of the Patrick family as found in The Golden Valle Pioneers.

Patrick also clerked in Heath's grocery store in 1911, then held office as sheriff. His wife was an invalid in a wheelchair.

Their sons, Hunter and Wayne, served in France during the War, while their father worked in Seattle. He leased the farm to Ben Simonson, whose son Erwin now holds the lease on the land.

Mrs. Patrick died in 1929, after not being able to walk for over thirty years. Patrick died in 1941 at age 79.

This was more information than I could have hoped for!

Without thinking, I asked her if she would mind scanning the page from her Golden Valley book and emailing it to me to use for the upcoming quiz. "No," she reminded me, "I can't do that, we don't have email."

"Then how about xeroxing it and sending it to me in the regular mail?," I asked. "You *do* have a Xerox machine, don't you?"

A few days later, an envelope arrived with a Beach postmark, containing a xerox of the page in the book with the information about the Patrick family.

We had guests most of that week and unfortunately when I went to look for the letter a few days later I couldn't find it. So I called the Historical Society back and asked Sandy a rhetorical question, "You remember me?" (Of course I thought, the call from that woman in California was probable on the front page of the local paper all week. They are probably still talking about it.)

I told her about my predicament and asked if she would kindly xerox the page again (I had already established they had a Xerox machine) and fax it to me. I thought to myself that a fax of a xerox would look pretty bad when it was posted at low resolution on our website, but I concluded that it would be better than nothing.

Well, it turns out this was not a problem at all. They don't have a fax.

Fortunately, I was able to find the letter. It was in my clothes basket.

CASE STUDY

This Photo Is OK!

= Remember to Look at the Back! = The Photographer =
= Don't Be Afraid to Contact the Experts =

A photograph can provide an interesting window into an ancestor's life. All too often, however, the ancestor has left no information about a picture, so that it is up to us to deduce its story. Fortunately, we have many resources to draw on to look for clues where, when, and why a photo was taken. These include both conventional materials such as city directories, and innovative resources such as eBay and Amazon.com. Sometimes the advice of an expert is only a mouse-click away.

The photograph in Figure 1 was submitted as a possible quiz photo by Linda Williams, one of our regular visitors to the weekly photo contests we host at www.forensicgenealogy.info. The picture is rich in detail and full of clues about its origin. It evidently depicts an event in a small town around the turn of the 20th century. It seems the crowd in the picture is waiting for a parade to begin. There are flags flying and two columns of men lined up in the middle of the street ready to start the march, each with a ribbon on his vest. Yet Linda did not know why it was among her great grandmother's papers nor what role, if any, her great grandmother's family played in the event. The back of the photo is shown in Figure 2.

Figure 1.

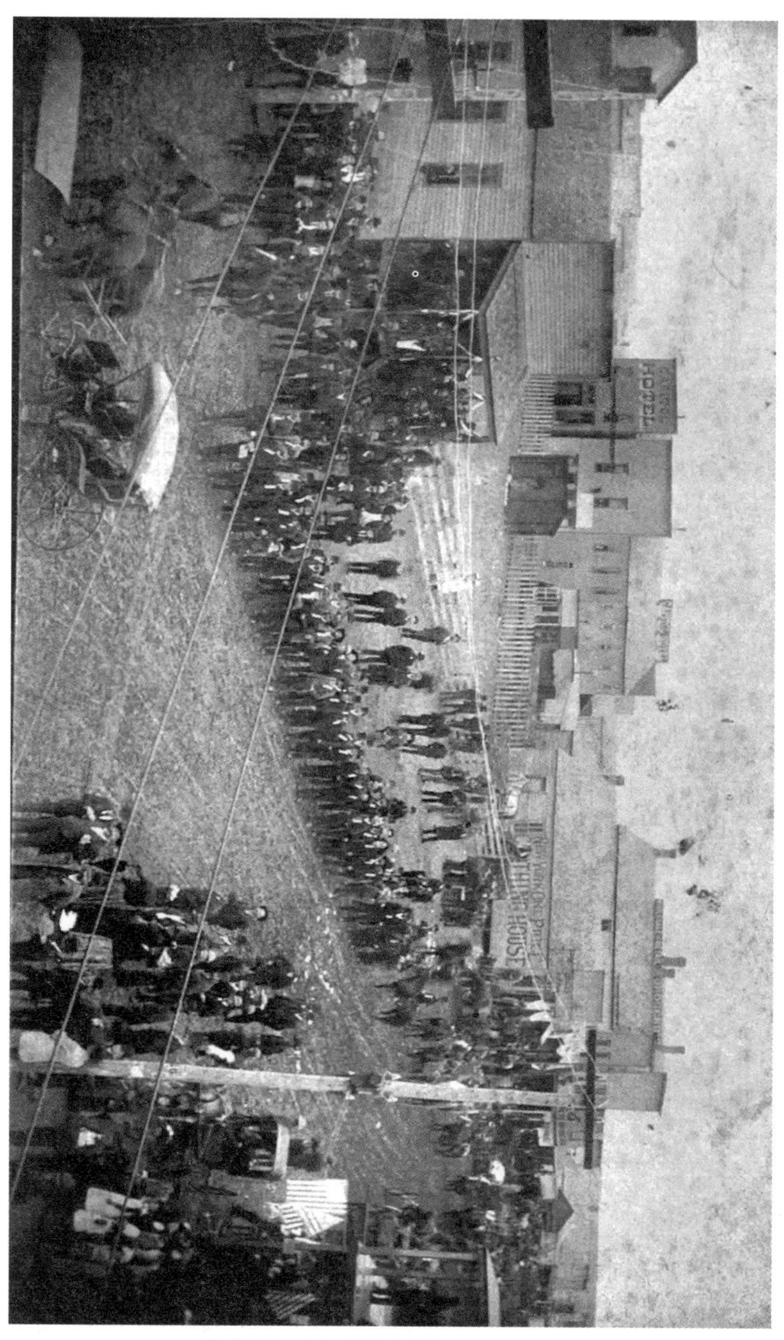

Used with permission of Linda Williams.

A good first step in analyzing a photograph is to note any writing that appears in or on the picture. The writing on our photograph offers a number of tantalizing clues. There are several buildings that can be identified: The New York One Price Clothing House, The Capitol Hotel, and a wholesale and retail grocery. A high resolution scan of the far right of the photograph reveals a sign reading 'stationery'. (See the enlargements in Figure 3.) There is also writing on the back that provides a specific location, at least for the photographer's studio: *Mitchell and DeGroff's Pioneer Photograph Studio, Harrison Ave., Guthrie, Ind. Ter.*

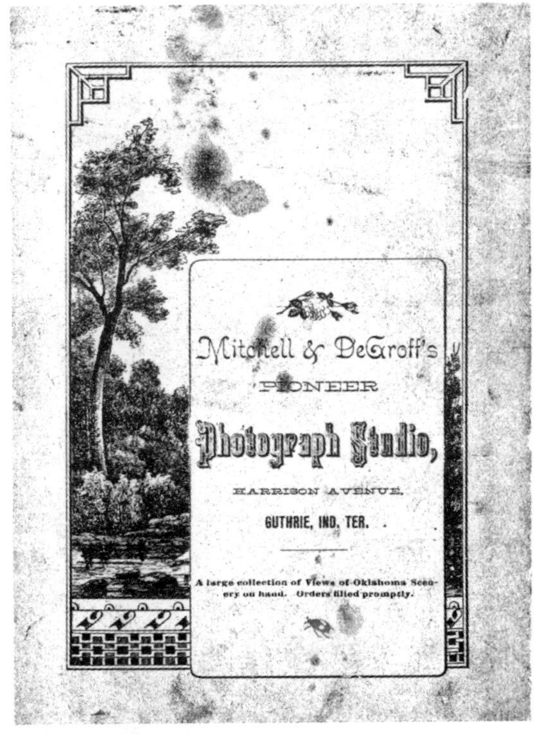

Figure 2.

Searching Google on the keywords *Guthrie* and *history* yields many websites describing Guthrie as a key town in the Oklahoma Land Run that occurred on April 22, 1889. Guthrie was soon to become the Oklahoma Territorial capital, and later first state capital.

For example, the website www.sandplum.com/guthrie/landrun.htm offers an historical background on the Land Run compiled by the Oklahoma Historical Society. The website says that on March 2, 1889, two days before he left office, President Grover Cleveland signed the Springer Amendment to the Indian Appropriations Bill, opening the Unassigned Lands of the Indian Territory to permanent settlement. The new President, Benjamin Harrison, set the date and the time for the land run as noon, April 22, 1889.

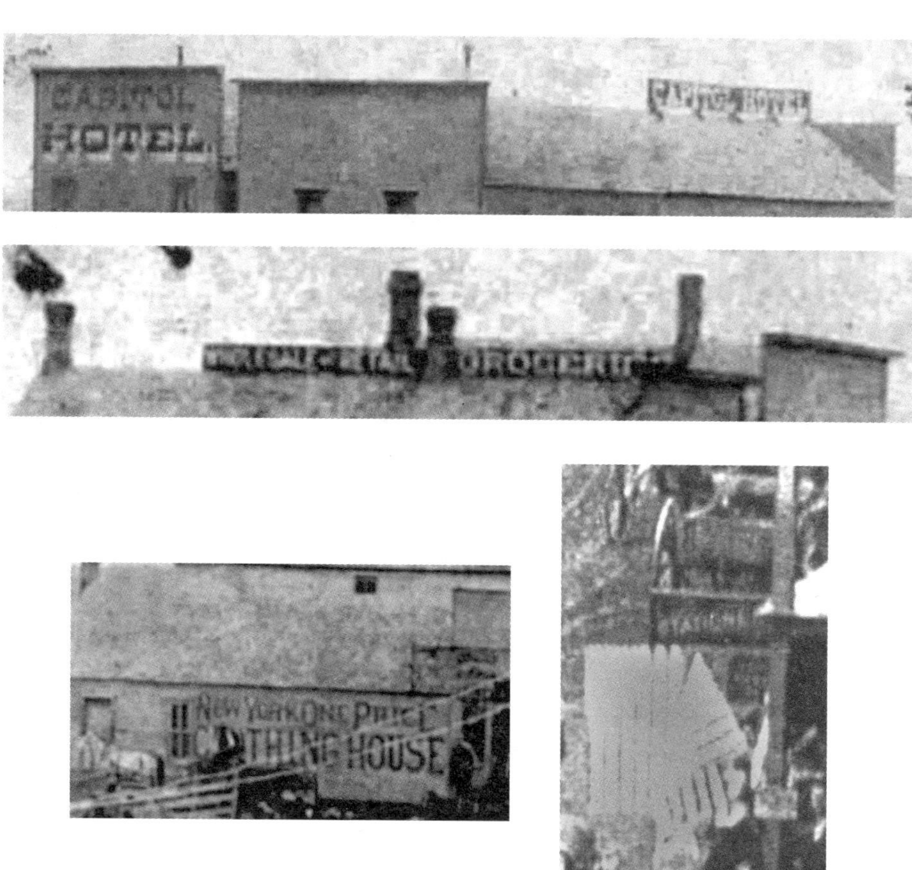

Figure 3. Building that can be identified from writing in the picture. Top: The Capitol Hotel; Second from top: Wholesale and retail grocery store; Above left: New York One Price Clothing Store; Above right: Stationery store.

The land was available to homesteaders on a first come, first served basis. Land-seekers were allowed to enter the district at that time, find a claim, and file at the U.S. Land Office in Guthrie or Kingfisher, approximately 30 miles to the west. These were the only locations designated under the Indians Appropriations Act until later in 1889 when one was established in Oklahoma city[1]. A picture of a typical claim is shown in Figure 4[2].

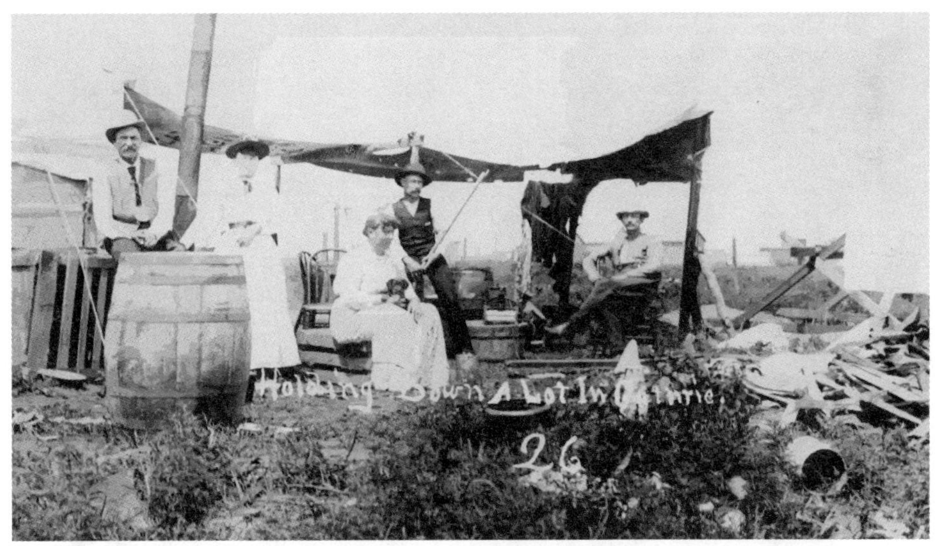

Figure 4. Holding down a lot in Guthrie, Indian Territory, 1889[2].

An estimated 50,000 to 75,000 people participated in the land run, entering the territory on noon of that day by foot, in covered wagons, on horseback, and by train. They joined a significant number who had illegally entered the territory earlier to get the best claims. These early arrivals were called 'sooners'. The population of Guthrie before the rush consisted of soldiers, deputy marshals, government officials, and railroad personnel; by nightfall it had swelled to 10,000 to 15,000 people living in tents or crude shacks. The earliest date the photo could have been taken was April 22, 1889, although the appearance of the town with streets and businesses implies that it was taken somewhat later.

Among the websites listed by Google were several that had photographs of early Guthrie. A picture on www.treasurenet.com/images/americanwest/westok.html (Figure 5) taken in 1893 from E. Harrison Ave. at 1st St. shows many brick and stone buildings. The structures in our photo are not as sophisticated, indicating that the picture was probably taken earlier. Further supporting this earlier date, the website homepages.rootsweb.com/~tammie/hotels/hotels.htm reports that the Capitol Hotel (seen to the left in our photo) burned down April 15, 1893. We now know the photo was taken between April 22, 1889 and April 15, 1893.

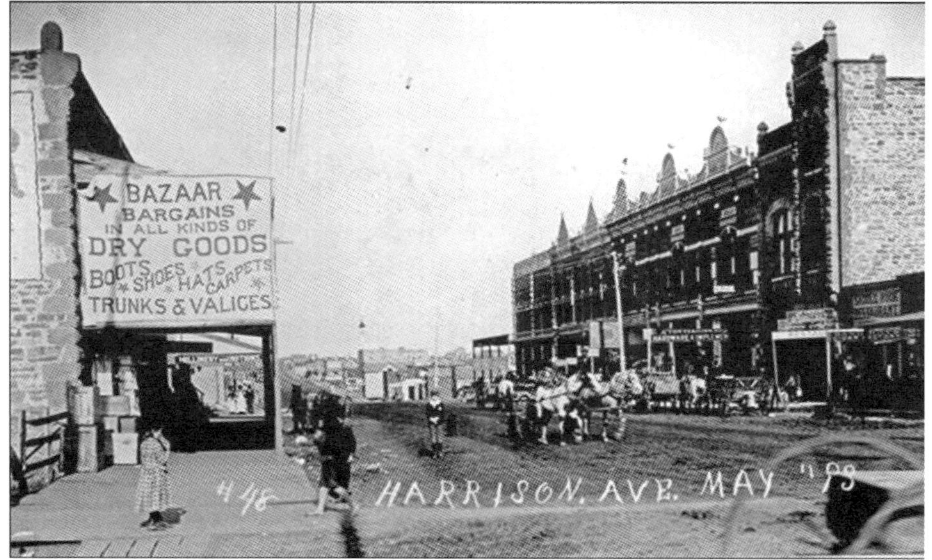

Figure 5. Photo of Harrison Ave. in downtown Guthrie taken in 1893[3].

Another website homepages.rootsweb.com/~tammie/logan.htm produced by Google offers several early Guthrie city directories that list some of the businesses in the picture. The 1890 directory includes the Capitol Hotel and Cohen and Strauss' New York Clothing House. The empty lot in the middle of the picture can be identified as part of the government acre and the crowded building to the left as the U.S. Government Land Office.

The locations given for these establishments allow us to draw a preliminary sketch of the layout of the town, shown below. Government acre was the rectangle bounded by 1st St. and 2nd St. on the east and west, respectively, and Oklahoma and Harrison Aves. on the north and south. (See Figure 6.) The U.S. Land Office was located at the northwest corner of the government acre, the Capitol Hotel on the southeast corner. The 1890 directory lists the NY Clothing House as being on the southwest corner. But according to other directories and city maps, the clothing store was located on the east side of Second St. between Oklahoma and Harrison and the Bluebelle Saloon was located at the southwest corner of the government acre, several buildings to the south of the clothing store. A modern map of downtown Guthrie[2] found on www.mapquest.com shows that the town still has the same layout today. Combining the information provided by the map with the identification of the various businesses in the picture using the city directories, we can say that the picture was taken from the second of two wooden frame structures that housed the Commercial Bank on the northwest corner of Oklahoma Ave. and 2nd St[3]. The photographer was facing south-southeast.

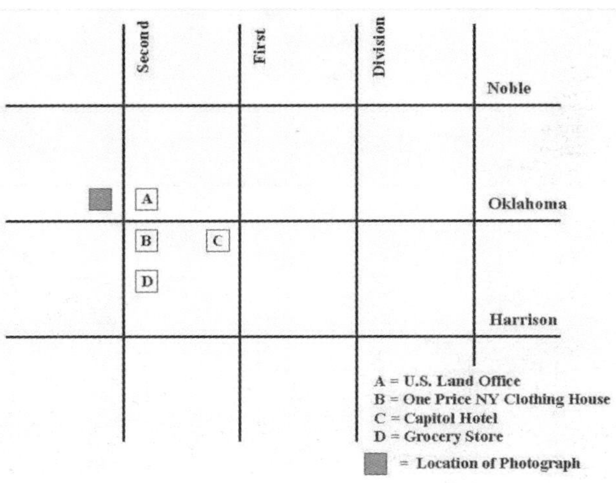

Figure 6. Sketch of downtown Guthrie.

Early Guthrie city directories sometimes omit businesses that were known from other photographs and historical accounts to be present in the early days of the town. This probably reflects the rapid and often chaotic changes Guthrie was experiencing. Some businesses are only listed by name or by their approximate locations between major streets. Yet the directories still provide enough information to identify establishments that appear in the mystery picture without legible signage.

The website www.amazon.com is a valuable research tool for identifying books on just about any topic. A search on Amazon for books on Guthrie[4] produced *Birth of Guthrie: Oklahoma's Run of 1889 and Life in Guthrie in 1889 and the 1890's,* by Lloyd H. McGuire, Jr. A search on Google produced contact information for the author on www.sandplum.com/guthrie/more.htm. Mr. McGuire has researched Guthrie for many years, and proved to be very generous in sharing his wealth of knowledge about the town.

Table 1. Listings for S 2nd St. in the 1889 Guthrie City Directory[5].

Last Name	First Name	Business	No.	Street
Way	John F.	lawyer	2	S. 2nd
Thomas	J. D.	boots & shoes	4	S. 2nd
Lindsay, Putnam & Widmer		lawyers	4	S. 2nd
Thomas	W. D.	seeds	4 1/2	S. 2nd
Lantz	N.	baker & confectnr	6	S. 2nd
Todd	H. D.	lawyer	6	S. 2nd
Blackburn & McCombs		real estate	6	S. 2nd
Shawhan & Churchill		cigars & tobacco	8	S. 2nd
Lauck & Lauck		lawyers	8	S. 2nd
Halley, Caruthers & Rucker		lawyers	10	S. 2nd
Willis & Rowe		lawyers	10	S. 2nd
Parker	C. C.	books & stationery	12	S. 2nd
Joy & Smith		cigars & tobacco	18	S. 2nd
Pye	James	merchant tailor	26	S. 2nd
Rhodes & Co.		cigars & tobacco	26	S. 2nd
Day, Driscoll & Co		real estate	28	S. 2nd
Arrell, Simms & Co.		real estate	28	S. 2nd

The August 1889 city directory found in Mr. McGuire's book provides the names of the businesses with the lowest street numbers along 2nd St. just south of Oklahoma Ave. seen in Table 1. The street numbers are all even since there were no establishments located across the street in the vacant area included in the government acre. There were other businesses on the east side of 2nd St. between Oklahoma and Harrison Aves., but they cannot be matched with the photo because they are listed in the directory without street numbers. These include Hamilton, Rowan and Co. stationers who might account for the sign to the far right of the photo.

The website www.sandplum.com/guthrie /hm03.htm offers a clue that our mystery photo was taken before the end of 1890 when the DeFord building was constructed at the original location of the NY Clothing Store. The wall of the DeFord building that would have been facing the camera is described as, "featuring contrasting-colored arched windows with worked wooden fans above corbelled brick, with a small turret marking the south". It is clear that the DeFord building had not yet been built, so that we can narrow the date of the photo to between April 22, 1889 when the land run occurred, and sometime in late 1890, before the NY One Price Clothing Store's frame building was torn down.

One clue that we have not used yet is the photographer's logo on the back of the photograph. Mitchell and deGroff photographers were listed in the 1889 Guthrie directory as one of the earliest photography studios in town, at 212 W. Harrison Ave. The address on the back of our photograph references Indian Territory. This could indicate that the photo was taken before May 2, 1890, when the settlers received word that the "Unassigned Lands" had been organized into the Oklahoma Territory. But it is also possible that the photographers had surplus card stock that was printed before this date that they continued using.

According to Mr. McGuire, Guthrie was originally laid out in 300 ft x 300 ft squares, with the location of the U.S. Land Office at the southwest corner of the intersection of Oklahoma and Division. However, it was soon realized that the Land Office was not easily visible to settlers arriving at the train depot, so that the office was moved 500 feet to the west, to the southeast corner of Oklahoma Ave. and 2nd St., moving 2nd St. 100 feet eastward and causing all blocks between 1st St. and 2nd St. to be shortened to 200 ft. Although the area bounded by Oklahoma, Harrison, 1st St. and 2nd St. became known as the 'government acre', it was 200 ft. x 300 ft., much larger than an acre (207.8 ft x 207.8 ft). The north half of the 'government acre' was an open space known as 'Hell's Half Acre'.

Guthrie was a very progressive new city that developed rapidly during its first few months. Wooden frame structures went up within a few days after the rush[6]. Guthrie's first brick building housing the McNeal Bank was

Used with permission of Lloyd McGuire, Jr.

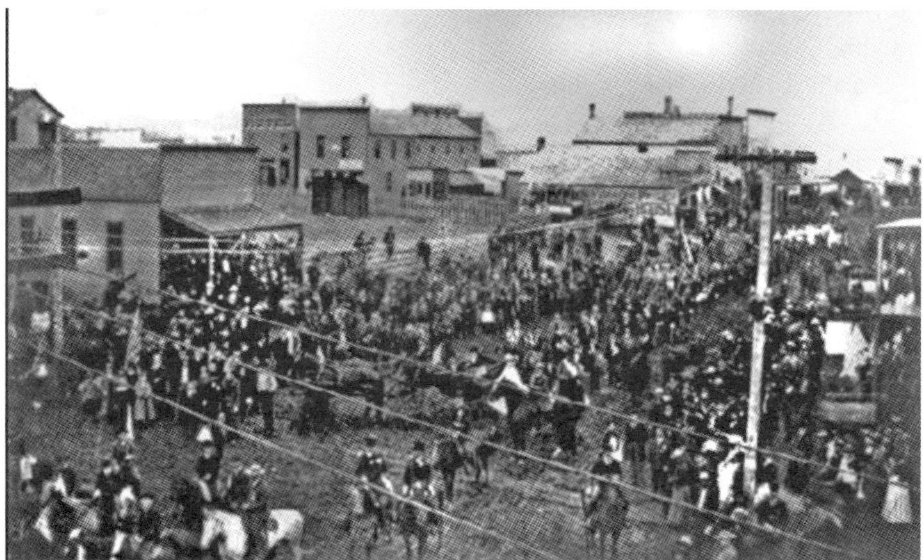

Figure 7. Looking southeast from 2nd St and Oklahoma towards the U.S. Land Office, Hell's Half Acre, Capitol Hotel and Blue Bell Saloon[2].

erected between May and August 1889 on the northwest corner of 1st St. and Oklahoma Ave. The Commercial Bank, the second brick structure in Guthrie, was completed in October 1889 on the northeast corner of 2nd St. and Oklahoma Ave. The bank was relocated to this brick structure from an earlier wooden frame building across the street on the northwest corner of the intersection[7].

Mr. McGuire's book has 180 photographs of Guthrie including 88 'then-and-now' photos. He contracted with Bob Bozarth, Guthrie photographer, for use of early day 'then' pictures from Mr. Bozarth's collection, and for Mr. Bozarth to photograph the modern-day 'now' pictures in matching locations.

Two of the early-day pictures might have been taken at the same event as the one in the picture we are investigating. The first photograph (Figure 7) apparently shows the same parade a few moments after our picture was taken, with many people standing in the same places.

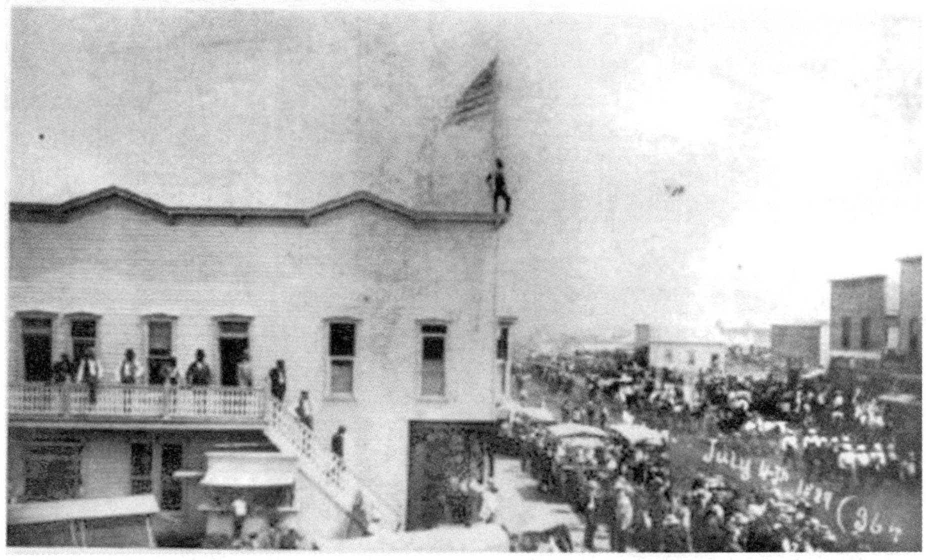

Figure 8. Looking north past Reeves Bros. Casino on left, and towards theU.S. Land Office at the end of the block with the 4th of July parade 1889, between. To the right, out of view, is the Blue Belle Saloon[2].

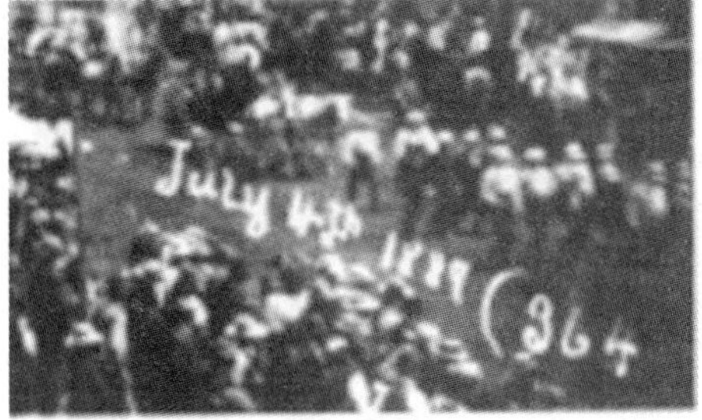

Figure 9.

The book also provides a picture of the Reeves Bros. Casino taken from a different location further down 2nd St. facing northeast. (Figure 8.) The writing in the corner of this casino picture states that it was taken on July 4, 1889. (Figure 9.) If we can show that the mystery picture and its twin feature the same parade as the casino picture, and if we can verify that the date on the casino picture is correct, we will have a date for our photo.

According to Mr. McGuire's book[9], there were four known parades held in Guthrie between the date of the Land Run in April 1889 and early to mid 1890, when the NY Clothing House frame structure was torn down. These were Decoration Day in May 1889 (now known as Memorial Day),

July 4th, 1889, April 22, 1890, the first anniversary of the run, and July 4th, 1890. While the organization of the Oklahoma Territory would also have been cause for celebration, none was held. On April 22, 1890, Guthrie's first anniversary, its citizens awaited a rider from the telegraph office at the train depot to bring word that Congress had made the 'Unorganized Territory' into an 'Organized Territory', thus creating the Oklahoma Territory with Guthrie as its capital. But no word came until May 2. Because it was not certain when the news would arrive, the town could not have held a parade on this date, eliminating it as a possible occasion for the picture[10].

The rapid construction of the town during its first few months provides a valuable timeline against which we can compare our three pictures to determine a date. Between May 1889 and July 1889 many new buildings were constructed. By July 1890, there was an enormous difference in the appearance of the town compared to its early days. If the same buildings (and *only* the same buildings) appear in the three photos, we can be reasonably certain that they were all taken at the same parade.

The views of the town offered by the two matching photographs and the Reeves Bros Casino photograph partially overlap, so that many of the buildings along the east side of Second Ave. between Oklahoma and Harrison are visible in all of them. In the Reeves Bros. Casino photograph, the U. S. Land Office, located on the northwest corner of the government acre, appears to the center right, the first building north of the gap on the opposite side of 2nd St. In the mystery picture and its twin, both the U.S. Land Office and the government acre are across the street from the photographer. These two photos show buildings of three different heights on the other side of the government acre along 2nd St., the smallest one identified as the New York Clothing House and the tallest one with the 'Wholesale and Retail Groceries' sign across the top. All three of these buildings (and no others) also appear in the casino photograph. Because the three photographs show the same number and arrangement of buildings (and the same paraders and spectators), it's reasonable to say that they were taken on the same date and depict the same parade. Now the task is to determine if the parade was the one held on July 4, 1889.

Confirming the date on the Reeves Bros.' casino picture as July 4, 1889 would probably be easier if more of the town were visible in the mystery picture or its twin. The brick Commercial Bank building was completed in October 1889 on the northeast corner of Oklahoma Ave. and 2nd St[11]. Being able to observe the stage of construction of the bank building could have given us an approximate date when it was taken, but the corner is just out of view to the left of the photograph. Also in 1889, the Merchants Bank was established on the southwest corner of the intersection across Oklahoma St. from the photographer. However, it is not visible either. The two-story porch-like structure seen to the far right of our picture is not a building in the process of being constructed, it is probably a viewing stand for the parade. The Merchants Bank building was already completed by July 4, 1889 and did not have a second story porch. See Figure 10 for a photograph[12] of the bank dated May 28.

There is still a clue we have not used. Some of the photographs in Mr. McGuire's book have numbers written on them along with the dates they were taken. Since they are all written in the same handwriting, they were

Used with permission of Lloyd McGuire, Jr.

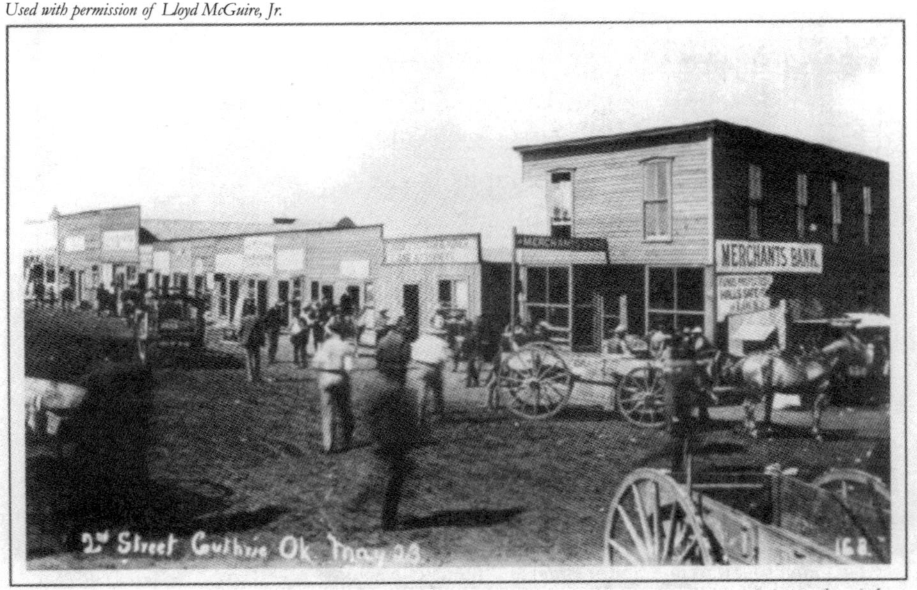

Figure 10. The Merchant Bank Building.

Numbers and Dates of Photographs

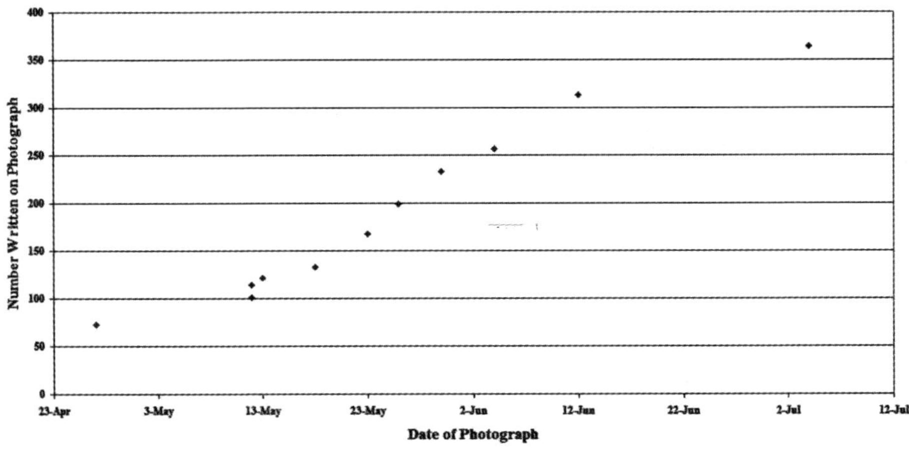

Figure 10.

probably all taken by the same photographer. Presumably these numbers represent the order in which the pictures were taken. By tracking the numbers on the photographs as a function of their dates, we can see if the number on the Reeves Bros.' photo is consistent with the July 4, 1889 date.

The graph in Figure 11 plots the numbers on the photographs versus their dates. It's clear that the date and number on the casino picture (July 4, #364) fit in well with those of the others. The photographer seems to have taken a large number of photographs in the first few weeks after the land run, but as the town settled in, the number seems to have tapered off along with the initial excitement. Even so, if the casino photograph had been taken at either of the parades in 1890, the number recorded on it would presumably have been much higher.

One last bit of interesting information that Mr. McGuire's book's photographs provide is the location of the photographer when he took the picture. The building listed on the northwest corner of Oklahoma and 2nd was the wooden building that housed the Commercial Bank before the Bank moved late in 1889 into its more permanent location across the street. The photographer must have taken the picture from the roof of this building. He was high above the street, on a level with the tops of the telephone poles, higher than the second stories of other structures. A picture of this building with a false front above its second story is seen to the far left in the photograph below[13].

Although our analysis of Linda's photograph has not produced any personal information about her family, it has given her an interesting link to an important and colorful chapter in American history. According to what Linda knows about her family, her great grandmother's brother lived in Oklahoma in the 1890s. Her great grandmother must have received the picture from him as a souvenir of the first 4th of July parade held in Guthrie in 1889. An interesting topic for further research would be to investigate the possibility that Linda's great great uncle was one of the settlers who participated in the Oklahoma Land Run of 1889.

References

1. Lloyd H. McGuire, Jr., telephone conversation.

2. www.mapquest.com

3. Lloyd H. McGuire, Jr. *The Birth of Guthrie, Oklahoma's Run of 1889 and Life in* Guth*rie in 1889 and the 1890s*, 2nd edition (2000), pp. 123 and 127.

4. www.amazon.com/gp/product/0967102316/104-4093127-3875949?n=283155.

5. Ref. 3, p. 280.

6. Lloyd H. McGuire, Jr., telephone conversation.

7. Ref. 3, p. 194.

8. These two and subsequent photographs are used with the permission of Lloyd H. McGuire Jr. See Ref. 3, pp. 126 and 129.

9. Ref. 3, p. 208.

10. Lloyd H. McGuire, Jr., telephone conversation.

11. Ref. 3, p. 194.

12. Ref. 3, p. 125.

13. Ref. 3, p. 128.

What's Wrong with This Picture?

Although the technology we use to take photographs has changed dramatically with the advent of digital photography and computer photo manipulation software packages, the "tricks" that can be used to produce a fake photograph have hardly changed at all. The two most common ways to fake a photograph are by manipulating its context or by changing its content. The only recent innovation in the way photos can be faked is that thanks to digital photography, these tricks can now be performed electronically.

All a digital photo really consists of is an array of numbers, each indicating the relative amount of light that has illuminated a pixel of the camera. (Hence the name *digital camera.)* The higher the number, the greater the amount of light associated with a pixel. Theoretically, a digital photo could be doctored by changing the value of different pixels, but this would be a very time-consuming task, considering the most popular digital cameras used at present have at least 3 megapixels (3 million pixels). For this reason, fake digital photographs are created using the same tricks used by conventional photography-by changing either the context or the content of a picture.

Types of Fake Photos

Changes in Context

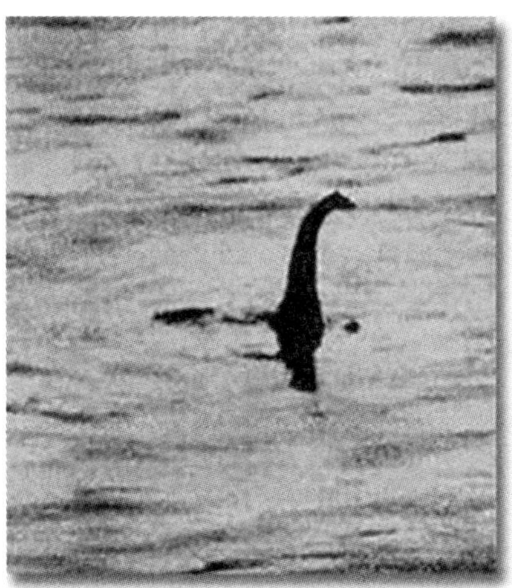

Figure 1. "Nessie" the Loch Ness Monster, 1934.

A photograph that has been faked by altering its context can be hard to detect, since it has not been physically or digitally doctored in any way.

Perhaps the most striking example of this is shown in Figure 1. This famous photo of the Loch Ness Monster was produced in 1933 near Invermoriston, Scotland by a surgeon from about half a mile away. The "monster" has a shadow, and a reflection. It is leaving a wake behind it as it moves through the water.

It was not until 1993 that the surgeon made a deathbed confession that the photo was a fake. The monster was really a piece of plastic wood fit over the conning tower of a toy submarine. The lack of perspective disguised the true dimensions of the object in the water. Although the "experts" claimed the neck of the monster was three feet high, it was only 8" in length[1].

Another famous example of photos that were faked by changing the context was that of the Cottingsley fairies. (Figure 2.) In 1917 Elsie Wright and her cousin Frances Griffiths claimed to have taken photos of dancing fairies near their home. The photos were examined by noted photographic experts who judged them authentic because they saw no evidence of double exposure nor evidence that the negatives had been altered. Even Sir Author Conan Doyle, creator of Sherlock Holmes, was convinced that the photos were genuine.

There are telltale hints that suggest that the photos are not what they are claimed to be. For example, although the shutter speed was slow enough that the waterfall is blurred in the background, the fairies in the first photograph are sharp and do not appear to be moving. Even though in 1978 it was found the fairies were from the 1915 book *Princess Mary's Gift Book* by Arthur Shepperson, the truth was not revealed until 1981, when the aging women confessed that the pictures of the fairies were nothing more than paper cutouts held in place by tacks[2].

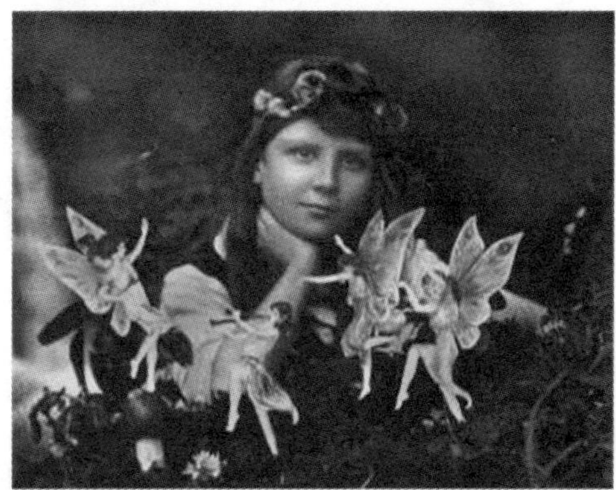

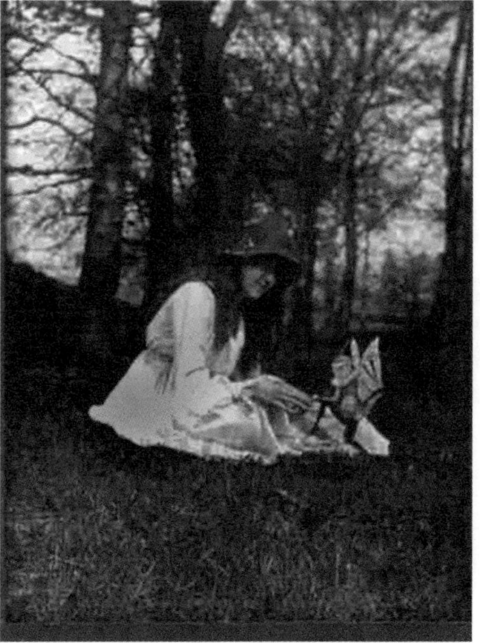

Figure 2. The Cottingsley fairies, 1917.

Change in Content

The content of a photo can be changed in a variety of ways to create an illusion. The most common ways of changing the content of a photo are (1) composite photos where multiple images are combined to make a single print, (2) multiple exposures where a conventional negative is exposed multiple times, and (3) photo collages where pieces of various photos are physically cut out and pasted together to create a single composition, which in turn can be photographed. (See for example www.photography-museum.com/phofictionsmontages.html.)

A well known example where the contents of a photo were altered to create a fake is that of a group of three American POWs that supposedly were shown to be alive in Cambodia in 1990. (Figure 3.) Eight families claimed to identify one of the men as a missing family member. It was subsequently discovered that the photo had appeared in a 1989 Khmer-language edition

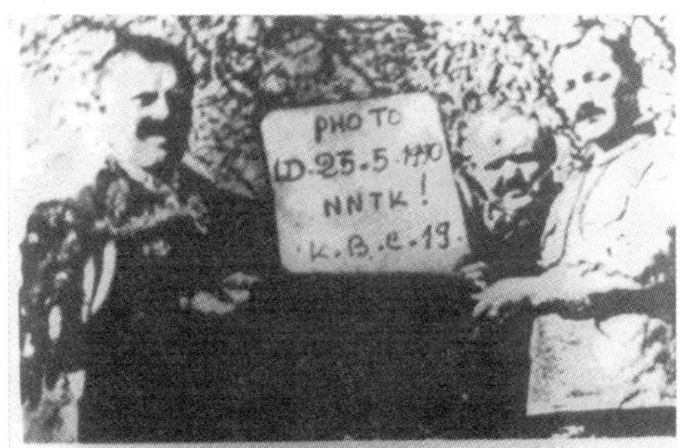

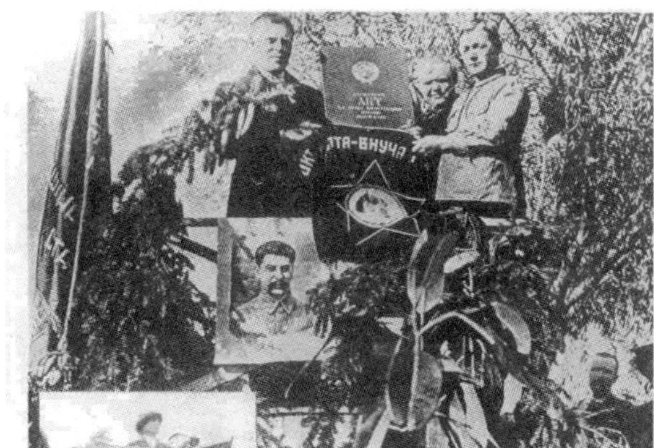

Figure 3. Vietnam POWs?

of the magazine *Soviet Life*. It is a photo of three Soviet farmers during the Stalin era celebrating a record harvest. The photo of the POWs was probably created as a photo collage and then rephotographed[3].

Spotting a Fake

So just how can you spot a fake photo?

A fake photo that is created by changing its context is the hardest to recognize, as it depends on subjective interpretation and not on any physical alteration of an original. Many photographs of UFOs fall into this category - by definition they are photographs of objects that are unidentified and open to judgment.

The best way to detect a faked photo whose context has been changed is by common sense and by comparing what the photo shows to what is otherwise known about the subject. Is there any other evidence that the Loch Ness Monster is real? Has anyone else ever photographed a fairy? Are their other pictures of the same UFO?

A photo that has been physically manipulated to change its contents is easier to detect. A rule of thumb in identifying a doctored photograph is to notice that something "is not quite right". The lighting, the contrast, the

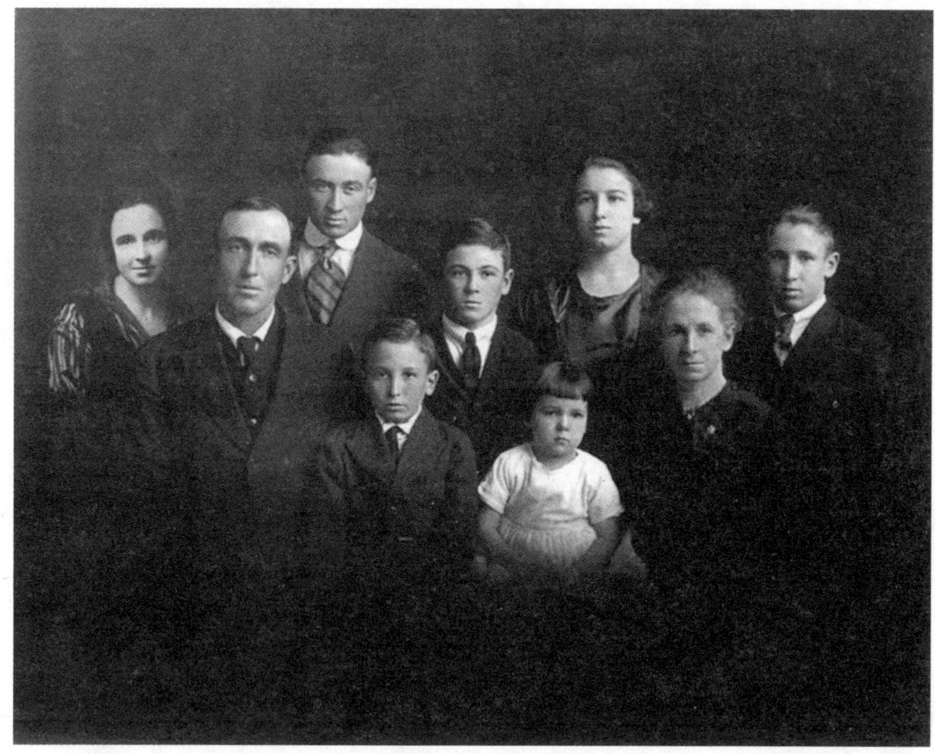

Figure 4. George and Jane Trollop Clark and family.

perspective, the size, and even the "noisiness" of the altered part of a photo are usually impossible to adjust simultaneously to match the original content. Sometimes it is possible to spot a fake photo based on your intuition alone.

Getting back to the picture of George Clark and his family that was shown in the first chapter *What is a Photo Really Telling You?* and shown again in Figure 4, one of the Clarks was not able to make it to the studio that day with the rest of the family. Who was it?

The answer is Millie, the Clark's 18 year old daughter on the left of the back row. Millie Clark died in childbirth at 18 years of age shortly before the picture was taken. When they posed for their portrait, the family left

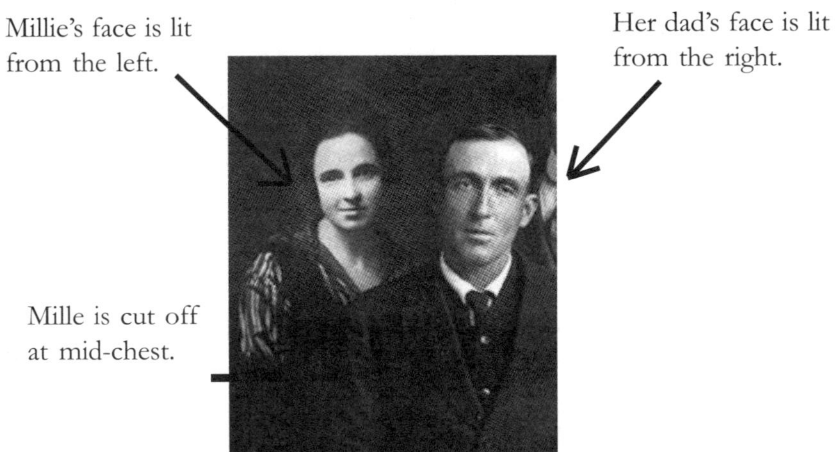

Millie's picture is also somewhat smaller than expected compared to her dad's.

Figure 5.

room for Millie. They added her high school graduation picture in the empty spot later, so that the whole family would be seen together.

There are several clues that Millie's picture was inserted later. Perhaps the most obvious one is that her face is lit from the left while the rest of the family members' faces are lit from the right. A mismatch in lighting like this is a common feature of most composite pictures, since it is almost impossible to match the lighting of a photographic "patch" with the picture it is pasted into.

Other noticeable differences between Millie and the rest of her family are that she is proportionally smaller than everyone else, and her picture is cut off below the chest. You might also notice the thin white line that appears around her head. These are all indications that she was pasted in. Other more subjective features are that Millie has a different expression on her face-she is smiling while the rest of the family is serious, and she is dressed somewhat more informally.

As we said at the very beginning of this book, it is important to know what a picture is really saying. If you did not know about Millie's tragic death, you would have to date the picture by other means. If you were aware that Millie had died, but did not notice that she was added later, you would think that the date of Millie's death was the *latest* date the photo could have been taken. However, if you knew Millie had died, and noticed that her picture had been inserted into the family portrait after the fact, you would realize that the date of Millie's death was the *earliest* the photo could have been taken.

Relative Amnesia

The back of this photo describes the terrible tragedy of a little boy who fell into a mill race and drowned. A mill race is the current or channel of a stream for conducting water to or from a water wheel or other device for generating energy to power a mill. The source of the water for a mill race is usually a pond or a stream that has been channeled downhill, sometimes with a restricted flow, to increase the water pressure sufficiently to drive a water wheel. (Figure 1.) According to

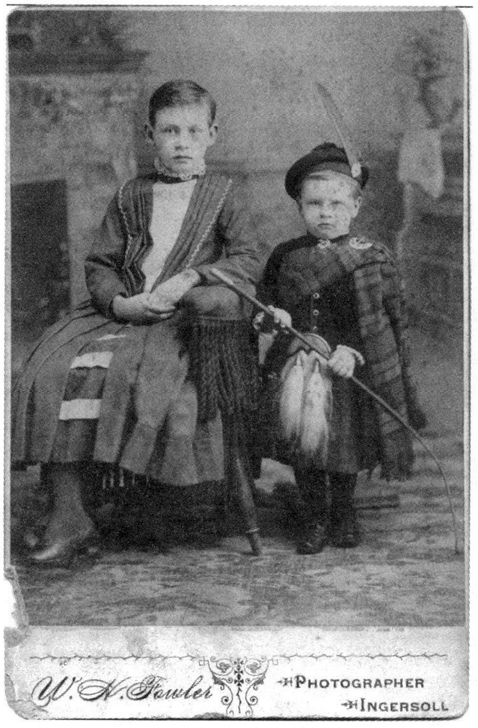

Aunt Mary McLeod
sister of George Mackay
her sons - Smallest drowned
in mill race at home in Ingersoll

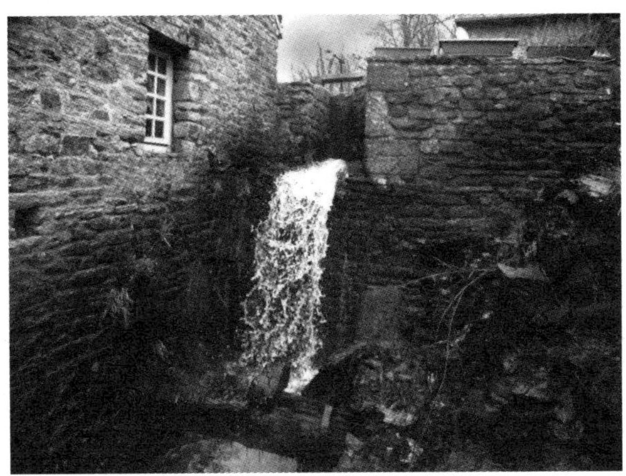

Figure 1. A typical waterfall at the end of a mill race[1].

the caption on the back of the photo, the younger son of Mary Mackay McLeod was swept away by the running water of a mill race in Ingersoll and drowned.

John Roberts is a founding member of the History Posse in Vermont. The Posse is a group in Vermont of avid photo-enthusiasts who are constantly on the lookout for interesting old photos that they can identify and return to their original families. John purchased the quiz photo from an antique store along with several other photos that were part of the estate of Mary Lick of Middlebury, VT. Mary left her estate to her alma mater Lake College in Ohio. The photos were evidently auctioned off to the antique dealer.

Ingersoll is located in the southern part of Ontario, where the border with Canada dips to the south between Michigan and New York. John's Plan A was to research Ingersoll, find THE mill, then find the McLeod residence nearby. Unfortunately, Ingersoll had scores of mills. A topographic map of the region suggests it is flat with Ingersoll the exception. Ingersoll had enough change in elevation to promote many mills. Furthermore, it was home to a huge Scottish immigrant population with MacKay and Mcleod being the Smith and Jones of the area.

John's Plan B was to research the local folklore. In John's words, "In my home town, if a boy drowned in a mill race, the incident would become legend. Mothers would chide their children to stay away from that mill or you'll wind up like that McKay boy. Children would spin it into ghost stories and dare each other to go there."

John's intention was to research Ingersoll history, find the legend, and trace it back to the facts. He caught his first break when he befriended Vicki Wahl, the librarian at the Oxford County Library in Ingersoll. The OCL is the center of genealogical research for the area, with an extensive archive of local newspapers that is accessible online[2].

But as thoroughly as Vicki searched, she could not find a trace of such a local legend. Ingersoll was a maze of mills. Each mill had its own story of founding, structural integrity, maintenance, and failure. Some of the failures were spectacular and would easily dwarf the story of a drowned child. For example:

From *Ingersoll: Our Heritage* provided by Vicki Wahl, p. 51:

The Flood of 1894

In May of 1894, there was a sudden melting accompanied by warm rains. The Harris Creek, which flows through central Ingersoll became badly flooded and three dams on this stream gave way. As water rushed through a conduit on King Street East, it washed away the foundation of the brick building on the eastside of the stream on the north side of King Street. This building was part of the brick block formerly known as the Jarvis Block, but at the time of the flood, it was known as the Campbell Block.

When the floodwaters washed out the foundation of the building adjoining the stream, the brick wall fell into the water, which caused the floors of the building to slope to the stream. The building was occupied by James McIntyre. Coffins, rough boxes and much furniture fell into the rough waters and were carried down to the Thames River. The river was high at this time, and many boats were tied up to the trees along the shore.

Young men got in the boats and took after the furniture and coffins. Much of the merchandise was pulled on shore at Paton's Sighting, three miles west of Ingersoll. Upholstered chairs were seen floating down river as far as Dorchester [about 10 miles away]. Water flowed over King Street and down Water Street a foot deep.

This story had a good juicy legend, floods, destruction, coffins, and furniture. If that wasn't enough to trump a drowning child, Vicki found a second story:

King's Mill was built in 1846, on the south side of King Street West, just east of Whiting Creek. This creek flows north into the Thames River. South of the mill was a 20-acre pond extending south eastward to Wonham Street S., which Mr. King used to operate his flour mill. He built what he called a mill-dam behind the mill.

When steam power was installed, the dam deteriorated. On April 4, 1887 at 7 o'clock in the morning, the dam broke. Beside Whiting Creek was a 4 dwelling apartment. This was totally destroyed by cordwood coming down the river, which was used at the mill to make steam. In the apartment were Mr. and Mrs. John Bowman and their three children; Mr. Bowman's father, John McLean and his 18 year old son, Alexander Laird, and his wife and child.

Mrs. Bowman and her youngest child were swept along holding onto a piece of furniture. Mrs. Bowman was saved, but she lost hold of her child who was drowned and never found. Mr. Bowman was bed-ridden and luckily floated to safety. The other members of the family escaped. The McLean boy's body was found among the cordwood. Alec Laird was drowned, his wife and child swept to the river. Mrs. Laird tried desperately to reach safely but her child slipped from her and was drowned. The dam was never rebuilt, however a small pond did remain.

In 1901, the Tillsonburg, Lake Erie and Pennsylvania Railroad was built through the pond bottom. The Chronicle states that in the 1870's, three mill-dams in the town gave way in the same manner when considerable destruction was caused but with no loss of life.

As legends go, a baby torn from its mother's arms and drowned, trumps a child drowning in a mill race. John was getting discouraged. In desperation, he tried a Googling a combination of McKay, Mcleod, "mill race," and Ingersoll. One of the returns yielded Oxford Library's "James McIntyre Poetry Contest", and the poem "A Providential Escape" from *Musings on the Banks of the Canadian Thames*, 1884 edition[3]. The items in bold are clues to what really happened.

A Providential Escape

Providential escape of Ruby and Neil McLeod, **children of Angus McLeod, Ingersoll, little Neil McKay McLeod, a child three years of age, was carried under a covered raceway**, upwards of one hundred yards, the whole distance being either covered over with roadway, buildings or **ice**.

A wonderous tale we now do trace,
Of little children fell in race;
The youngest of these little dears,
The boy's age is but three years.

While **coasting o'er the treacherous ice—**
precious pearls of great price—
The **elder Ruby, the daughter,**
Was rescued from the ice cold water.

But horrid death each one did feel
Had sure befallen poor little Neil;
Consternation did people fill,
And they cried "shut down the mill."

But still no person yet could tell
What had the poor child befel [sic];
The covered race, *so long and dark,*
Of hopes there scarcely seemed a spark.

Was he held fast as if in vice,
Wedged 'mong the timbers and the **ice**,
Or, was there for him ample room
For to float down the narrow flume?

Had he found there a watery grave,
Or been borne on crest of wave?
Think of the mothers agony, wild,
Gazing through dark tunnel for her child.

But soon as **Partlo** *started mill,*
Through crowd there ran a joyous thrill,
When he was quickly borne along,
The little hero of our song.

Alas! of life there is no trace,
And he is black all over face ;
Though he then seemed as if in death,
Yet quickly, they restored his breath.

Think now how mother she adored
Her sweet dear child, to her restored,
And her boundless gratitude
Unto the author of all good.

Swept through dark passage 'neath the road,
Saved only by the hand of God,
No wonder Father now feels proud
Of little **Neil McKay McLeod**.

Having found the poem, John's further research on "Niel McKay McLeod" produced the following:

Ingersoll Chronicle & Canadian Dairyman

Thursday, October 02, 1884

Death Notice

McLEOD—*In Ingersoll, on the 25th ult., Neil MacKay, son of Angus McLeod, aged 3 years and 4 months.*

James McIntyre was the undertaker/furniture manufacturer mentioned in the first flood story from *Ingersoll, Our Heritage*. He is remembered for his really bad poetry, for example, his *Ode to a Mammoth Cheese Weighing 7,000 Pounds*. His furniture store jingle was "Please to let me go, Ma, to McIntyre's to get a sofa." He had the good business sense not to write a jingle for his undertaking business. (Figure 2.)

Nevertheless, bad poetry does not grant enough poetic license to alter the outcome of a drowning. According to the newspaper, and the photo annotation, the boy drowned. John decided Niel must have survived the drowning and died later of complications. Hence the poem. Vicki found another tidbit:

Ingersoll Chronicle

Feb 21, 1884, p3 c2

A MIRACULOUS ESCAPE

A Child Falls into a Mill Race, and Is Carried Under the Street

On Thursday afternoon an accident occurred in town which happily did not result fatally, although the escape may be said to be almost miraculous. Two children of Mr. Angus McLeod — a boy and a girl, aged respectively five and three years, were being drawn on a hand sled by another child on the sidewalk down King Street East, and when opposite Mill Street the sled was overturned precipitating its occupants into the mill race, running under the street from the pond to Partlo's Mill. (Figure 3.)

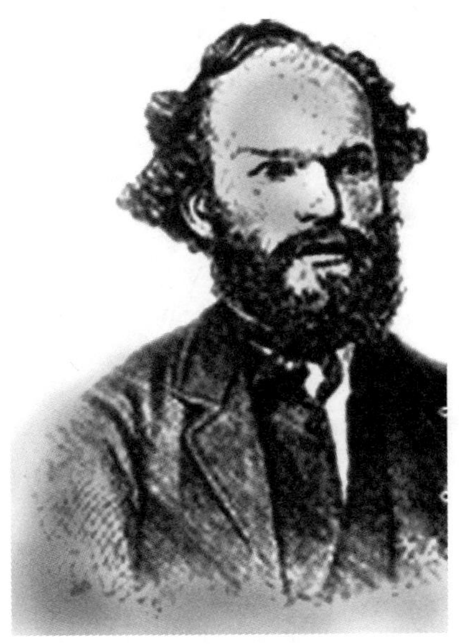

Figure 2. James McIntyre, the Cheese Poet Laureate of Ingersoll[3].

The little girl caught hold of a projecting plank and was rescued without sustaining any serious injury. The boy, however, was not so fortunate, but was drawn in by the swiftly flowing current and carried out of view, passing under the street a distance of 200 feet to the gate of Partlo's Mills (Figure 4), *when after being in the water for nearly ten minutes he was rescued in an insensible condition, and to all appearances drowned, the face being black. Restoratives were administered and after considerable rubbing the child was brought*

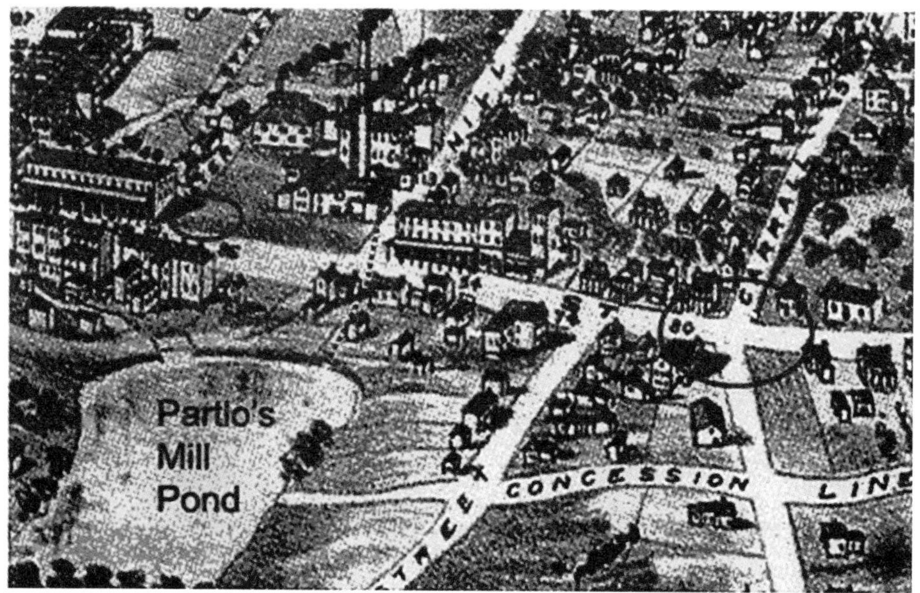

Figure 3. Partlo's Mill c. 1897. The large oval to the right is where Angus and Mary McLeod lived. Within the same intersection, on the opposite corner, lived James McIntyre, fellow Scottish immigrant, fellow Masonic lodge member, and fellow Oddfellows Lodge member to Angus McLeod. It would be difficult for them not to know each other. The small oval on the left is where McIntyre had his furniture, and ndertaking enterprise. It was washed away in the 1894 flood, but in 1884, it stood near Partlo's Mill. The dotted line shows the approximate path Neil took on his near fatal ride. Clearly, McIntyre was in the thick of the action and decided to immortalize the incident in a poem in spite of his critics.

back to consciousness and is now as well as ever beyond a feeling of soreness in his limbs, after his involuntary underground voyage.

John thought the mystery had been solved. He survived, but did he die the same year? Vicki came through again:

Ingersoll Chronicle

Oct 2, 1884

SAD BEREAVEMENT

Many families in our town have been visited by sorrows of various kinds, but we can think of none parallel to that which has overtaken our esteemed fellow townsman, Angus McLeod. It is not many months ago that we were called upon to relate a most wonderful escape from drowning, it being the occasion of poor little Neily McLeod having fallen into the race running under King Street to Partlo's Mill and now we are called upon to chronicle the death of the poor little boy by an accident almost unprecedented.

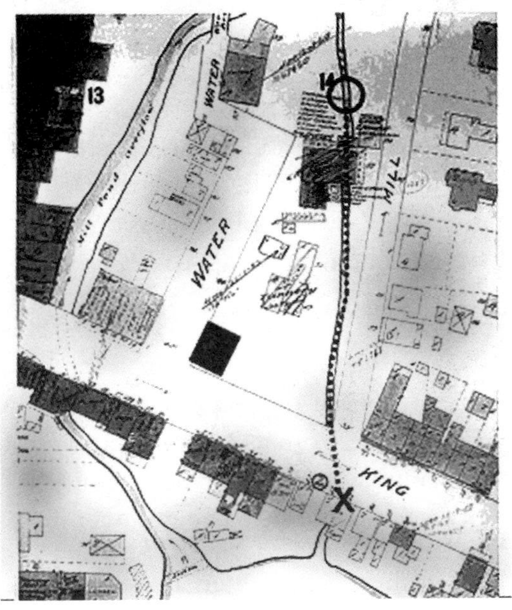

Figure 4. Neil's approximate path. McIntyre's shop is the solid rectangle to the left of Neil's path. The Odd Fellows Lodge is in one of the buildings on the left.

While visiting a friend north of the river with his mother, poor Neily with some other children were amusing themselves in a swing and he was thrown back against a pot of lye and unfortunately lost his balance and fell backward into it, his body being very much burned, and from the consequences of which he died the same night.

The funeral took place on Sunday afternoon from the residence of Mr. McLeod on King Street to Putnam. Though the rain was incessant a large concourse of friends assembled to show their sympathy and respect to the family. Both Mr. and Mrs. McLeod have long had the respect and esteem of a large section of the community. As an Oddfellow and Mason, Angus has enjoyed the fullest confidence and brotherly love of both bodies to a very large degree, having been a most active member in both lodges. The members of Oxford and Samaritan Lodge, IOOF, gave a vote of sympathy to himself and family at their last meeting.

We sincerely trust they may never have to pass through another affliction of this kind. To one like our Angus who has so well filled the station of a man and brother in his daily walk of life, we must all feel to mourn with him in this his hour of deep anguish.

John decided to investigate Angus and Mary's other son, George Angus McKay. Neil and George were born four years apart, but Neil never lived to age four. Therefore, they could never have shared the earth together —let alone a photo session. This photo was failing the "smell" test. If it was a hoax, it was perpetrated over a hundred years ago and for what purpose?

John blames this on something he calls "Relative Amnesia." Relatives forget details in direct proportion to their distance from each other and their distance from a common ancestor. His parents often swapped his sisters' names. Aunts and Uncles confused him with his brother James, but slipped him a dollar, so he got over it.

In this case, the general story is there. Mary was George's sister and had two sons. One of them fell into a mill race and died (though later).

Vicki, the librarian, found that the photographer, W. K. Fowler, operated in Ingersoll only between 1888 and 1890. However, Neil died in 1884. In spite of the great story, this can't be Neil in the photo. How about George? He would have been between four and six years old in that time frame. So what became of him?

Ingersoll Chronicle

December 28, 1893

DROWNING ACCIDENT

The first drowning accident of the season occurred on Smith's Pond better, shortly after dinner, by which George, the 8 year old son of Mr. Angus McLeod, lost his life. The unfortunate youth in company with some companions was skating on the ice, which was perfectly safe with the exception of a strip at the south end of the pond, which had only been frozen over the night before. It was at this point the lad broke through and sank at once to the bottom. (Figure 5.)

There were only a couple of other small boys near by at the time, and they being unable to rescue their companion quickly spread the alarm. A large number were soon on the spot including the agonized father, and the body was recovered about half an hour after the accident occurred. The remains were immediately conveyed to the parents residence, where every known means were made use of to bring about resuscitation but without avail. The deceased was a bright intelligent lad and his sudden death will be a terrible blow to his parents who have the deepest sympathy of the community.

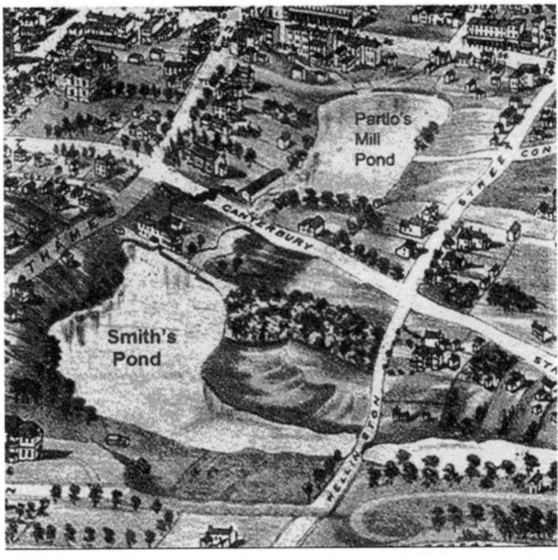

Figure 5. Location of the pond where George Angus McLeod drowned in 1893.

Ingersoll Chronicle

Jan 4, 1894

GEORGIE M'LEOD

Perhaps no event that has taken place in Ingersoll has called forth a more universal outpour of sympathy, from all classes of the community, than the sudden taking off, by drowning of Georgie McLeod, only son of Angus McLeod, who together with his good wife have long been well known and highly esteemed in Ingersoll.

From the time the poor little fellow was brought home on Wednesday, until the day of his funeral [Saturday afternoon], Mr. McLeod's dwelling was visited by scores of deep sympathizers of the bereaved. The neat little coffin which held all that remained of a darling little boy, was literally covered with flowers, sent and brought in by friends far and near. Rev. Mr. Hutt conducted the services, and his tender and loving remarks must have given great consolation to the grief-stricken parents.

Nearly all of the employees of the Noxon foundry marched at the head of the funeral procession, through the town, followed by a large number of carriages containing the mourners and citizens of Ingersoll, who were assembled on this more than ordinary occasion to express their sympathy and kindly feelings. It must have been comforting to the bereaved ones to know how fully their great sorrow was participated in by the community at large.

The Next Chapter

John became convinced that the smaller boy in the photo was George Angus Mcleod. Relative amnesia could easily take the phrase "one boy fell in a mill race, and one boy drowned." to "One boy fell in a mill race and drowned." Since both boys died in childhood, having no heirs, he decided to seek Ruby's descendants to find the photo a home.

From the vital statistics of the Oxford County Library:

Groom: Manson, David A.
Bride: McLeod, Ruby
Date of Marriage: March 8, 1910
License or Banns: L
Place of Marriage: Ingersoll

Groom's Occupation: Merchant	**Bride's Profession:** Organist
Groom's Martial Status: Bachelor	**Bride's Martial Status:** Single
Groom's Age: 27	**Bride's Age:** 28
Groom's Religion: Presbyterian	**Bride's Religion:** Presbyterian
Groom's Residence: Collingwood	**Bride's Residence:** Ingersoll
Groom's Father: Manson, John	**Bride's Father:** McLeod, Angus

Bride's Father's Profession:
Carpenter

Groom's Mother:
Jardine, Jessie

Bride's Mother:
MacKay, Mary

Groom's Witness: McLeod, Mary
Residence of Groom's Witness: Ingersoll
Bride's Witness: Manson, Thomas
Residence of Bride's Witness: Collingwood
By Whom Married: Bright, Alfred
Date of Registration: April 6, 1910

Of the witnesses, Thomas Manson was David's brother, and Mary was Ruby's sister.

Ingersoll Chronicle & Canadian Dairyman

Thursday, March 10, 1910

Pg: 6, Col: 2

MANSON-McLEOD—*Last evening at the home of Mr. and Mrs. Angus McLeod, King St. E., the marriage of their eldest daughter, Ruby, to Mr. David G. Manson of Collingwood, took place. The wedding was very quietly solemnized in the presence of relatives and immediate friends of the family, at the request of her mother, who is critically ill. The Rev. Alfred Bright, BA of St. Paul's Presbyterian Church, officiated. The bride was given away by her father. She was charmingly attired in white mull elaborately trimmed with lace and insertion. Miss Mary McLeod, sister of the bride was bridesmaid and Mr. Thomas Manson of Collingwood, was groomsman.*

Miss McLeod has been organist of St. Andrews, Collingwood, for some time and at one time was organist of Chalmers Church, Woodstock, where she rendered most excellent service. Her many friends in Ingersoll, Woodstock, Collingwood, unite in wishing her many years of happiness, health and prosperity.

As for Jessie Jardine, David's mother, John found:

The Collingwood Enterprise

January 25, 1923

Died: last Thursday, Mrs. John MANSON, at the home of her son David MANSON, daughter of the late John JARDINE. She was born in Nottawa Village in 1854. She was brought up by her grandparents, Mr. & Mrs. David JARDINE. Married in 1880. Buried Duntroon Cemetery.

Ruby married on March 8, 1910. John found that her mother, Mary, died shortly afterward on March 17. Ruby was listed among the survivors. *"Besides the husband, she leaves to mourn her loss, three daughters, Mrs. David G.[sic] Manson of Collingwood and Misses Katie and Mary."*

Her father, Angus, died July 18, 1913. Again Ruby was listed, *"The deceased who was aged 67 years is survived by three daughters, Mrs. D. Manson and Miss Katherine, of Collingwood and Miss Mary at home."* Her Aunt Jean MacKay, another sister of George MacKay, died February 28, 1933. Ruby is listed under her maiden name. Could it be a typo, or did she divorce? *Surviving are three nieces, Ruby McLeod of Collingwood; May[sic] McLeod, Erie, PA; and Kate McLeod, Erie, PA."* This is the last trace John had of Ruby.

A Major Breakthrough

Bob and JoAnne Craig, who are regular visitors to our website, came up with the missing pieces of the puzzle. One source of information they found was the 1911 Ontario census, which listed Ruby (Robena) with her husband, her brother-in-law, and her mother-in-law. Then by consulting the records for the borders crossings into the US, the Craigs found that Mary McLeod (Ruby's sister), moved to North East, PA, when she was 17. She listed her profession as a Phone Operator. On one of Mary's (Ruby's daughter) crossings, she listed her place of visit as her Uncle Fred Evans. The 1930 US census shows a Fred and Mary Evans and their children, a boy, 7 year old George, and a girl, 1 year old Marjorie, living in North East, PA. Mary's place of birth, her age, and her father and mother's places of birth were correct.

Table 1.

1911 Ontario Census		
Name	**Date of Birth**	**Occupation**
David Alex Manson	March 1883	Piano Merchant
Robena (Ruby) Manson	1889	
Thomas Manson (Brother)	1889	Piano Merchant
Jessie Manson (Mother)	1854	

A further search of the border crossings showed that in 1943 David and Robene (Ruby) immigrated to the US (Pennsylvania) to live with their daughter Mary (Manson) Lee (b. 29 Aug 1913). She and her husband Robert M. Lee, lived in North East, Erie County, PA.

John's Response:

Amazing detective work. You all have taken me past a stumbling block that has stopped me for a year. I did not know that Ruby's name was Robene, that she had a daughter, Mary, or that they settled in North East Borough, Pennsylvania.

I'll let you in some things I did know. The photo references George McKay and describes Mary McKay McLeod as his sister. I have photos of George McKay including the one I've attached here. (See Figure 6.) *George had a partnership in a milling company called Blaine, McKay, Lee. He must have been close to his partners, because he named one of his sons George Blaine McKay and they referred to him as Blaine. It's not a stretch to believe that he was close to his other partner, John Lee, and that his niece would marry his partner's son. Lo and behold, John Lee had a son, Robert M. Lee. Further, the Lee's lived on Lake Street near George's son-in-law, Walter Lick.*

I can't find Robert and Mary in the 1930 census, but they may have had a child by then. Have you had any luck? Attached is the photo of George McKay with the anecdotal information on the back. I found John Lee as a railroad clerk in Cook County, Illinois,

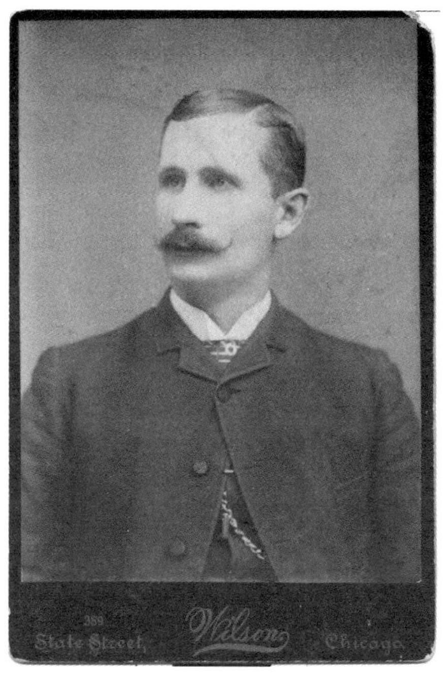

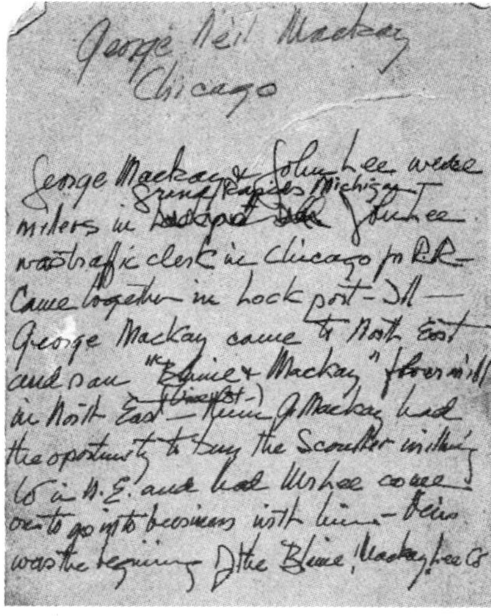
George Neil Mackay
Chicago

George Mackay & John Lee were
millers in Grand Rapids Michigan John Lee
was traffic clerk in Chicago for R.R.
Came together in Lockport - Ill -
George Mackay came to North East
and saw "Blaine & Mackay" flour mill
in North East (Vine St.) — G. Mackay had
the opportunity to buy the Scouter milling
Co in N.E. and had Mr. Lee come
on to go into business with him — this
was the beginning of the Blaine, Mackay, Lee Co

Figure 6. George Neil McKay, Chicago. George McKay and John Lee were millers in Grand Rapids, Michigan. John Lee was traffic clerk in Chicago for R.R. Came together in Lockport, Illinois. George McKay came to North East and saw "Blaine & McKay" flour mill in Noth East (Vine St.). G. Mackay had the opportunity to buy the Scouter Milling Co. in N.E. and had Mr. Lee come on and go into business with him. This was the beginning of the Blaine, Mackay, Lee Co.

living in North East, PA, on Lake Street as a Manufacturer, Flour Mill. Seven year old Robert M. is part of the family. See Series T624, Roll 1343, Page 37. In 1920, seventeen year old Robert M. is with his parents at the same location. See Series T625, Roll 1567, Page 215. Can you find Robert and Mary in the 1930 census? By the way, North East, Pennsylvania is paradoxically in northwest Pennsylvania. The name refers to the North East borough of Erie, Pennsylvania.

I have a very good friend Dick Tefft from that area.

Ever grateful,
John Roberts

Hello Dick,

I am seeking a descendant Robert M. Lee and Mary Manson. Robert was the son of John Edward Lee, partner of the Blaine, McKay, Lee Co. Robert's parents lived on South Lake St. in North East, PA. In 1943, his in-laws moved in with them. They were David and Robene (Ruby) Manson. I hope is to return a family photograph to their descendants. I would be grateful for any information you could provide.

Yours very truly,
John Roberts

*****

John,

I believe this is the man you are looking for. I went to school with him and he lived on South Lake St.. Robert Lee, 2106 North Cascade St., Colorado Springs, CO 80907.

Dick Tefft

*****

Dick,

I'm grateful for the address you provided and excited that this research may be drawing to a close. All of this searching revolves around a photograph that I bought in Vermont over a year ago. You can see a scan of the photograph at www.forensicgenealogy.info/contest_130_results.html.

Colleen Fitzpatrick is a forensic genealogist and the web site's owner. I submitted the photograph for her photo contest, and she graciously posted it. I believe the younger boy in the photo is the brother of Ruby McLeod Manson. Ruby was Robert M. Lee's mother-in-law. The Robert M. Lee I'm referring to was born around 1903 in Illinois; the son of John E. Lee. The family appears in North East in the 1910 census. If you went to school with Robert Lee, could it have been a son, Robert Jr, perhaps? If you have this man's phone number, I would be grateful if you would share it with me. Otherwise, I will write to him soon.

Ever grateful,
John Roberts

*****

Hi John,

According to one of the private databases I subscribe to, the Robert Lee that Dick went to school with is:

Robert D. Lee
b. 08/17/1945
2106 N Cascade Ave
Colorado Springs, CO 80907
*Tel: (719) 471-****

Possible Relatives:
Wright, Kira Lee (Age 34)
Lee, MARY M.
Lee, Kristin Michelle (Age 32)
Lee, Beverly S. (Age 61)

Regards,
Colleen

*****

Dear Colleen,

I researched one of the associated names returned with Robert D. Lee's phone number. By her age, Beverly Lee is likely his wife. I homed in on Kira Lee Wright. She has a very unique name with lots of "net spoor" for tracing. I believe she's Robert D.'s daughter. It seems she married a man named Peter Wright, and they're living in Portland, Oregon with two daughters. I left a contact message for his wife on his blog.

J. R.

*****

Hello Kira,

As a hobby, I indulge in some aspects of forensic genealogy. (See www.forensicgenealogy.info/contest_130_results.html). Lately, my research has led me to Erie County, Pennsylvania. I am seeking a descendant of Robert M., and Mary (Manson) Lee of North East Borough, PA. I have found enough clues to suspect that they were your grandparents. If this is your lineage, I encourage you to reply. I have information to share with you.

Ever grateful,
John Roberts

*****

Hello John,

Those are indeed my grandparents. I'd be interested in what you have to share.

Kira

The End of the Story

John sent the photograph to Kira, who was delighted to have a picture of her great grandmother's family. In spite of a bad case of relative amnesia, we successfully identified the young boy in the picture as George Angus McLeod, son of Angus McLeod and Mary Mackay McLeod. He was Kira's great great uncle, the brother of her great grandmother Rubena McLeod Manson. But who was the other child?

At first, judging by the hairstyle, we believed the older child was male, and estimated his age as about 10 years old. Yet we could not find any evidence that Angus and Mary McLeod had a son who was older than poor little Neily who drowned. We could only account for one older sibling, Ruby, b. 1889, who was two years older than Neily.

On closer examination, however, in spite of the short hair, the older child might be a girl. He/she is wearing a dress - hardly surprising for a male or a female child from around the turn of the 20th century. (And after all, in a Scottish community, even grown men wore skirts.) But the slippers and feet could be those of a girl, as could the hands. By the time the photograph of the two children was taken between 1888-1890, Ruby would have been between 9 and 11 years old, which is consistent with the appearance of this child. Though it is impossible to be certain, we believe the older child in the photo is Ruby, the older sister of the unfortunate Neily and George McLeod, and the great great grandmother of Kira Lee.

References

1. www.leahy-hill.com/images/France/Moulin/March%202003/Water/Mill%20Waterfall.jpg

2. www.ocl.net

3. www.ocl.net/projects/poetrycontest/aboutjames.shtml

The History of Photography Part I

What Took It So Long to Be Invented?

Introduction

A photo detective has a lot to be gained from knowing the history of photography. For example, being able to tell if a photograph is a Daguerreotype or an ambrotype will give you a better idea of when it was taken.

However, there is more to the story than the advent and decline of different types of photographs. Other aspects of photography can be at least as important in analyzing a picture, yet are often neglected - the invention of different kinds of lenses, for example. Noticing that the Sheboygan Dead Horse Picture was taken with a wide angle lens gave us the earliest possible date for the photograph. We'll talk more about this a little later in the chapter.

The history of photography can be roughly divided into two eras, before and after the introduction of the Brownie camera in 1900 by George Eastman. Before the Brownie came along, taking pictures was the domain of the skilled technician and the wealthy. After the Brownie appeared, anyone could become a photographer.

The 19th century saw much progress in the *science of photography*. Daguerrerotypes on silver-coated copper plates made way for less expensive ambrotypes on glass that in turn were replaced by tintypes that were much cheaper and less fragile. The discovery of albumen as a binding agent for photosensitive chemicals led first to the development of the glass negative in 1848 and then the albumen print in 1850. For the first time, many copies of a photograph could be printed from a single negative, decreasing the cost of production and making them more widely available to the public. The most popular forms of the albumen print, the Carte de Visite and the later cabinet card, account for the majority of 19th century photographs that survive today. Yet photography itself was still out of the reach of the common man. Cameras were large and bulky, and processing was still complicated and messy.

In the late 1880s, thanks to George Eastman, the *engineering of photography* began to take on importance. Eastman pushed to make photography more convenient by simplifying the processing and reducing the size and complexity of the camera. His inventions in 1880 of dry processing plates, followed in 1883 by roll film were the first steps in this direction.

The first Kodak camera, introduced in 1888, measured three and three-quarter inches high, three and a quarter inches wide, and six and a half inches long. It sold for $25 and came loaded with enough roll film for 100 exposures. When the roll was finished, the whole camera was sent to Eastman Kodak in Rochester for processing. The film was developed, prints were made from the negatives, and the camera was returned loaded for another 100 exposures. All for $10.

Yet a camera was still out of the price range of the common man.. A price tag in 1888 must be multiplied by a factor of 20 to obtain its equivalent in today's dollars. In 1888, the cost for having one set of prints made, not including the camera, would be $200 today. If you include the cost of the camera, the total was $35, or $700 today.

Yes Eastman saw the potential of the mass market and continued with his vision of making photography available to the most people at the lowest price. In 1896, the 100,000th Kodak camera was manufactured, and film was being produced at the rate of 400 miles per month. But even at $5 ($100 today), the Kodak pocket camera was still too pricey for most would-be photographers.

Eastman's introduction of the Kodak Brownie camera in 1900 changed all this. The Brownie started a revolution in personal photography that still continues in digital form today. Not only was the Brownie easy to use, it was cheap, with a price tag of $1 - or about $20 in today's dollars. Kodak's slogan "You push the button, we do the rest" said it all. For the first time, everyone could take pictures in his own home, without advanced technical knowledge. Over 1,000,000 Brownie cameras were made during the first five years of production with more than 100 different models of the Brownie introduced during its first eighty years on the market. The phrase "Kodak moment" became a permanent part of the English language.

And the rest, as they say, is history.

The Beginning

The elements that make up photography, light-sensitive chemicals, a optional lens to collect light, and a box to hold it all, have been around for a long time. So what took photography so long to be invented?

The Box

The simplest method of imaging a scene, called camera obscura (Latin for dark room), was familiar to philosophers, mathematicians, and artists for centuries. Camera obscura is an enclosure, usually a box or a room with a small hole in one wall that allows light through, forming an inverted image of a scene on the opposite wall. The smaller the hole, the sharper the image, until the hole gets so small that diffraction becomes important.

Camera obscura was first described by Mo-Tzu, a Chinese philosopher who lived around 400 BC. Mo-Tzu was aware that light travels in a staight line and explained why a camera obscura image is inverted using the analogy to an oar in an rowlock[1]. Aristotle later used camera obscura to safely observe a solar eclipse.

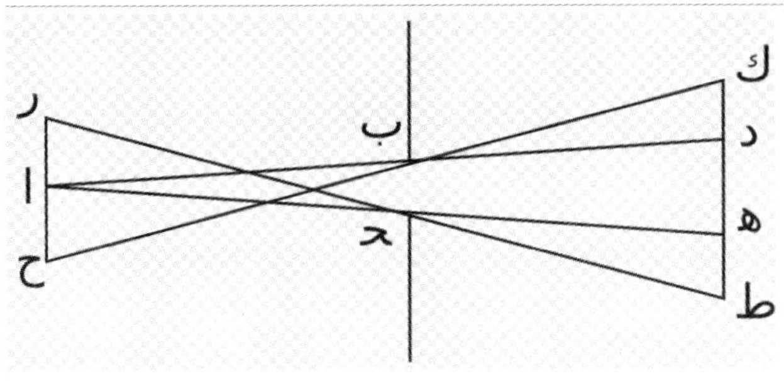

Figure 1. How an inverted image is created by camera obscura. From the 10th century *Book of Optics* by Ibn al-Haitham[3].

The first accurate description of the principles of camera obscura was given by the 10th century Persian mathematician Abu Ali Al-Hasan Ibn al-Haitham (known in western cultures as Alhacen). See Figure 1 for a drawing from his *Book of Optics* (1011-1021)[2]. Alhacen was also the first to understand that the human eye imaged light in a similar fashion. Vermeer is said to have used camera obscura

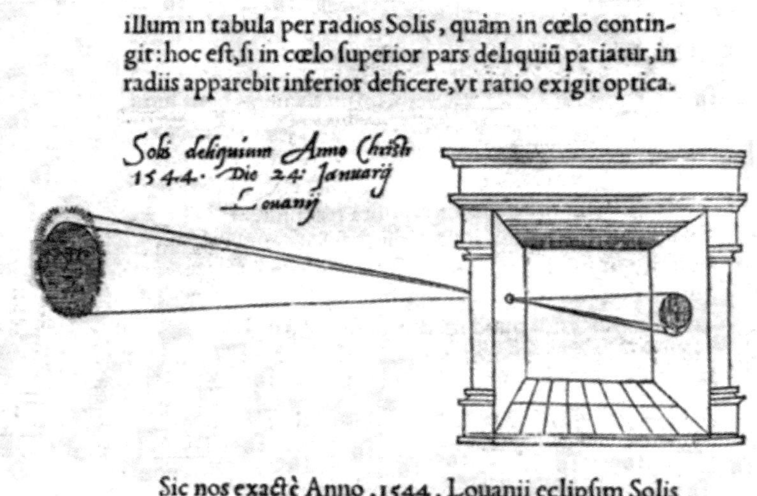
illum in tabula per radios Solis, quàm in cœlo contingit: hoc eſt, ſi in cœlo ſuperior pars deliquiũ patiatur, in radiis apparebit inferior deficere, vt ratio exigit optica.

Sic nos exactè Anno .1544. Louanii eclipſim Solis obſeruauimus, inuenimuſq; deficere paulò plus q̃ dex-

Figure 2. **Reinerus Gemma-Frisius**, observed an eclipse of the sun at Louvain on January 24, 1544, and later he used this illustration of the event in his book *De Radio Astronomica et Geometrica*, 1545. It is thought to be the first published illustration of a camera obscura[3].

to paint his *View of Delft* in 1659-1660. Many other scientific and artistic applications of camera obscura have been documented through the centuries. (Figure 2.) Even today, we have a version of a camera obscura that is a component of a number of modern imaging techniques. You may have heard of it. It's called the camera.

The Lens

The invention of photography was not waiting on the invention of the box to put everything in. So what about the lens? Was the lens responsible for the hold-up?

Because camera obscura requires a very small aperture to produce a sharp image, only a very small amount of light is available to do so. If the aperture is too large, its light collecting ability increases, but the image becomes fuzzy. To remedy this problem, photographers commonly use a lens on the front of the aperture of a camera to allow more light in while still producing a sharp image.

There's an easy way to understand this. If you remove your eyeglasses, the world around you appears blurred. You can regain the sharpness of the image by looking at your surroundings through a pinhole made with your fingers. If you want to see just as clearly, but not have to walk around with a pinhole in front of your eye, you could take the pinhole away and just put your glasses back on.

Your eye is very sensitive, so that your ability to see is not taken away by the reduction of the light reaching your eye through your finger pinhole. This is not generally true for recording materials, which require a certain threshold of illumination to function. The smaller the pinhole, the longer the exposure required to collect enough light to form an image. If the exposure time is too long, it is practically impossible to take a picture. So why not reduce the exposure time to a reasonable level by increasing the size of a camera's aperture to make sure there is enough light, while placing a lens over the aperture to prevent the image from becoming fuzzy?

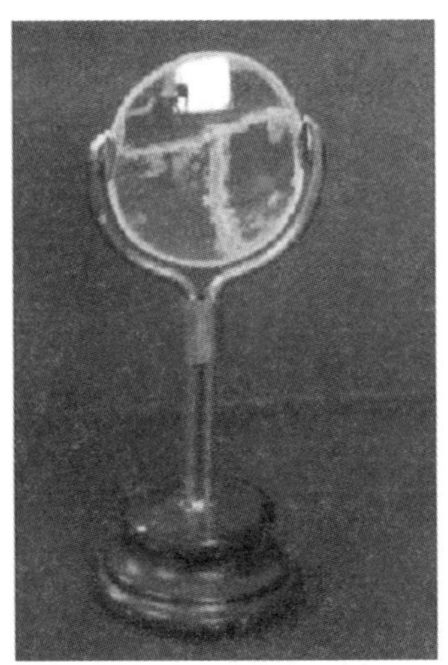

Figure 3. The first known lens, a crudely formed plano-convex lens dating to the 7th century BC[4].

The word *lens* refers to any transparent material that can manipulate the path of light. Even a drop of water can be used as a lens. The earliest known lens still in existence is a piece of rock crystal dating to the 7th century B.C. found in excavations at Ninevah by the British archaeologist Sir Austin Henry Layard in 1847[4]. (Figure 3.)

. The earliest written record of lenses dates to Ancient Greece. Aristophanes' play The Clouds (424 BC) mentions a burning-glass used to focus the sun's rays to produce fire. The Romans were also familiar with lenses. Pliny the Elder mentions the magnification produced by a glass globe filled with water[5].

The first lensmaking activities were probably trial and error shapings of rock crystal or other transparent materials, or the creation of water lenses like those of the Romans mentioned above. About 984 AD the Arabian mathematician Ibn Saul first formulated the law of refraction (now known as Snell's law) in his *On Burning Mirrors and Lenses* where he described how to construct mirrors and lenses to bend and focus light[6]. The foundation of geometrical optics is credited to Alhacen, whose *Book of Optics* (1011-1021) is regarded as one of the most influential contributions in the history of physics. It is believed that lens making techniques that we regard as "modern" might have been discovered long ago but lost during the last 500 yrs. Aspheric lenses from the 11th to 12th century found in the Viking town of Fröjel, Gotland, Sweden have imaging quality comparable to those fabricated in the 1950s[7].

The Recording Materials

So lenses have been around for a long time, and lens design and lensmaking were underway by the 11th century AD. And actually, a camera does not even need a lens if a photographer can wait long enough to obtain the exposure he needs. So the invention of photography was not waiting on the lens, nor on the box to put everything in. The remaining possibility is that the birth of photography was waiting for the formulation of the appropriate photochemistry.

The key word is "appropriate". The fact that certain chemicals changed color when exposed to light was discovered in 1694 by Wilhelm Homberg. What photography required was more control over such chemicals. Photography was waiting on the discovery of photosensitive materials that could respond to the range of exposure levels normally existing in a projected image. For a photosensitive material to be useful, it had to be fast enough to record the gradient of light and dark levels in an image, but not so slow or so fast that the image would be underexposed or overexposed with all areas affected to the same degree. In modern terms, the sought-after material had to have a gamma curve that was not too flat nor too steep.

And of course, the end product had to be visible. Simply recording a latent image was not enough. You had to be able to see it. Then once an image was recorded, early photographers had to find a way to keep it from disappearing. In other words, the photograph had to be developed so you could see the picture, then fixed so it wouldn't go away.

In 1816 Joseph Nicéphore Niépce began experiments to capture images in a camera obscura using silver chloride on paper. He had some success in recording images, but he was unable to prevent them from fading[8]. In 1822, he discovered a method for fixing an image. Two years later, he recorded the first permanent images - contact copies of engravings and drawings on glass and stone. About this time, he made a recording of a camera obscura image of a view from his window. The recording required a five day exposure. It was done on stone, with the goal of producing an etched plate for the mass production of lithographic prints. It is believed that this first permanent recording of a camera oscura image has not survived.

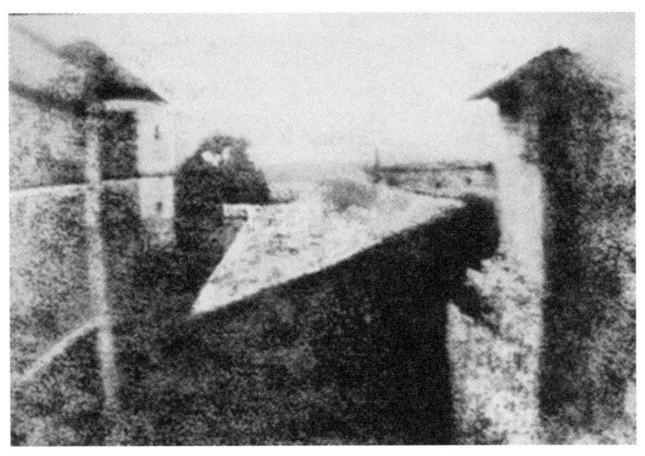

Figure 4. The first photograph of the rooftops of Paris taken by in 1826 by Joseph Nicéphore Niépce.

Finally in 1826, Niépce produced what is regarded as the first photograph. He used a polished pewter plate coated with a type of asphalt called *bitumen of Judea* dissolved in lavender water. Bitumen permanently hardens when exposed to light, unlike other photographic materials that darken. The exposure created a latent image, which Niépce developed by washing the plate and removing the unexposed bitumen. The result was a direct positive image, the hardened areas of bitumen representing the exposed light areas of the image, with the darker areas of bare pewter representing the shadows. Niépce called his invention *heliography*, or sun writing.

Niépce's first photograph, *View from the Window at Le Gras*, is shown in Figure 4. The exposure took eight hours. This was such a long exposure that the sun passed overhead, illuminating both sides of his courtyard. Even so, the plate was underexposed and the image was very faint.

Niépce took the photo by placing his light sensitive pewter plate inside a camera obscura. Aware that a camera obscura reverses an image right to left, Niépce used a prism in front of his lens to reverse it back. The exposure was made from an upper rear window of the Niépce family home in Burgundy, in the village of Saint-Loup-de-Varennes. From left to right, the structures seen in the picture are the upper loft or pigeon house of the family home; a pear tree with a patch of sky showing through an opening in the branches; the slanting roof of the barn with the long roof and low chimney of the bake house behind it; and, on the right, another wing of the family house[8]. Niépce's original photograph is on display as part of the permanent collection of the Harry Ransom Center at the University of Texas at Austin.

The Daguerreotype

Niépce continued to search for a more practical means of producing a photographic image. He found that by exposing silver and silver-coated copper plates to sodium iodide fumes, a layer of photosensitive silver iodide was formed that could be used to record a latent image.

In 1829, Niépce formed a partnership with Louis Daguerre, a French theatrical designer famous for his invention of the Diorama, a form of theatre based on changeable backdrops. Daguerre was initially interested in using Niépce's technology to improve his theatrical presentations.

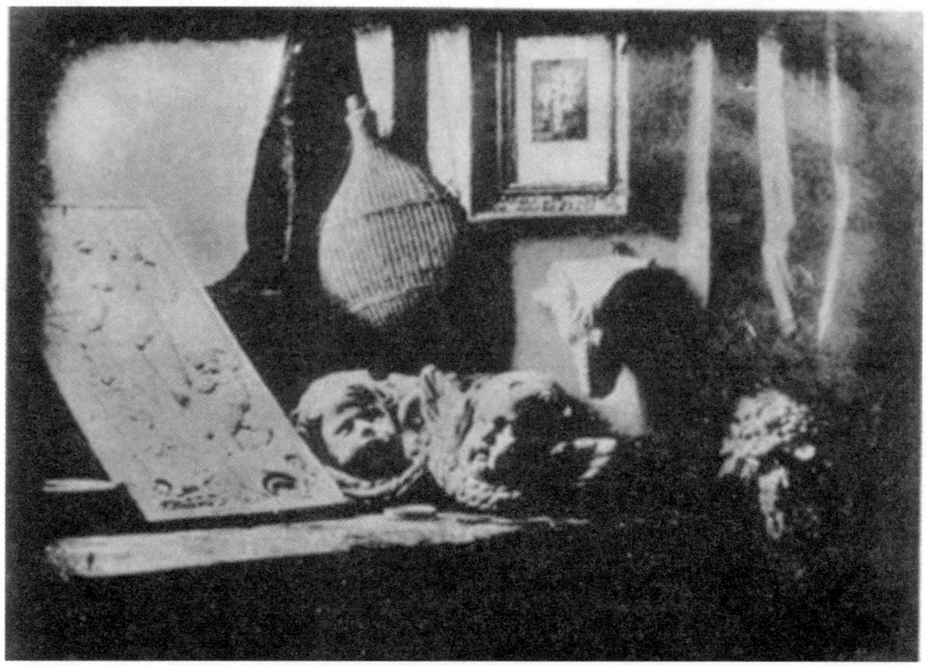

Figure 5. The first Daguerreotype.

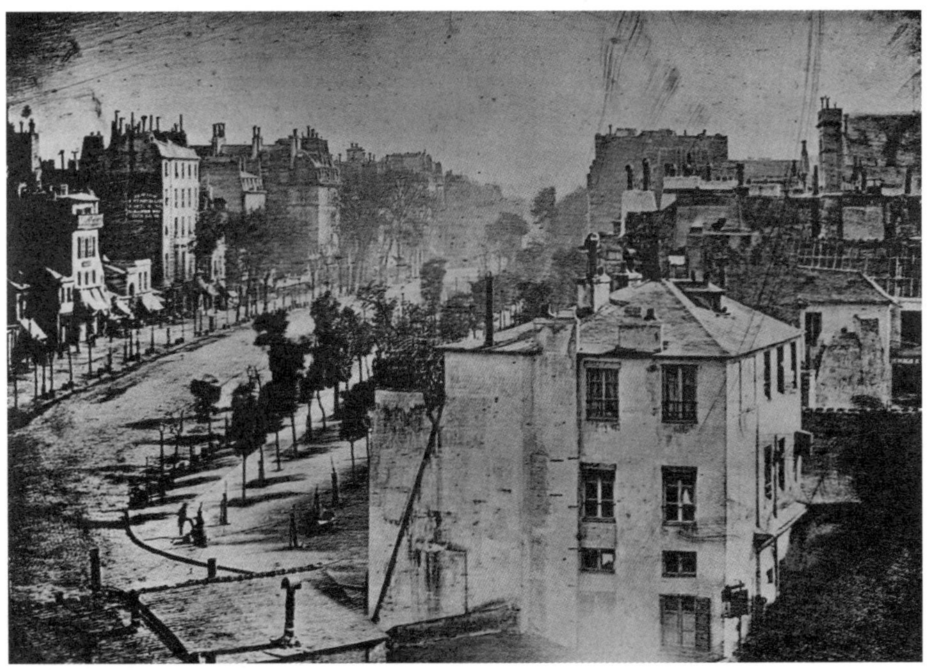

Figure 6. The man to the lower left probably never knew that he made history by getting his shoes shined. He became the first person ever to have his picture taken.

When Niépce died suddenly of a stroke in 1833, Daguerre continued experimenting with various substrates and photographic chemistries. He discovered that he could develop the latent image formed on a sensitized silver-coated copper plate using fumes of warm mercury vapor. In 1837, he discovered the image could be fixed by rinsing the plate in salt water, although later he improved the process by using thiosulfate of soda as a fixing agent. With his new method, Daguerre reduced the time required to produce a photograph to about 30 minutes. Daguerre did not invent photography, but he was the first to make it commercially viable. The earliest surviving Daguerreotype is shown in Figure 5.

Samuel Morse, inventor of the telegraph, was surprised that Daguerreotypes of street scenes did not show people until he realized that due to the long exposure times, all moving objects became invisible[9]. However, in one exposure of a street scene of Paris taken in late 1838 or early 1839, seen in Figure 6, a man getting his shoes shined remained in place long enough to show up in the picture. This was the first photograph of a person, albeit accidental.

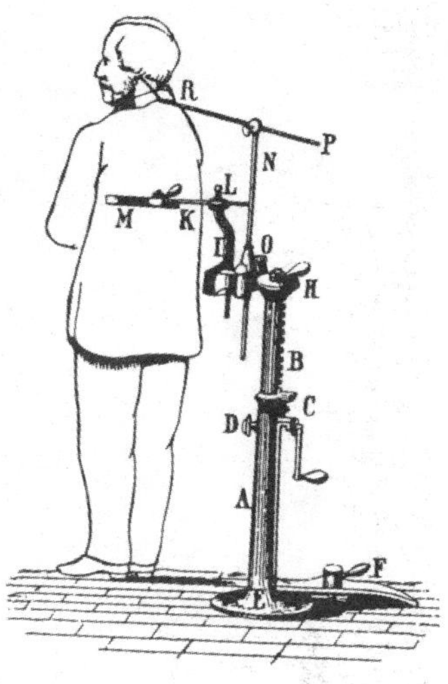

Figure 7. A posing stand[6].

Morse's observation that a subject needed to remain still to have his picture taken represented an important challenge to commercializing photography. Street scenes were great, but the real money was in selling photographic portraits. But this meant that a subject had to be kept motionless for as long as half an hour. To accomplish this, Daguerre fixtured his subjects using head clamps and posing stands[10]. See Figure 7.

Daguerreotype images usually exhibit fine detail associated with a small aperture camera lens and high resolution, long exposure recording materials. (Figure 8.) They became popular during the late 1840s to early 1850s. After the early 1860s, they were replaced by the less expensive ambrotypes and tintypes.

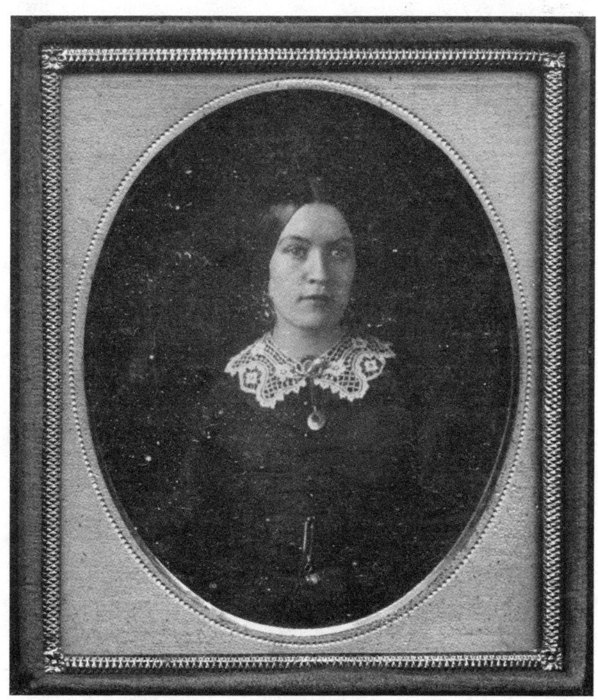
Figure 8. A typical Daguerreotype.

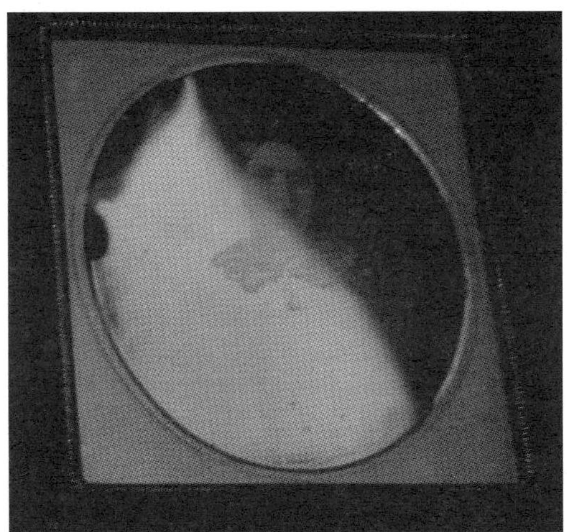

Figure 9. The left half of this Daguerreotype appears in the negative because the light reflecting from it is outside the range of its viewing angle.

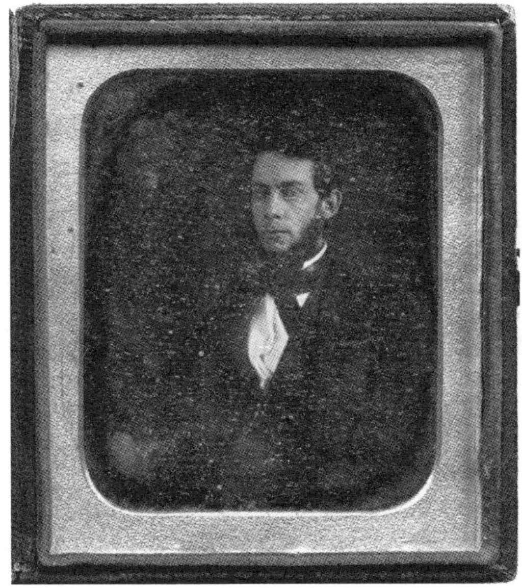

Figure 10. The damage to a Daguerreotype starts at the edges and proceeds towards the center.

Daguerreotypes were made by coating a layer of silver onto a highly polished copper plate, and then exposing the surface to sensitizing chemicals such as iodine or bromine vapor. This created a light sensitive silver halide skin on the surface of the silver coating. Exposing the plates to light reduced the silver halide in the exposed areas to metallic silver, which formed silver mercury amalgam when developed with mercury vapor. The silver halide remaining in unexposed areas was washed away in a final rinse with a fixative to prevent further development. The result was a positive, monochromatic mirror image of the original scene, with more highly exposed areas appearing bright due to the diffuse light scattering properties of the silver mercury amalgam, and unexposed areas appearing dark from the off-axis reflection of the underlayer of bulk silver. Each Daguerreotype was one-of-a kind.

The image of a Daguerreotype can only be seen through a limited range of viewing angles. Outside this range, the image appears as a negative with the bright areas appearing relatively dark and the dark areas appearing much brighter. This happens because outside of the viewing range the mirror-like reflection from the silver substrate visible in unexposed areas of the image causes them to appear much brighter than the diffusely reflecting silver-mercury amalgam created in the exposed areas of the image. Note in Figure 9 that the lace on the right side is light on a dark background but the lace on the left side is dark on a light background, the negative.

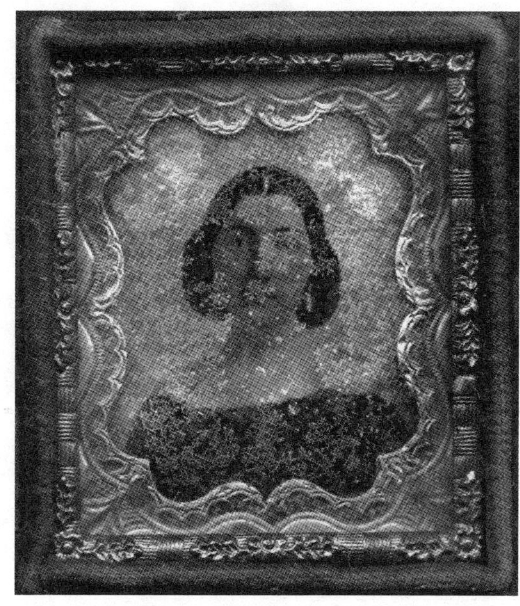

Figure 11. Mercury vapor can be deposited on the inside of the coverglass of a Daguerreotype.

Figure 10 shows a Daguerreotype whose seal has been broken open so that the image has been exposed to the elements. It is a good example of how a Daguerreotype image deteriorates from the edges inward. The Daguerreotype in Figure 11 exhibits another type of damage experienced by Daguerreotypes. The small deposits that can be seen on the inside glass surface come from the outgassing of mercury vapor that , in amalgam with the silver, is responsible for the bright parts of the image[11].

The damaged Daguerreotype in Figure 12 shows the parts of its assembly. First, a brass mat or a piece of tape was placed around the edges of the plate to serve as a shim to support a protective cover glass. A metal mat was placed over the glass, and the assembly was sealed in a metal or cardboard frame or a small box. Also shown is the copper surface of the back of the Daguerreotype plate.

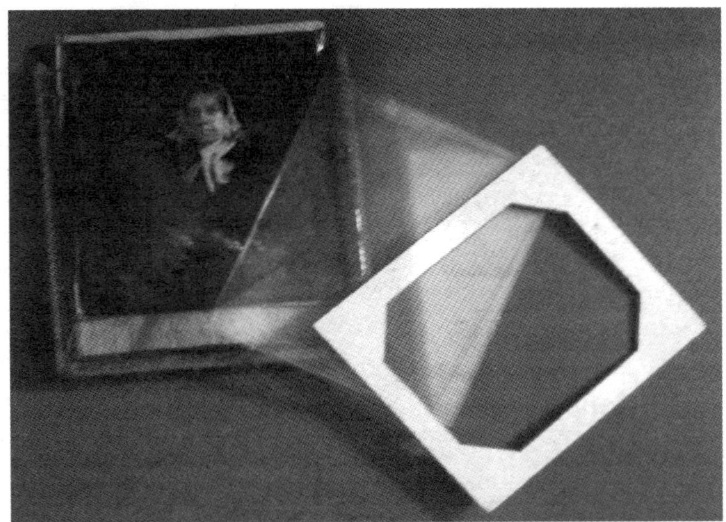

Figure 12. A damaged Daguerreotype showing the parts of its assembly.

Daguerreotypes can be identified by:

- Narrow viewing angle
- Image appearing as a negative outside of the viewing angle
- Image reversed left to right
- Copper back
- High resolution
- High contrast
- Glass cover protecting image
- Deterioration usually starting from the edges

Outdoor Photography

The Daguerreotype shown in Figure 13, supposedly produced in 1840, was originally identified as the only known photograph of Constanze, the wife of the Austrian composer Wolfgang Amadeus Mozart. It is known that the photograph was taken in the Bavarian village of Altoetting in front of the home of her old friend Maximillian Keller. It was allegedly two years before Constanze's death in Salzburg at the age of 80. Constanze was

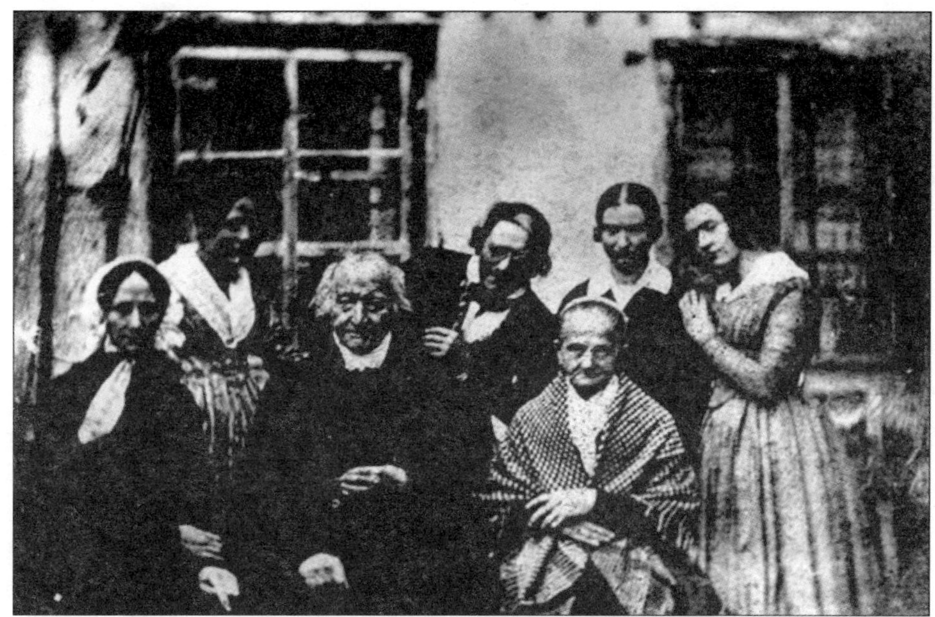

Figure 13. Mozart's wife?

said to be the woman on the left in the front row next to Max Keller. Keller's wife Josefa is on his right. Behind them are (from left to right) are the family cook, Keller's brother-in-law Philipp Lattner, and his daughters Josefa and Luise[2]. Over the years, this photograph has received much attention in the music community as potentially the only picture of the wife of the famous composer.

Much of the debate on the identification of the woman as Constanze has relied on historical information. In 1840, Constanza was crippled with arthritis and probably unable to travel to see Keller. There was no evidence that she had been contact with him since about 1826[3]. Furthermore, although the composer's wife kept meticulous diaries of her activities, there is no mention of a trip to Bavaria, which would have been a major undertaking for her.

More objectively, the story is inconsistent, not with what we know about Constanze, but rather with the history of photography.

Daguerreotypes were first produced in 1839, so it would not be out of the question to find one dating from 1840. However, *outdoor photographs of people* were not possible until 1841 when Joseph Petzval invented the Petzval lens for correcting chromatic aberration.

When sunlight passes through a glass prism, it is broken into the colors of the spectrum. A single element glass lens has the same property so that different wavelengths of light focus at slightly different positions along the optical axis. Each individual color image might be sharp in its respective focal plane. However, the only plane of importance in photography is that of the recording material, and in this plane, all but one of the colors will be out of focus. The result is an image that is blurred and surrounded by colored halos. This is called chromatic aberration.

We've already discussed that an early photographer didn't need a lens to produce photographs using camera obscura, as long as he was willing to pay the price of very long exposure times. If he wanted to speed things up,, he could open his aperture and use a lens to focus the image while reducing exposure times to only a few minutes. The aperture used was still relatively small, so that chromatic aberration was not a problem.

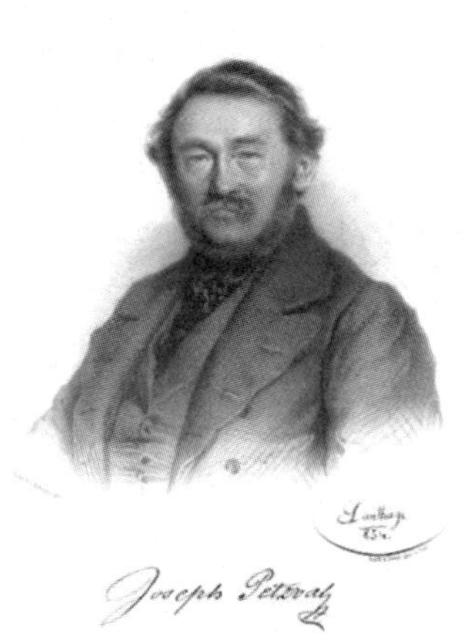

Figure 14. Joseph Petzval[12].

This was a good fix for photographs taken in a studio, where a subject could be kept both somewhat comfortable and stationary for many minutes. However, this was not a solution for taking pictures of people outdoors. Even though a lot more light was present outside, exposures could still be several minutes long, a very long time for a person or group of people to sit still in strong sunlight. It was also impossible to take pictures of outdoor activities, one of the primary motives for taking pictures of people outdoors in the first place.

The previous remedy of further opening the aperture to let more light in to reduce the exposure time did not work for taking pictures in sunlight. When the aperture exceeded a certain size, pictures taken outdoors became blurry as chromatic aberration manifested itself.

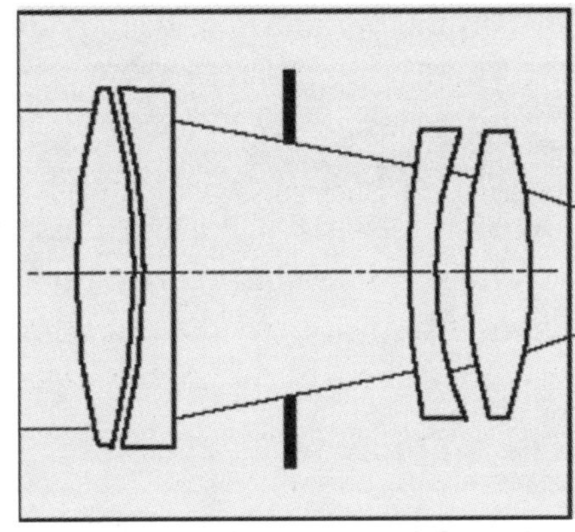

Figure 15. Diagram of a Petzval lens[13].

Outdoor photography had to wait for the invention of the Petzval achromatic lens in 1841. Its inventor Joseph Petzval was a famous Slovak mathematician, inventor and physicist best known for his work in optics. (See Figure 14.) Petzval is considered to be one the founders of geometrical optics, modern photography and cinematography. Among his inventions are the Petzval portrait lens and opera glasses, both still in common use today[12].

The Petzval lens was the first mathematically designed lens. Since all calculations were done by hand it took over a year of mathematical labor to formulate the design.

The Petzval lens is a compound lens that corrects for chromatic aberration present in a single lens. A Petzval lens consists of four lens elements grouped into two doublets. See Figure 15. More modern variants sometimes added a fifth lens.

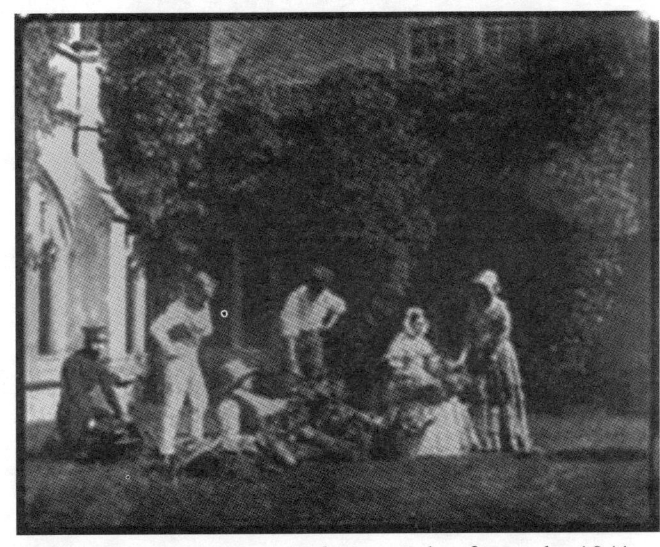

Figure 16. First outoor photograph of people, 1841.

By eliminating chromatic aberration, this lens allowed the larger apertures (and therefore shorter exposure times) required by outdoor photographs. Petzval's design (f/3.7) was ten times faster than earlier lenses (typically around f/14 or f/17), so that it gathered more light than other lenses available in the 1840s[14]. The amount of time subjects had to remain motionless was drastically reduced. The first outdoor photograph of people, taken by Henry Fox Talbot in 1841, is shown in Figure 16.

The Ambrotype

Ambrotypes were introduced by Frederick Scott Archer in 1851. (See Figure 17.) Archer experimented with collodion in the hope of producing a photographic negative on ordinary glass plates. Collodion, a thick and syrupy liquid, is made by dissolving nitrated cotton in a mixture of alcohol and ether[15]. It is still widely used as a liquid bandage owing to its strength and adhesion. It is also a high explosive known as "gun cotton".

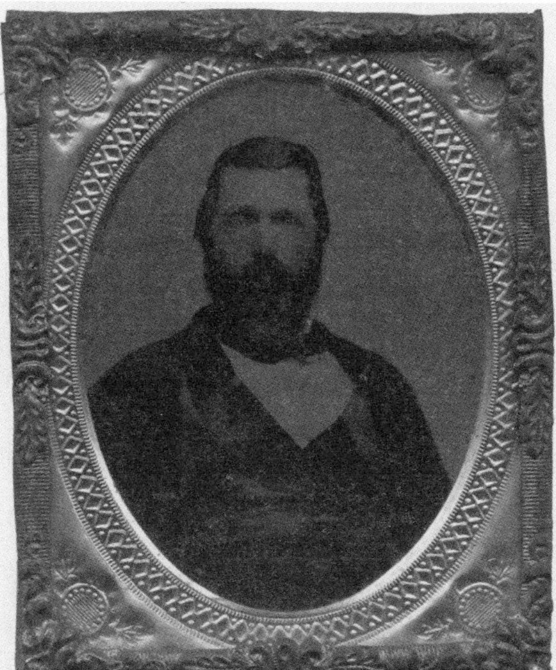

Figure 17. A typical ambrotype.

The processing of an ambrotype was similar to that of a Daguerreotype. A photographer coated a glass plate with potassium iodide suspended in collodion immediately before use. The alcohol and ether were allowed to evaporate, after which the plate as bathed in silver nitrate to create a layer of light sensitive silver iodide. The plate had to be used while it was still wet, hence the name "wet plate" processing.

After exposure, the plate was developed in an acidic solution of ferrous sulfate, after which it was fixed in a dilute solution of potassium cyanide. Since larger silver halide crystals could be suspended in the collodion layer of an ambrotype than those attached to the surface of the silver-covered copper plate of a Daguerreotype, a shorter exposure time was possible with an ambrotype but with a reduction in resolution.

The end result was an underexposed negative image of the original scene. Unexposed areas of the image were removed during processing, so that they appeared transparent and light. This was the opposite of the result obtained for a Daguerreotype, where removal of the emulsion in unexposed areas revealed the layer of silver plate underneath, causing them to appear dark. In other words, because an ambrotype was created on glass, it was a negative image while a Daguerreotype was a positive image. Since the appearance of an ambrotype depends on the diffuse reflectively of the collodion remaining after the plate has been developed, unlike a Daguerreotype, an ambrotype can be seen through a wide viewing angle.

Archer's development of the photographic negative achieved the goal of creating a photographic negative that could be used to create multiple copies of an image on paper. However, the first commercial application of the technology used the negative itself as an ambrotype, a one-of-a-kind photograph that was the successor to the Daguerreotype.

The negative image of an ambrotype gave it an advantage over the Daguerreotype. The negative image on glass could be backed by black velvet so that the clear (unexposed) areas appeared black, causing the image to convert to a positive. The plate could also be positioned face down on the backing, so that the final product would not be reversed left to right and the image would be protected on the underside of the glass.

One of the primary causes of damage to an ambrotype is the degradation or removal of its black backing. Unexposed areas that appeared dark return to appearing clear without the backing. Exposed areas that are opaque are not affected when the backing is removed.

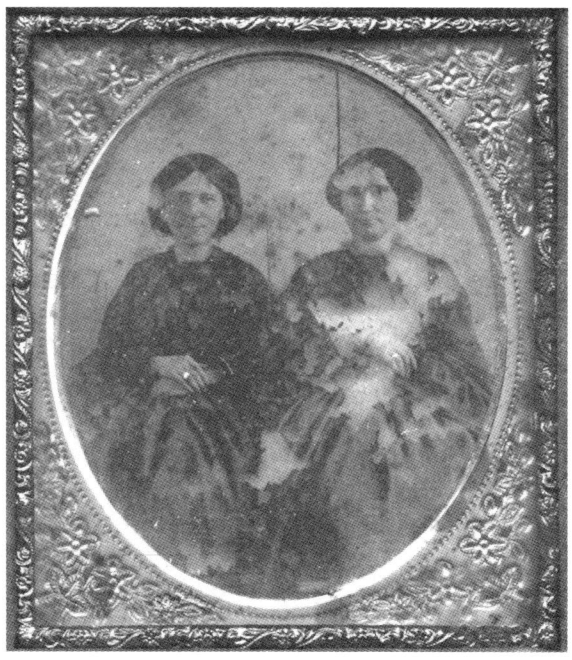

Figure 18. The black cloth backing has deteriorated on this ambrotype.

The damaged ambrotype shown in Figure 18 gives insight to the structure of this type of photograph. The woman on the right is wearing a dark-colored dress, and has her hand on her lap. The area of her dress where the black cloth on the back of the glass has disappeared is transparent. The appearance of her hand remains unchanged, so that it looks like a disembodied shape on the clear glass. (See Figure 19.)

Part of the black cloth on the left side of the same woman's head has torn away. In a close-up of this area, you can see where her hair is clear instead of black because of the missing cloth. Part of the cloth behind the oval of her face is also missing, making it look somewhat lighter than where the cloth is still intact. (See Figure 20.)

Ambrotypes can be identified by:

- Positive image visible through a wide viewing angle
- Not reversed left to right
- Glass substrate
- Black background in the form of black paint, metal, or fabric
- Without black backing, image appears as a negative
- Relatively low contrast

Ambrotypes became popular because glass plates were cheaper and more rugged than the thin silver-coated copper plates used for Daguerreotypes. Ambrotypes were also more convenient to produce, requiring shorter exposure times. Ambrotypes reached their peak popularity between 1855 and 1860. They died out after the introduction of the Carte de Visite (CdV) in the early 1860s, which were printed on paper and could be reproduced in quantity, driving down production costs.

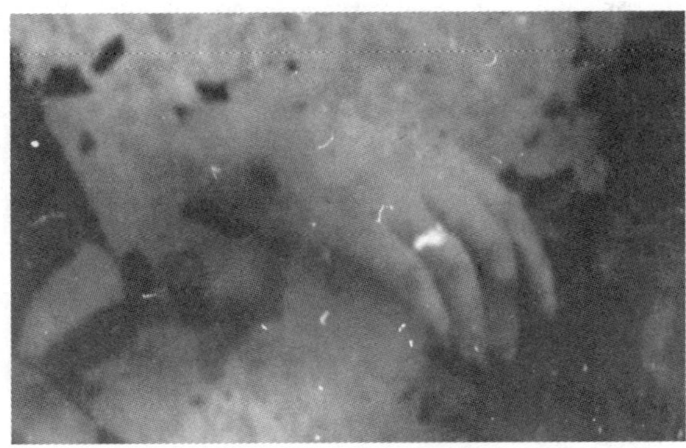

Figure 19. Enlarged area of hand of woman on right where black cloth is absent.

Union Cases

Because Daguerreotypes and ambrotypes were fragile, they were usually enclosed in a small case to protect them from light, moisture, and fingerprints. A case also made it safe to carry a photograph around. Early cases were simply wooden boxes covered with leather or cloth. A case was held together with a metal hinge or a cloth or velvet spine, and latched shut with a simple clasp. The photograph,

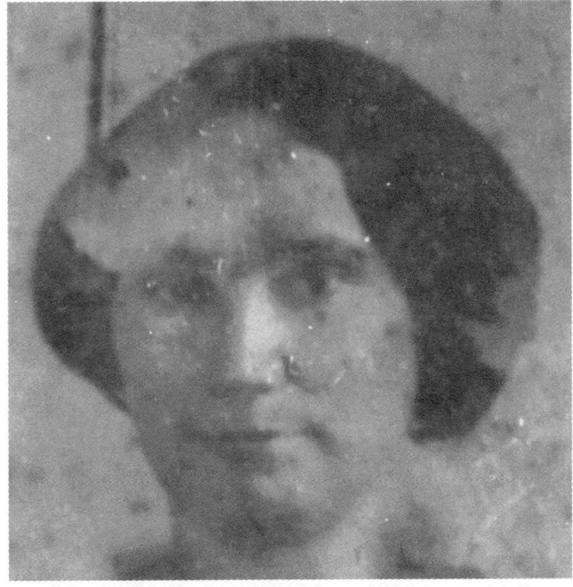

Figure 20. Note differences in skin tone where cloth is is present and cloth is absent.

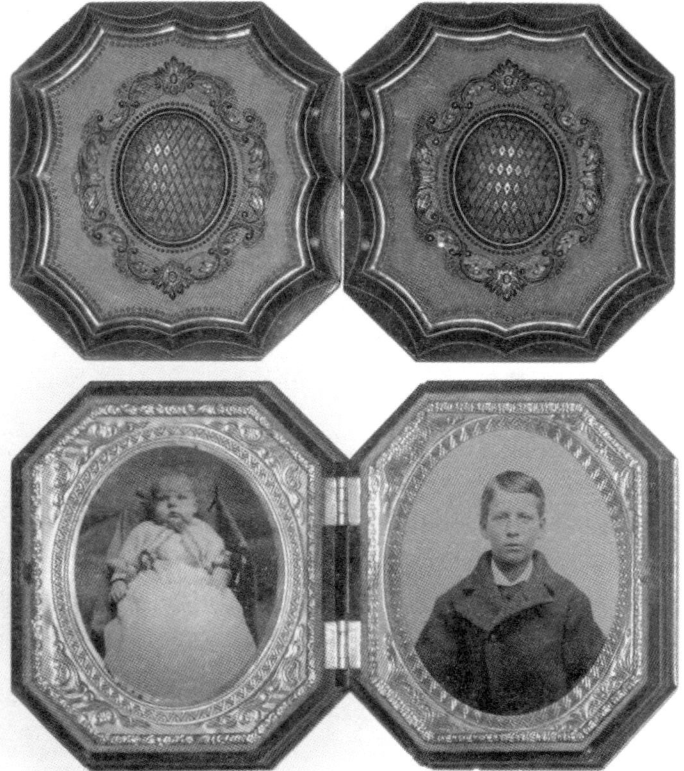

Figure 21. The interior and exterior of a Union case with an octagonal shape.

protected by glass and a mat made from a brass alloy called pinchbeck, was snugly inserted into the back portion. The inside of the top half was fit with a velvet or silk cushion that was occasionally replaced with a second photograph. (See Figure 21.)

In 1853, Samuel Peck introduced a new type of thermoplastic case called the "Union Case". The term "Union" was derived from the union of the components i.e. gum shellac, wood fiber or other fibrous material and a color dye which, when heated and mixed together, produced the thermoplastic compound[16]. The term Union case was created specifically to describe the thermoplastic case, but over the years it has taken on a more generic meaning. All cases or boxes that were produced to enclose early photographs are now called Union cases.

As the demand for Daguerreotypes and ambrotypes soared during the 1850s, the demand for cases to protect them also soared, with a large number of manufacturers producing their own variations. Unfortunately the majority of these manufacturers did not mark their products, so that it is impossible to determine the date and place a case was produced. However in a few instances, a manufacturer's name can be found either inside the top cover or hidden beneath the photograph. The portraits themselves do not present too many details for further examination, but the frames and their cases certainly do. The case shown in Figure 22 was manufactured by Littlefield, Parsons & Co. The inscription inside the case shown in Figure 23 indicates that it was manufactured by A. P. Critchlow & Co.

The manufacture of Union cases was a highly competitive and volatile industry, where very few companies survived. Of these, Scovill Manufacturing Co., Samuel Peck & Co., and Littlefield, Parsons & Company were the most well known. Knowing a little about these companies can help to date the cases they produced.

Samuel Peck was a daguerreotypist from New Haven CT, who held several patents relating to the display and storage of Daguerreotypes. In November 1850 he closed his Daguerreotype gallery and became a manufacturer of Daguerreotype cases. On October 3, 1854 Peck was issued Patent #11,758 in which he detailed a method for strengthening the structure of the thermoplastic case[17]. Even though he did not claim thermoplastic material as his own invention in the patent, because of his detailed description of the thermoplastic manufacturing process he provided, he is usually credited as its inventor[18]. Starting in 1855, Samuel Peck & Co. was a prominent manufacturer of thermoplastic cases. Peck sold out to the Scovill Manufacturing Co. in 1857, although he continued to be listed in the local directory under the same business name until 1860. Scovill was a prominent manufacturer of Daguerreotype plates and after 1866, furnished the United States Mint with copper nickel, and bronze blanks for U.S. coins[19].

At the same time that Samuel Peck was perfecting his version of the Union case, Arthur Critchlow was working on his own. On October 14, 1856, he was granted Patent #15915 'Hinge for Picture Cases'[20]. Although

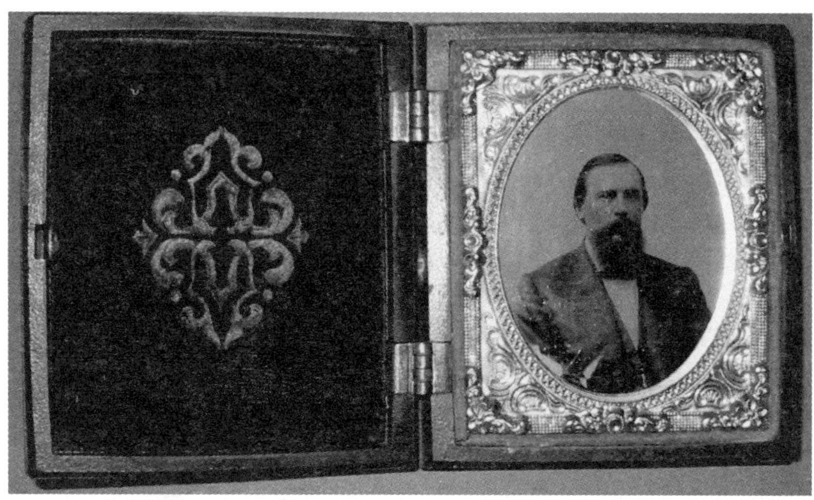

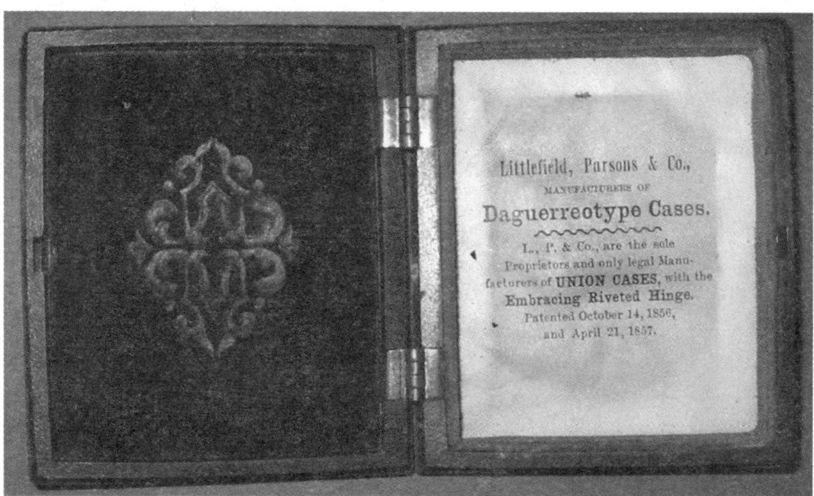

Figure 22. The manufacturer's label, printed in silk, was revealed when the ambrotype was removed from this Union Case. The inscription reads: Littlefield, Parsons & Co., Manufacturers of Daguerreotype Cases. L. P. & Co. are the sole Proprietors and only legal Manufacturers of UNION CASES, with the Embracing Riveted Hinge. Patented October 14, 1856 and April 21, 1857.

Critchlow only vaguely mentioned thermoplastic molding material in his patent as a "compound as being composed of various materials, well known to those whose business it is to manufacture such cases" he claimed his company to be the inventors of the "original composition for the Union case". (See Figure 23.)

Critchlow entered into partnership with Samuel Hill and Isaac Parsons in 1853 as A. P. Critchlow & Co.. In 1857, David Littlefield became a partner[21]. When the popularity of Union Cases was approaching its peak, Critchlow sold his interest in the business and its name was changed in 1858 to Littlefield, Parsons & Company. However, by the mid 1860s, tintypes and paper photographs had greatly diminished demand for Daguerreotypes and ambrotypes. The need for the Union Case was gone. In 1866, Littlefield,

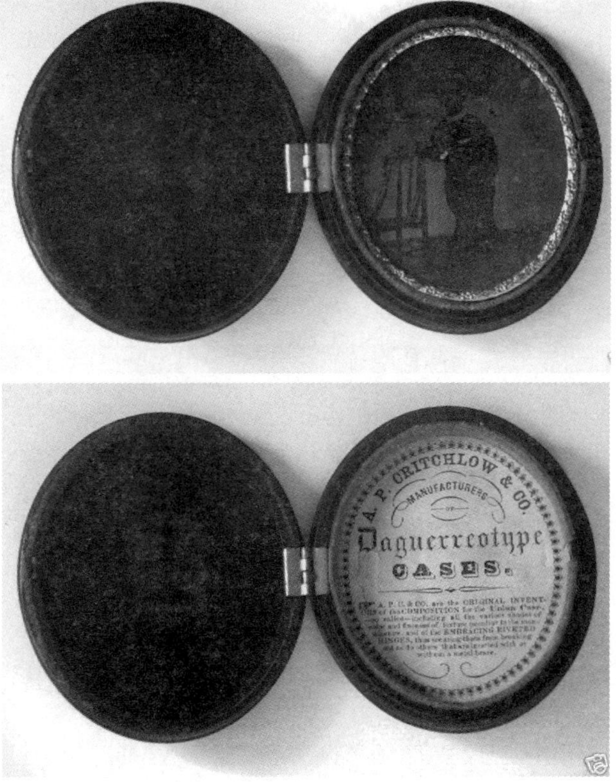

Figure 23. Ambrotype enclosed in a Union case. The inscription reads: A. P. Critchlow & Co., Manufacturers, Daguerreotype cases. A. P. C. & Co. are the ORIGINAL INVENTORS of the COMPOSITION for the Union Case - so called - including all the various shades of color and fineness of texture peculiar to the manufacture and of the EMBRACING RIVETED HINGES thus securing them from breaking out as do others that are inserted with or without a metal brace.

Parsons & Co. changed their name to the Florence Manufacturing Co. and produced a number of beautiful shellac hand mirror and brush sets[22].

From this discussion, the Union case shown in Figure 22 labeled Littlefield, Parsons & Co. was produced between 1858 and 1866. It was manufactured between 1853 and 1858, before the company changed its name.

So far, over one thousand one hundred seventy nine different thermoplastic cases have been recorded[23]. Unfortunately, aside from the presence of a manufacturer's logo, the products of all manufacturers are indistinguishable.

Tintypes

Tintypes, sometimes called ferrotypes, were invented by Adolphe Alexander Martin in 1853 as a less expensive and more rugged alternative to the ambrotype (Figure 24.) The construction of a tintype was very similar to that of its predecessors, except that an iron (not tin) sheet was used as the substrate material. The black blacking that was characteristic of the ambrotype was replaced by a coating of lamp black applied to the surface of the metal prior to the application of the collodion film. A tintype, like an ambrotype, was produced using wet-plate processing, where an image was formed in a silver halide-carrying collodion layer that was applied to the surface immediately before use. Both sides were coated by varnish to protect the image from scratches and the metal from corrosion.

Many of the properties of ambrotypes are shared by tintypes. Tintypes are low contrast, direct positive images, reversed left to right. A tintype can be seen over a wide viewing angle. Each plate was one-of-a kind although it could contain up to 12 images. A tintype can be identified through its attraction by a magnet.

Tintypes became popular during the Civil War because it was possible for soldiers to send them to their families through the mail. They were less likely to break than the glass plates of ambrotypes or the copper plates of Daguerreotypes. In addition, up to twelve images could be produced on a

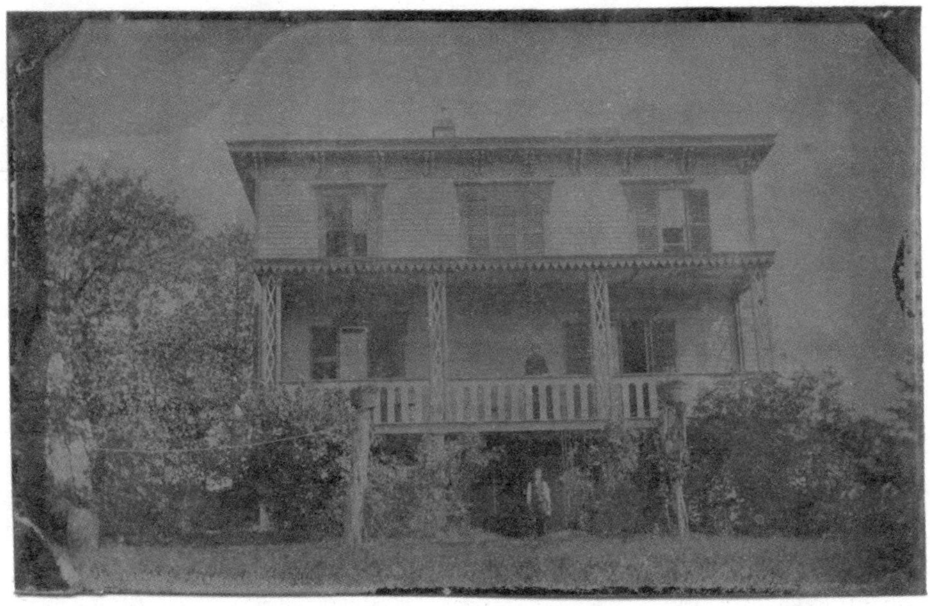

Figure 24. A typical tintype.

plate in a single exposure with a multiple lens camera. It is said that the tintype got its name from the tin shears used to cut individual images from the multiply exposed sheet.

Brown or chocolate tintypes were popularized by the Phenix Co. during the years 1870 through 1885. Another development was the 'rustic' look introduced around 1870 which made use of painted backgrounds of rural themes[24]. Tintypes were popular until the late 1880s, when they were superceded by gelatin dry emulsion plates, although in more rural areas they were produced until much later.

Tintypes experienced a resurgence in popularity in the late 1890s, as a type of cheap and quick photograph sold at carnivals and boardwalks. The last tintypes were produced in about 1930. Tintypes are hard to date because they were produced over such an extended period of time.

A tintype can be identified by:

- Attraction by a magnet
- Wide viewing angle
- Image reversed left to right
- Whitish gray appearance of relatively low contrast

In the Meantime...

Aerial Photography

As photography advanced, many new applications were found for it. The first aerial photograph, for example, was taken in 1858 by Gaspard-Félix Tournachon, better known as Nadar, using a tethered balloon over the Bievre Valley, France. However, this photograph has been lost[25]. The old surviving aerial photograph was taken on October 13, 1860 by James Wallace Black from a balloon at an altitude of 1,200 feet over Boston. Many features of downtown Boston from 150 years ago are still recognizable in a modern satellite photo of the town[26]. See Figure 25.

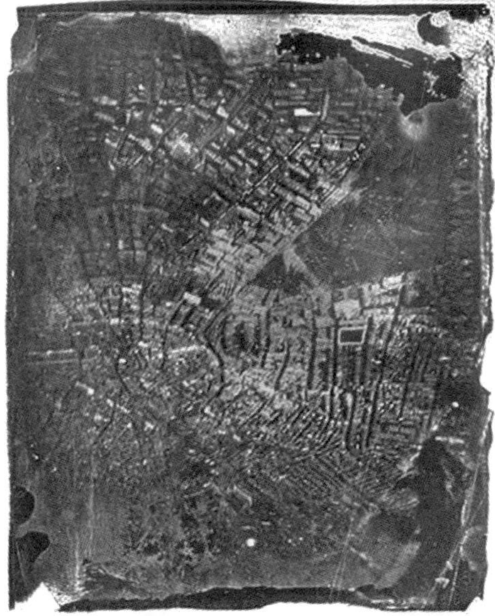

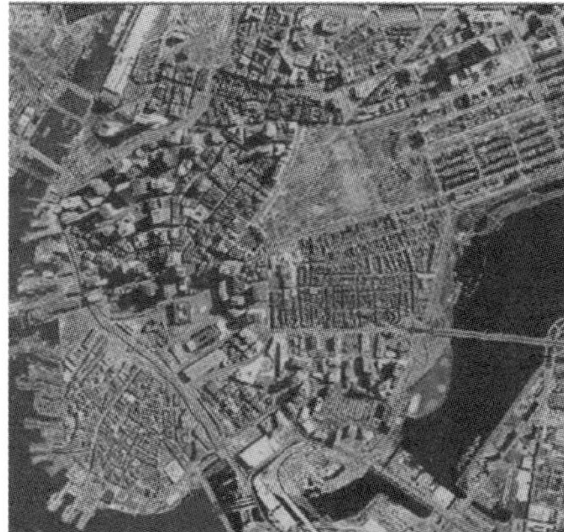

Figure 25. (Left) Oldest surviving aerial photograph, Boston, 1860; (Right) Satellite image of Boston today. today.

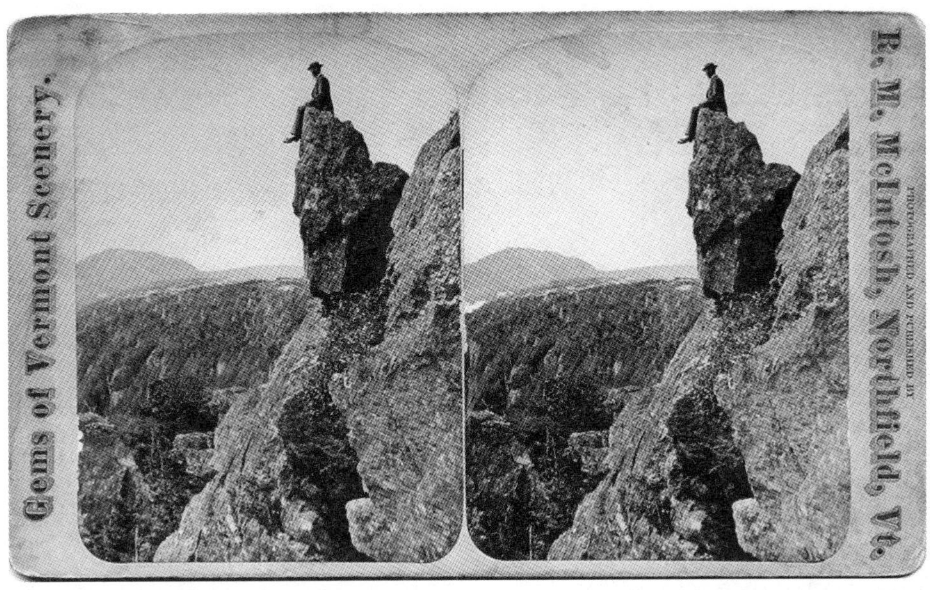

Figure 26. Stereoview of Vermont scenery produced in the late 19th century.

Stereoviews

Stereoscopic images are two dimensional drawings or photographs that show slightly different viewing angles of a scene, such that when one image is presented to the left eye and the other to the right, a three dimensional image results. (Figure 26.) In the modern version, two images can be viewed stereoscopically by projecting them with light of crossed polarizations or with two different colors, allowing the viewer to view them stereoscopically through polaroids or colored glasses.

Yet stereoscopic images preceded the invention of photography by two hundred and fifty years. Binocular drawings were first produced by Giovanni Battista della Porta in the late 1500s or early 1600s. These drawings were probably viewed as stereoscopic images by crossing one's eyes. It was not until 1838 Charles Wheatstone presented to the Royal Scottish Society of Arts a device he called a stereoscope to view binocular drawings using prisms and mirrors[27].

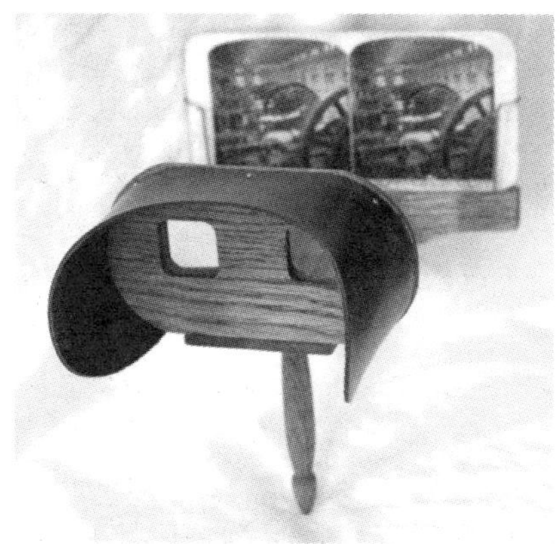

Figure 27. A reprouction Holmes stereoscope[31].

Eleven years later, in 1849 Sir David Brewster described a stereoscopic camera by substituting lenses for the earlier mirrors. In 1850, Jules Dubosq, a French optician and instrument maker, took the first stereoscopic photographs, Daguerreotypes of a spark produced by an electric arc, for which he won medals at the World's Fair in London in 1851[28].

The popularity of stereograms soared when Queen Victoria was presented with a stereoscopic viewer made by Dubosqc at the Crystal Palace Exhibition in London in 1851. As an indication of the demand for stereograms in the mid 19th century, The London Stereoscopic and Photographic Company listed over a hundred thousand stereoviews in their 1858 catalogue. The company was founded in 1850 and stayed in business for seventy years[29].

Stereoview Daguerreotypes, ambrotypes, or tintypes are rare. The production of stereo photographs in quantity had to wait for the invention of photos printed on paper (the albumen print, see next chapter). Their popularity in the US exceeded their popularity in Europe with the invention of a compact, inexpensive viewer by Oliver Wendell Holmes in 1861. See Figure 27. By the close of the 19th century, every middle class home had a stereoviewer and Underwood and Unerwood of New York, one of the largest producer of stereoviews, was selling about 25,000 of them a day[32]. Stereoviewers had become the 19th century's equivalent to the 20th century's VCR.

Underwater Photography

The first underwater photograph is attributed to an Englishman William Thompson. Believe it or not, Thompson took the photograph in 1856 in Weymouth Bay using a 4" x 5" plate camera whose shutter was opened and closed by a string from the surface. The negative plate was prepared on shore in a developing tent, after which it was loaded into the camera that had been prefocused at 10 yards. Although the camera leaked during the 10 minute exposure, Weymouth was able to salvage the image, since the seawater had only left a line at the height the water reached while the camera was submerged[33]. The image was not satisfactory, however, and evidently was not preserved for posterity.

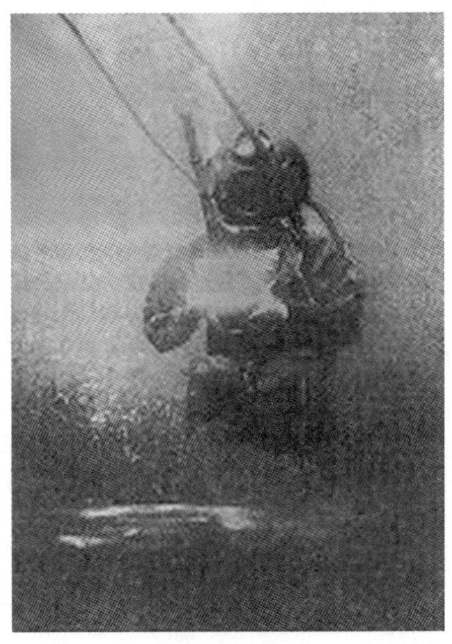

Figure 28. First underwater photo made with hard hat diving gear, 1893.

The first photograph made using surface-supplied hard hat diving gear is attributed to a Frenchman Louis Boutan. See Figure 28. He trig-

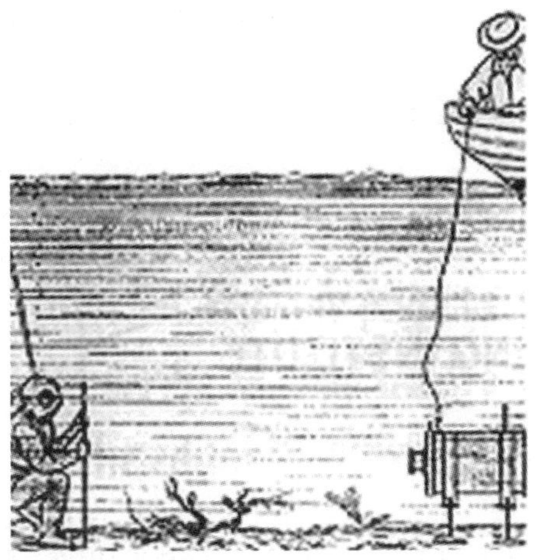

Figure 29. The method Louis Bouton used for unerwater photograph in 1893.

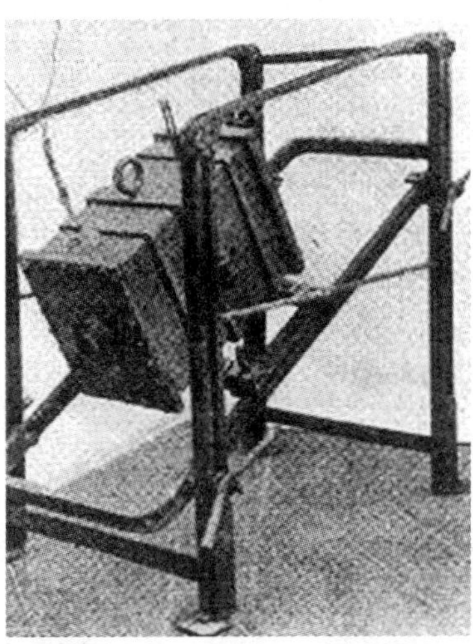

Figure 30. Bouton's 400 lb camera.

gered his 400 lb camera with a string from the surface using 30 minute exposures. A sketch of this arrangement is shown in Figure 29[34]. Good thing this was all done underwater. His camera weighed 400 lbs! See Figure 30.

References

1. www.acmi.net.au/AIC/CAMERA_OBSCURA.html

2. en.wikipedia.org/wiki/Camera_obscura

3. Gernsheim, Helmut and Alison, The Origins of Photography: From the Camera Obscura to the Beginning of the Modern Era, New York, McGraw Hill, 1969.

4. www.usal.es/~histologia/aplicacion/english/museum/microsco/micros01/micros01.htm

5. en.wikipedia.org/wiki/Lens_(optics)

6. en.wikipedia.org/wiki/Ibn_Sahl

7. Ref. [5] op cit.

8. www.hrc.utexas.edu/exhibitions/permanent/wfp/

9. en.wikipedia.org/wiki/Louis_J.M._Daguerre

10. The Daguerreotype Process, www.photohistory-sussex.co.uk/dagprocess.htm

11. The Daguerreotype in America, Beaumont Newhall, Courier Dover Publications, 1976, p 134.

12. Joseph Petzval, en.wikipedia.org/wiki/Petzval

13. hyperphysics.phy-astr.gsu.edu/HBASE/geoopt/mulens.html

14. PhotoNotes.org, Dictionary of Film and Digital Photography, photonotes.org/cgi-bin/entry.pl?id=Petzvallens

15. "Wet Plate" Collodion Photography, William Dunniway & Co., www.collodion-artist.com/History/

16. Luminous Lint, For Collectors and Conoisseurs of Fine Photography,, History of the Miniature Case, www.luminous-lint.com

17. The Daguerreotype in America, Ref. [11] op cit, pp 129-130.

18. Ref 16, op cit.

19. A Brief Historical Profile of the Scoville Manufacturing Co., www.thelampworks.com/lw_companies_scovill.htm

20. American Photographic Patents, 1840-1880, p. 9.

21. The Daguerreotype in America, Ref. [11] op cit, pp 131

22. www.plastiquarian.com/critchlo.htm

23. Luminous Lint, op cit.

24. www.city-gallery.com/learning/types/tintype/index.php

25. www.neatorama.com

26. en.wikipedia.org/wiki/James_Wallace_Black

27. www.rleggat.com/photohistory/history/stereosc.htm

28. en.wikipedia.org/wiki/David_Brewster

29. ancestorville.com/stereoviewphotographs.html

30. Ref. 28 op cit.

31. commons.wikimedia.org/wiki image:Holmes_stereoscope.jpg

32. xroads.virginia.edu/~MA03/staples/stereo/stereographs.html

33. "The first underwater photograph, Briton Beats Boutan", by Brian Pitkin, *In Focus*, The British Society for Unerwater Photographers Newletter, August 1985. www.bsoup.org/Articles/First_UW_Photo.php

34. www.divermag.com/archives/dec96/gilbert1_dec96.html

History of Photography Part II

The Glass Negative and Paper Photographs

The Birth of the Paper Photograph

Daguerreotypes and ambrotypes were one-of-a-kind photographs; multiple exposures could be made on a single tintype plate but none of these three types of photographs could be easily reproduced. The next innovation for photography was the invention of a method to produce multiple, high quality, inexpensive copies of a photograph on paper.

The first step was the invention of the photogenic drawing by Henry Fox Talbot in 1834. A photogenic drawing was a negative image created on photosensitive paper either by contact printing objects such as leaves, or by exposure to sunlight in a small camera called a "mousetrap camera". Talbot used the same process to create the first photographic prints from his negatives. These were called **salt prints**.

To create a negative or a salt print, paper was photosensitized by dipping it in a salt solution and then floating it on a solution of silver nitrate. A negative was exposed to sunlight and then washed with water and fixed with sodium thiosulfate. A salt print was processed the same way, but it was contact printed by exposure to sunlight through a negative. A salt print or its negative is an example of a photograph where the photosensitive chemicals are soaked into the paper, and not coated in an emulsion on its surface.

Salted paper is a type of printing out paper that forms an image directly through the reaction of light on photosensitive chemicals. It does not need a developer.

Talbot improved on the photogenic drawing with his calotype process, where a latent negative image was produced in the camera, and then made visible during subsequent development. Calotypes were made on developing-out-paper that needed a chemical developer to make a latent image visible. The production of the latent image allowed for shorter exposure times, enabling portraiture. Salt print processing could then be used to make prints from a calotype negative. Talbot's calotype process defined the basis for taking pictures that we still use today - the creation in a camera of a negative that can be developed and fixed to produce any number of positive prints of an image[1].

Since salt prints were formed by absorption of the photosensitive chemicals into the paper, the surface features of the paper appeared as part of the final image, reducing the resolution. Although the salt print could produce multiple copies of the same image, its resolution could not compete with that of the Daguerreotype. Salt prints tended to fade easily so that very few have survived. Daguerreotypes were sharp, high resolution images, but they were labor-intensive to make, and could not be easily reproduced. What photography needed was a method that combined the advantages of the two techniques. What emerged was a glass negative that could be used to print a large quantity of high resolution copies of a photograph on paper.

It was known that an increase in the resolution of a printed photograph could be accomplished by using a glass negative, but it was difficult to find a binder which would adhere to a glass surface. Many substances were tried, even snail slime. In 1848 Abel Niépce, the nephew of Nicephore Niépce, solved the problem by using albumen (egg white) salted with potassium iodide. After the suspension was applied to the glass surface, it was sensitized by exposure to a silver nitrate solution and after exposure, developed with gallic acid. However, albumen plates required too long an exposure time to be of practical use.

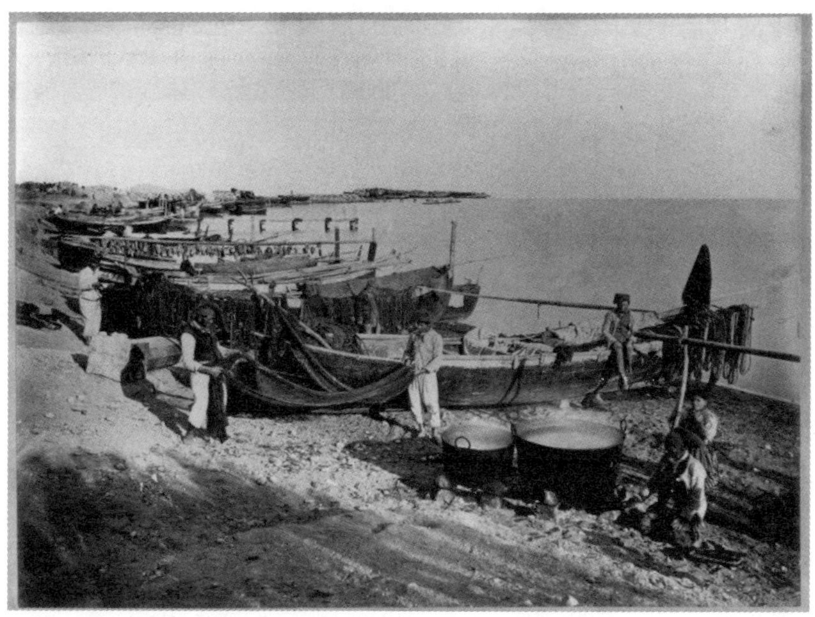

Figure 1. An albumen print.

Two years later, Blanquart-Ervrard perfected albumen printing paper. The advantage of albumen prints over salt prints was that images were produced on coated paper, with an emulsion filling the space between the fibers on the paper surface. This resulted in improved resolution. Albumen prints also required shorter exposure times than salt prints. With the development of the collodion glass negative by Frederick Scott Archer in 1851 , the stage was finally set for the mass production of high-resolution paper photographs.

A typical albumen print is shown in Figure 1.

Albumen prints can be identified by:

- Glossy surface
- Traces of surface features of the paper in the image
- Fine cracks in the surface seen under low magnification
- Strong tendency to curl
- Most are attached to card stock

- Yellowing of bright areas
- Loss of details in bright areas
- Fading inward from the edges
- Inability to produce true back and white tones

Cartes de Visite and Cabinet Cards

Two very popular forms of the albumen print that deserve special mention are the **Carte de Visite** (**CdV**) and the **cabinet card**. Initially, CdVs were more popular and dictated the style of the cabinet card. In later years, when their popularity was reversed, the cabinet card set the standard for the CdV.

As indicated by its name, the Carte de Visite (or visiting card) was the natural successor to the calling card of the 1850s with an embossed or a printed name replaced by a photograph. The Carte de Visite was introduced in 1854 by Andre Adolphe Disderi when he patented a technique to produce eight negatives on a single 8" x 10" photographic plate. This allowed the production of eight 2 1/2" x 4" photographs each time a negative was printed.

However, it was not until 1859 that the CdV's popularity took off. There is a legend, largely discredited, that the CdV owes its popularity to the Emperor Napoleon when he stopped to have his photograph taken in Disderi's studio on his march to Italy. The craze quickly spread to the U.S. where CdVs were introduced in New York late in the summer of 1859, probably by C. D. Fredericks[2].

The Civil War greatly boosted the popularity of CdVs in the U.S. Like tintypes, they were small, inexpensive, and could be sent by mail to a sweetheart or a family waiting for a soldier to come home. Soldiers could also carry pictures of their loved ones into battle. Many famous Civil War personalities were the subjects of CdVs and cabinet card portraits, including Abraham Lincoln and Ulysses S Grant.

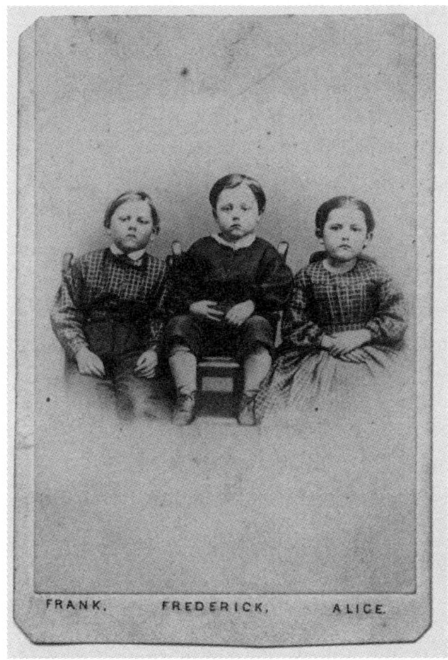

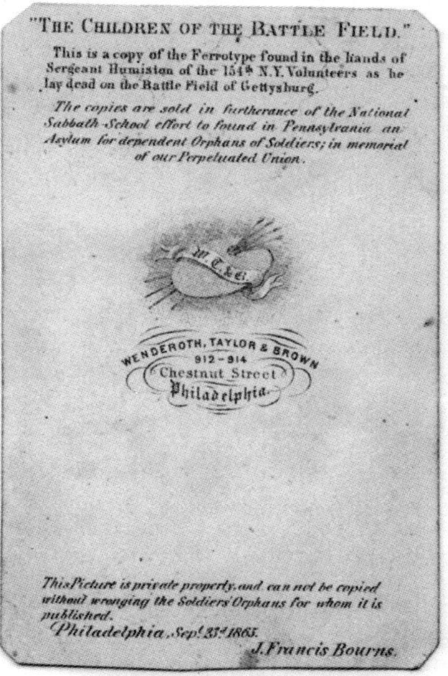

Figure 2. A well-known Carte de Visite from the Civil War-*The Children of the Battleield.* The inscription on the back reads: This is a copy of the ferrotype found in the hands of Sergeant Humiston of the 154th volunteers as he lay dead on the Battlefield of Gettysburg.

CdVs were also produced as copies of older photographs. The CdV in Figure 2 is copy of the tintype "The Children of the Battlefield" that was found clutched in the hand of Amos Humiston, a Union soldier who died at Gettysburg. The card prompted a national search for the soldier's widow Philinda and his three children Frank, Frederick, and Alice[3]. Revenues from sales of the card were used to finance the National Soldier's Orphan Home in Gettysburg, PA for children of fallen Union soldiers.

CdVs of famous people were called "sure cards" because they were sure to make a small fortune for the photographer. Hundreds of millions were sold in England during the 1860s. Queen Victoria was an avid collector, owning over a hundred albums. Within a week of the death of His Royal Highness Prince Albert, the Royal Consort, on December 14, 1861, at least 70,000 of his CdVs were ordered[4].

Cartes de Visite are albumen prints that are typically 2 1/8" x 3 1/2", mounted on 2 1/2" x 4" card stock. Prints can deviate somewhat from this standard size because each print had to be cut by hand from the original multiple-image master print. However, the card stock is more regular since it was usually bought by the photographer from a commercial supplier. Upon the introduction of the photo album in about 1860, the standard size of the CdV was slightly reduced to be compatible with album pockets. Because the photographer attached a print to the card stock himself, the image is sometimes crooked.

CdVs were popular throughout the Civil War because like tintypes, they could be sent through the mail without being broken. CdVs reached their peak in popularity in 1866, after which they were gradually replaced by the cabinet card until production died out in the early 1880s.

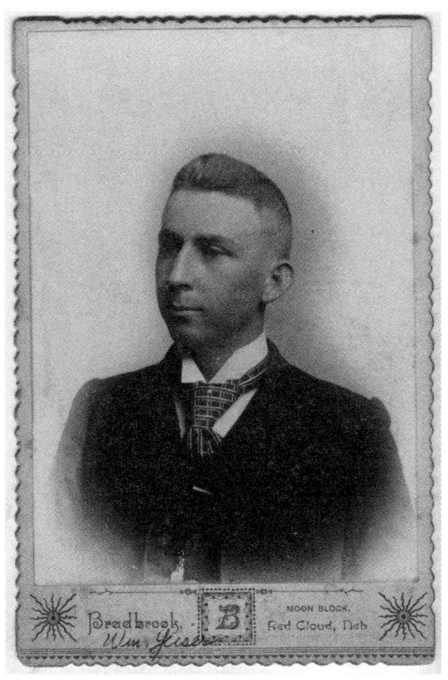

Figure 3. A typical cabinet card from the late 19th centry.

The **cabinet card** was introduced as a larger format albumen print by Windsor & Bridge in London in 1863. (Figure 3.) The name "cabinet card" was applied to this type of picture card because it was too large to fit in a photographic album, so that it was usually displayed in a cabinet. A standard cabinet card consists of a 4" x 5 1/2" image mounted on 4 1/4" x 6 1/2" card stock. Because of the larger size, retouching became a necessary part of the photographic process. Usually a test print was made first to identify changes and corrections to the negative from which final prints were made[5]. Cabinet cards were popular 1870–1890, but by the end of the century were declining in popularity in favor of the snapshot (an unmounted paper photography)[6]. Cabinet cards continued to be produced until the early 1920s.

Cartes de Visite and cabinet cards are notoriously difficult to date. The features usually used to date them - the style of the photographer's logo, the size and the style of the photograph, and the size and the design of the mounting board, changed independently and irregularly over time and location. The news of a new style or a new technical development took time to spread, and was not necessarily accepted right away. Photographers in urban areas were more likely to have access to the latest innovations and to accept them quickly in order to stay ahead of the competition. A photographer in New York City would probably be more willing to adopt a new style than his counterpart in Tickfaw, Louisiana, especially if it required the upgrade of his photographic equipment.

To make matters worse, each of these main features can be considered a composite of sub-features that changed on their own schedules. A style of mounting board or mat is usually characterized by its size, thickness, border style, the use of square or rounded corners, and so on, all of which changed at different times in different locations. It is difficult to pin down when and where a CdV or a cabinet card was produced, although it can be helpful to compare it to one of a similar style of known origin.

However, as it was pointed out in Chapter 1, Remember to Look at the Back, the Edges, the Shape, the Paper, the Mat......, the type of material the card is mounted on can provide an unambiguous clue to an earliest date it could have been produced. If the mount is made of cardboard or pressboard composed of several thin laminated layers, the photo was produced after 1870, when the technology for manufacturing cardboard was first introduced. On the other hand, if the mount is one solid layer of Bristol board, it is not possible to say when it was produced and other features must be used to date it. There are CdVs and cabinet cards produced in the 1860s through the late 1890s that are mounted on single-layer Bristol board.

To quote again from the website www.city-gallery.com/?q=node/17: "Card stock [of cabinet cards] is thicker than [that of] the Carte de Visite

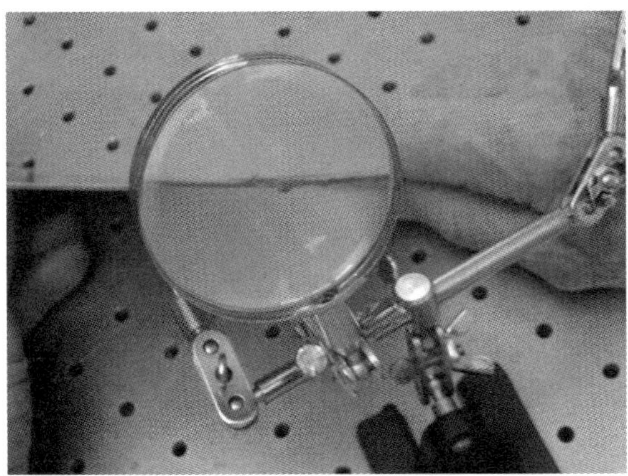

Figure 4. Under magnification, the separation of the layers of cardboard is evident, especially at the corners.

with earlier cards being made of Bristol Board, gradually giving way to various types of press board...or cardboard (paper made from pressed layers of paper like a sandwich)...throughout the 1880's and 1890s as technology for manufacturing cardboard advanced. Cards showing evidence of separating layers on the edges are definitely made after the introduction of pressboard and cardboard technology (after 1870) replacing the Bristol Board (a single layer card stock) of the 1860s." See Figure 4.

We'll limit the discussion primarily to cabinet cards, since CdVs had greatly decreased in popularity by the 1870s. However, it would not be surprising to find CdVs produced after 1870 that are on cardboard mounts. Although the CdV and the cabinet card can be distinguished by size, both types of cards were mounted on whatever paper stock was commercially available. Therefore, both types of cards must have experienced the same increase in thickness in cardboard mounting and in the number of layers the cardboard was composed of.

To test whether the thickness of its cardboard mount could be used to date a cabinet card, we used a micrometer to measure a collection of cards that were produced between 1875 and 1900. See Figure 5. The cards were from our personal collection; all but one were produced by photographers in Red Cloud, NE. We only used a card if it was marked with a date. While these cards represent only a small sampling of the variety of cards produced during the 19th century, they provide insight into the changes in format and style experienced by cards produced elsewhere in the country.

Our results (Figure 6) show that the thickness of card stock gradually increased over time so that it can be used to obtain a fairly accurate date for a cabinet card. In the early to mid 1870s, card stock was just below 20 mils. From about 1880 through 1895, the thickness increased gradually to nearly 30 mils. From 1895 forward, the thickness of the cardboard mount increased very rapidly to almost 70 mils in 1900. We believe this was due to an improvement in cardboard manufacturing technology, but we are still researching this.

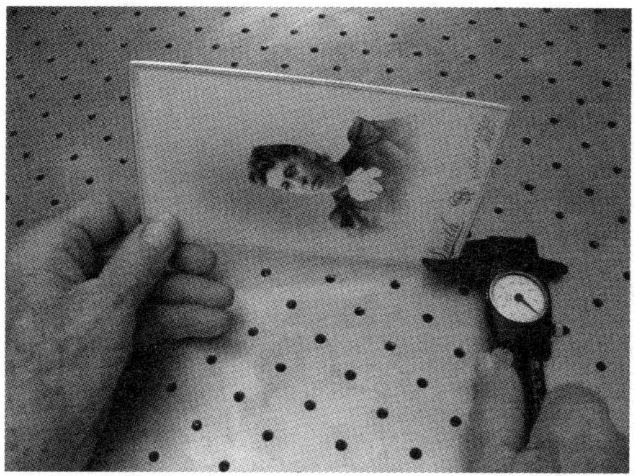

Figure 5. How to measure the thickness of cabinet card mounts.

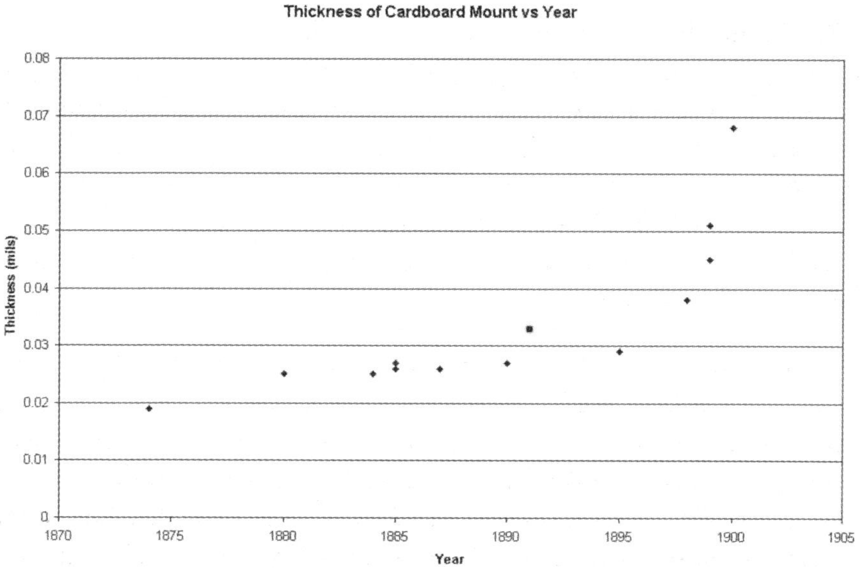

Thickness of Cardboard Mount vs Year

Thickness (mils): 0, 0.01, 0.02, 0.03, 0.04, 0.05, 0.06, 0.07, 0.08

Year: 1870, 1875, 1880, 1885, 1890, 1895, 1900, 1905

Figure 6. Thickness of Cartes de Visite and cabinet cards as a function of the year they were produced.

We only found one cabinet card that did not fit in with the rest. It was produced in 1891 in San Francisco and is shown by a square on the graph. It would be interesting to compile data on cards from a variety of locations. The steady increase in the thickness of available card stock was undoubtedly common everywhere, with some photographers having access to new and improved stock while others continued to use old, thinner stock until their supply as exhausted. It might be possible to date a card by comparing the thickness of its stock to that of cards of known dates produced in the same city.

It must be noted that the date derived for a card from its mount is not necessarily the date the image was produced. Commercial card stock was sometimes stored and used at a later date to mount a print. It is also not uncommon to find an earlier Daguerreotype, ambrotype, or tintype that was copied later as an albumen print. For example, the Carte de Visite shown in Figure 2 of "The Children of the Battlefield" was copied from an earlier tintype.

The fact that a copy of a card was produced at a later date than its original can be deduced if the cards were produced by different photographers. If the same photographer made both and they were produced between August 1, 1864 and August 1, 1866 during the Civil War, the original and the copy can be distinguished by the relative value of the tax stamps on the back. Items including photographs were taxed during the War according to how much they sold for. A copy was less expensive than the original, so that the value of the tax stamp on the back of a copy will be less than that on the back of the original. (See the section Sun Picture Tax Stamps below for more information on tax stamps.) Cabinet cards can also be copies of earlier Cartes de Visite. See Figure 7.

An extensive matrix for dating CdVs has been developed by Bill & Glenna Jo Christen. It is based on data obtained from William C. Darrah's *Cartes de Visite in Nineteenth-Century Photography,* for which he examined forty thousand cards[7]. The matrix provides information on dating CdVs according to type of card stock, stock thickness, decorative features on the front of the card, backmarks and imprints, print medium, and image or pose for cards produced from 1858 through 1870. Because many features appeared over a broad range of years, it is suggested that a combination of features should be used to narrow down the date for a CdV. The reader is referred to the website in Reference 7, as the matrix is too extensive to include here.

To supplement the Carte de Visite Matrix with information on cartes produced from 1858 through the turn of the 20th century, we include additional information from www.PhotoTree.com, a popular website dedicate to 19th century photography[8]. This information is said to specifically apply to CdVs, although the last were produced during the 1880s. However, because the styles of the CdV and the cabinet card followed the same trends, the descriptions pertaining to CdVs produced after 1880 can also be applied to cabinet cards.

Several of the guidelines that appear on PhotoTree.com are shown in Tables 1, 2, and 3. We include information for dating a CdV by the thickness of its mount to give the reader a complete set of information from this source. Note that the PhotoTree information is consistent with our

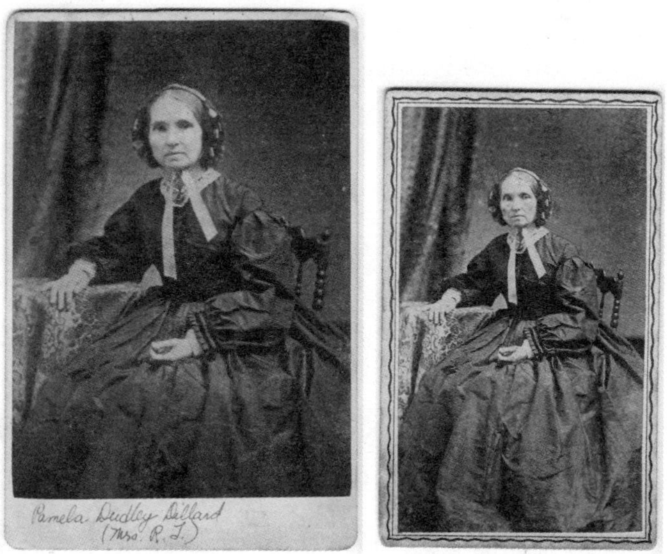

Figure 7. A cabinet card (left) from 1874 that was copied from an earlier Carte de Visite (right).

own measurements presented earlier. As a summary, the *Quick Identification Chart* appearing on the PhotoTree website is given in Table 4.

Card Thickness: We've already discussed the thickness of a card as a function of the year it was produced. The information contained in Table 1 is reasonably consistent with our measurements, considering we used a sample that was small compared to the variety of cards produced through the end of the 19th century.

Table 1. CdV thickness according to year

Thickness	Year
0.01" - 0.02"	1858 - 1869
0.02" - 0.03"	1869 - 1887
0.03" - 0.04"	1880 - 1900

Card Corners: Card corners were mostly square until about 1870. After this, corners became rounded to make them less prone to wear and tear. Older cards might appear to have rounded corners, but close examination will reveal that corners that were originally square have become rounded through handling. Square corners that have been damaged in this way are generally more ragged than corners that were originally round.

Image Size: Image size gradually became larger due to the improvement of photographic equipment. This improvement did not relate to the technical ability to take larger photographs. It related to the technical ability to take larger photographs with higher quality and adequate resolution, since the larger the image, the more noticeable an imperfection. In general, the smaller the photograph, the earlier it was produced, with dime-sized photographs dating from before 1865. (Table 2.)

Table 2. Image sizes according to year

Image Size	Year
< 3/4"	1860-1864
About 1"	1862-1867
1 1/2" - 1 3/4"	1865-1872
2 1/8" - 3 1/2"	1874-1910

Borders can be used to date a CdV according to how many lines were used and how wide they were. A rule of thumb for dating a CdV according to its borders is that the fewer the lines used to border the photograph, and the thinner these lines are, the earlier the CdV was produced. (Table 3.)

Table 3. CdV borders according to year

Number of Lines	Year
None	1860-1863
One or Two Thin Lines One Wide and One Thin Line	1863-1869
Wide Lines	1874-1880

Props, backgrounds and card styles developed in parallel, starting from the very basic and ending with the ornate and imaginative. Early props and backgrounds consisted only of a chair or a table that the subject could lean on. Initially, card stock was white with straight edges. But around 1870, backdrops became much more inventive, and from about 1874 forward, colored card stock appeared sometimes with gilt and beveled edges. After 1863, CdVs were sometimes displayed behind a rectangular or oval mat.

For a quick identification guide for identifying CdVs, see Table 4[8].

The styles of cabinet cards have not been researched as thoroughly as those of CdVs. However, a cabinet card can be recognized at first glance by its larger image and, for cabinet cards produced after about 1880, the photographer's logo and address at the bottom of the mat. As we have discussed, if a cabinet card mount is made of cardboard, it was produced after 1870.

A rule of thumb for dating cabinet cards is that the more elaborate the style of the card, the later in the century it was produced. In the 1880s and 1890s a number of colored card stocks were used, and by 1885 gold beveled edges were in style. In the 1890s scalloped and notched edges appeared, with elaborate patterns on the back. Until about 1895, cabinet cards were albumen prints, from 1895 through 1905, gelatin silver printing-out prints, and from 1905 forward, gelatin silver developing out print[10]. (See the section on Three Layer Collodion and Gelatin Prints below.) Cabinet cards from the 1890s often resemble later black and white photographs, printed on matte collodion, gelatin or gelatin bromide paper[11].

One of the most often quoted references on dating cabinet cards is Willis, *Photography as a Tool in Genealogy*[12]. The information shown in Table 5 reproduced from Willis is not quite consistent with that above for CdVs, it is one of the few sources available.

Sun Picture Tax Stamps

Faced with the growing cost of the Civil War, the U. S. government issued the Revenue Act of 1862, placing a tax on a variety of items. The act also created the Department of Internal Revenue to oversee the monies generated by the tax. Nearly every kind of document was taxed, including deeds, insurance policies, telegrams, and stock certificates. Revenue stamps were designed to affix to these various items proving that the tax had been paid. Manufacturers of luxury goods such as matches, medicines, perfumes, and playing cards took advantage of the 5 to 10% discount allowed for producing their own stamps, and regarded them as an opportunity for ad-

Table 4. Quick Guide to Dating Cartes de Visite[8].

Feature	59-62	63-66	67-69	70-73	74-77	78-81
Card						
Square Corners	X	X	X			
Round Corners			O	X	X	X
Thin Stock	X	X	O			
Thick Stock			O	X	X	X
Tax Stamps (Sep 1, 1864 - Aug 1, 1866)		X	X			
Colored Cards				O	X	X
Gilt and Beveled Edges					X	X
Border						
2 Thin lines	X	O	O			
1 Thick, 1 Thin Line		X	X	O		
1 Very Thick Line					O	X
Image Size						
Small	X	O				
Medium		X	X			
Large				X	X	X

Table 5. A guide to dating cabinet cards[9].

Card Colors	
1866-1880	White card stock of light weight
1880-1890	Different colors for face and back of mount
1882-1888	Face buff, matte-finished; black glossy, creamy yellow
Borders	
1866-1880	Red or gold rules, single or double lines
1884-1885	Wide gold borders
1885-1892	Gold beveled edges
1889-1896	Rounded corner rule of single line
1890-1892	Metallic green or gold impressed border
1896	Impressed outer border wtihout color
Corners	
1866-1880	Square, lightweight mount
1880-1890	Square, heavy board with scalloped edges

vertising. These stamps are found in *Scott U.S. Specialized Catalog* and are known as 'Private Die Proprietary Stamps', or 'Matches and Medicines'[13].

Manufacturers of goods such as matches, medicines, perfumes, and playing cards took advantage of the 5 to 10% discount allowed for producing their own stamps, and regarded them as an opportunity for advertising. These stamps are found in *Scott U.S. Specialized Catalog* and are known as 'Private Die Proprietary Stamps', or 'Matches and Medicines'[13].

The tax on photographs was also called the 'sun picture' tax, after one method used for printing the most popular (and therefore the most tax-worthy) albumen prints. The tax covered all types of photographs, including copies of engravings and artwork, photos used as book illustrations, and photographic portraits. It was paid in the case of an individual portrait by affixing one or more stamps to the back. See Figure 8.

On June 30, 1864 Congress placed a new tax on "photographs, ambrotypes, daguerreotypes or any other sun-pictures." From August 1, 1864 through August 1, 1866, photographers were required to affix a properly denominated revenue stamp on the back of the image and cancel it upon use.

Photographers opposed the tax, and refused to print their own stamps. They felt it was not worth the discount for the relatively small volume of photographs they produced, nor did they need the advertising, as the stu-

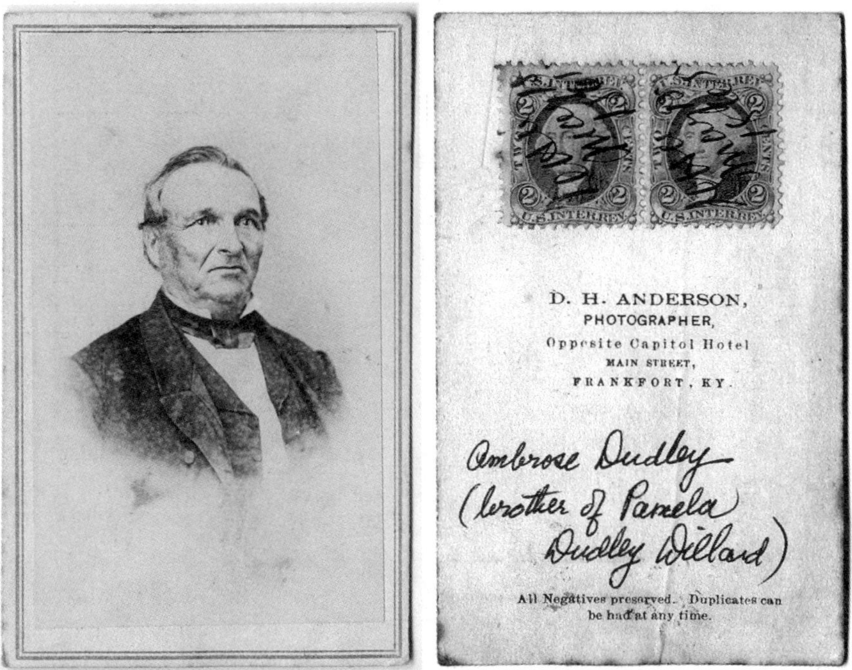

Figure 8. Both of these two-cent George Washington stamps were canceled with the initial of the photographer and the date the photo was taken-May 15, 1865.

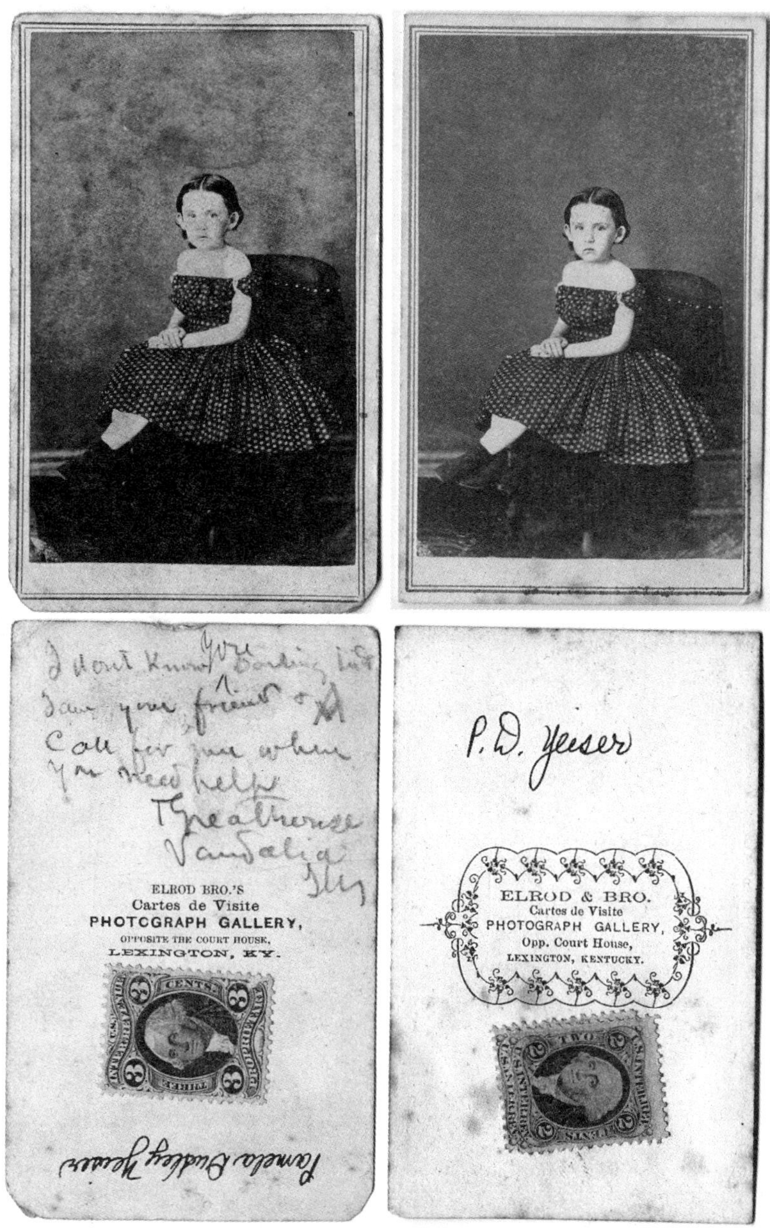

Figure 9. A copy of a CdV can be distinguished from an original by the value of the tax stamp on the back. The original bearing a three cent stamp is on the left, and its copy with a two cent stamp is on the right.

dio logo could be printed on the back of the mount. For this reason, there are no equivalent private die stamps for photography studios. Photos from this era carry official government-issued tax stamps on their reverse sides.

A stamp was canceled immediately upon use. Some stamps were canceled by a simple pencil mark. Others were marked with the cancelation date or the initials of the photographer as in Figure 8. Stamps can be used to identify which of two identical photos is the original and which is the copy. The original cost more, so that it will carry a more expensive stamp. Many photograph tax stamps have survived because photographs were the only items exempt from the stipulation that stamps be destroyed when opening a package[14].

The amount of tax on a photograph depended on the value of the item. See Table 5. The majority of images, particularly CdVs and tintypes, cost between 25 and 50 cents. You will most likely find 2 or 3 cent stamps affixed to them. Most of these stamps feature the head of George Washington, and are found in orange, red, blue, or green.

As it as noted earlier, it is possible to determine which of two identical CdV is a copy and which is the original by the value of their tax stamps. The original cost more, so that a higher value tax stamp was required. Figure 9 shows two cards with the same photo. The one on the left (with the logo Elrod Bro.'s) is the original because it carries a three cent green George Washington stamp on its back. The tax on the copy (on the right with the logo Elrod & Bro.) was only two cents.

Some stamps are quite rare. The blue Playing Card stamp was used only during the summer of 1866[15], shortly before the tax was repealed. The rarest is the red one cent "playing card" stamp, and the most common is the orange two cent "playing card" example[16]. In March of 1865, there was a reduction of tax to one cent on images that sold for under 10 cents.

Stamps were most commonly placed on ambrotypes, tintypes, and CdVs. It is rare to find a cabinet card bearing a tax stamp, since they were not prevalent during this time period. Because Daguerreotypes were not commonly produced during this period, they were not included in the tax.

Table 5. Civil War Tax Rates for Photographs

Value of Item	Tax
Less than 25 cents	2 cents
25 to 50 cents	3 cents
50 cents to $1	5 cents
>$1	5 cents per additional dollar or fraction thereof

Three-Layer Collodion and Gelatin Prints

Towards the end of the 19th century, photography was almost in its modern form. To take a picture, a photographer loaded a glass plate coated with photosensitive material into a box called a camera that was outfitted with a lens. By opening and closing a shutter, the photographer recorded the scene on the plate. The plate was removed and developed in a darkroom, where a negative was produced that could be used to print many copies of the photograph on paper.

So what were the final innovations that brought the science of photography into the 20th century?

The remaining problem to be solved was that a collodion plate lost its sensitivity after it dried, so it had to be prepared immediately before it was exposed and developed immediately afterwards. The equipment required for this was cumbersome, the equivalent of a small chemistry laboratory. It was very difficult for a photographer using a collodion emulsion to work outside of a studio.

The invention of dry gelatin plates was the significant breakthrough that opened the possibility of pre-packaged photographic materials. Although gelatin had been suggested by Robert Bingham in 1850 for producing a glass negative, it was not until 1871 that Dr. Richard Leach Maddox demonstrated that gelatin could be used as a binder for photographic materials[17].

Gelatin is a translucent, colorless, nearly tasteless protein extracted from the collagen inside animals' connective tissue. Gelatin plates had the big advantage that they were used dry so that they could be mass produced and distributed in quantity. At first, gelatin emulsions were much slower than collodion, but in 1878 Charles Bennett announced a new gelatin dry plate process. This was a major breakthrough since Bennett's process enhanced the sensitivity of the emulsion, reducing the exposure time to one tenth of that required for collodion[18].

The dry plate process was very popular, and manufacturers could not keep up with the demand. In April 1880, seeing a business opportunity, George Eastman was granted a patent for a "method and apparatus for coating plates for use in photography" and began commercial production of gelatin dry plates[19]. Five years later, Eastman introduced the first transparent flexible film, followed in 1888 by the first Kodak camera. The stage was set for 20th century photography. Although collodion continued to be used for print paper into the 1920s, gelatin is now used to hold silver halide crystals in an emulsion in virtually all photographic films and papers. Despite some efforts, no suitable substitutes with the stability and low cost of gelatin have been found.

During the manufacture of gelatin and collodion print paper, an extra layer of barium sulfate, called the baryta layer, is added to buffer the emulsion from the irregularities in the paper surface, resulting in a smooth, glossy surface and a higher resolution photograph. The baryta also increases paper whiteness.

This is important in identifying gelatin and collodion prints. The three layer structure gives these prints a glossy, smooth texture. Unlike albumen prints, it is not possible to see paper fibers using a magnifying glass or a microscope. Highlights in an albumen print turn yellow, and fade in non-image areas first, whereas gelatin and collodion prints fade uniformly, if at all. See Figure 10 for a comparison of the type of fading exhibited by an albumen print compared with the fading of the gelatin silver chloride print. Figure 11 compares the same silver chloride print to a silver bromide print of similar subject matter and about the same age.

There is a simple test you can do to distinguish an albumen print from a collodion or a gelatin print. It must be performed very carefully to avoid major damage to the photograph. If a photograph has already been damaged over the years, the type of damage might be the key to identifying its type.

The test involves placing a VERY small drop of water on the photograph in an inconspicuous place, possibly near the edge close to the mount. After a minute, blot the drop and observe whether it has affected the photograph. If the drop causes the emulsion to swell or to crater, the photograph is a gelatin print.

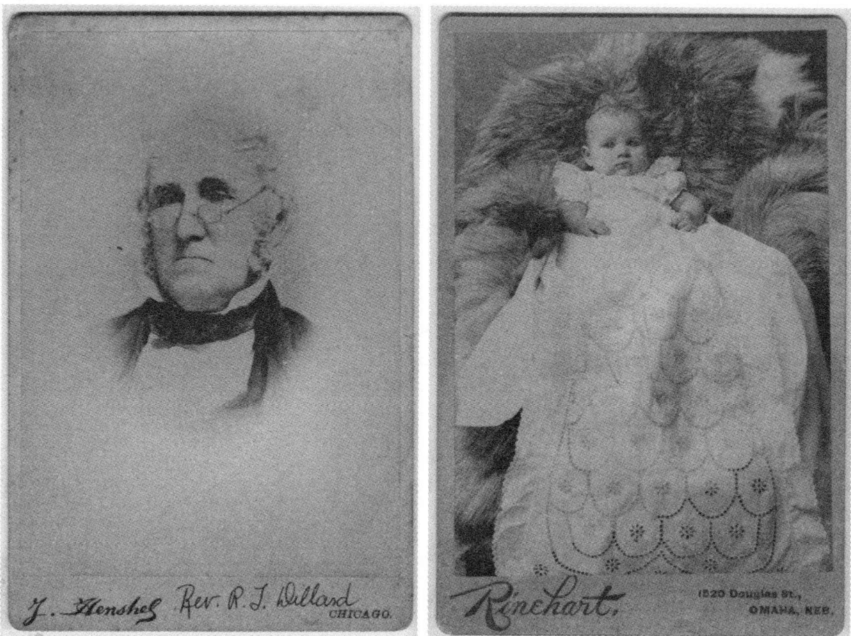

Figure 10. An albumen print (left) loses detail as it fades, a gelatin silver halide print (right) does not.

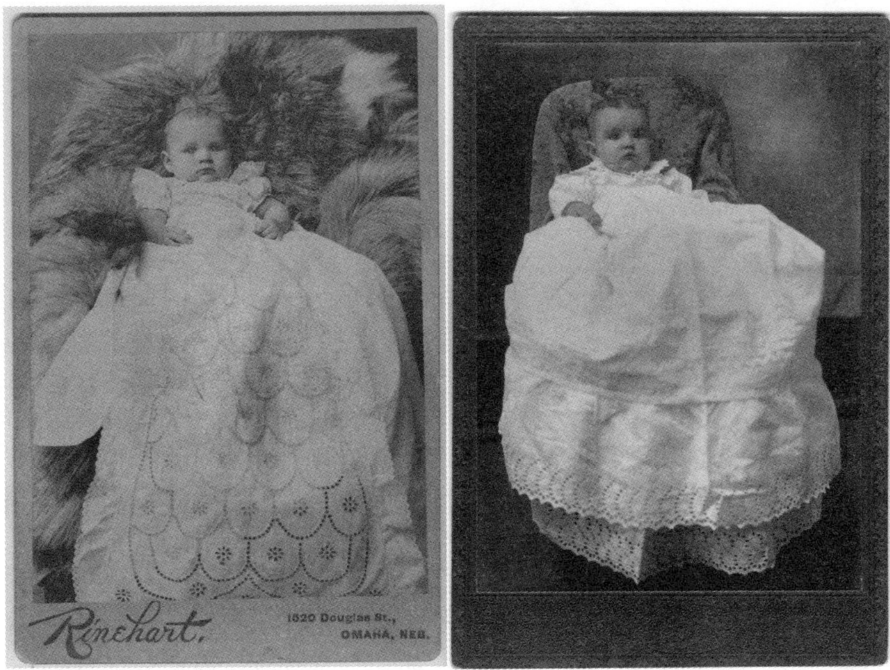

Figure 11. Two types of gelatin print. (Left) Gelatin silver chloride print (Right) Gelatin silver bromide print.

Repeat the same test with a VERY small drop of wood alcohol in another area of the photograph. If the emulsion is affected, the photograph is a collodion print.

If neither water nor alcohol affects the emulsion, the photograph is an albumen print.

If the photograph exhibits spots, examining them under a magnifying glass will indicate if the emulsion has been dissolved or distorted. If so, it is quite likely the spots were made by drops of water, and the photograph is a gelatin print.

Collodion prints and gelatin prints can be identified according to Table 6, taken from The Northwest Conservation Document Center's Preservation Leaflets that can be found on the website mentioned in Reference 20.

Table 6. Guide to identifying collodion and gelatin prints, taken from Reference 48.

Type	Date	Characteristics
Collodion	**Glossy:** late 1880s–1920s **Matte:** 1894 – 1920s	Glossy surface (sepia, purple color) or matte surface (gold or platinum toned, black color), very stable image, rarely faded; easily abraded; usually mounted; paper fibers not visible. Glossy collodion prints often exhibit a subtle rainbow effect on their surface when viewed under fluorescent lights
Gelatin Silver Chloride	c. 1880 – c. 1910	Warmer in tonality than gelatin silver bromide; usually very glossy; often faded to yellow; paper fibers not visible.
Gelatin Silver Bromide	c. 1880 – present	Appears black and white unless image deterioration has occurred; matte, glossy or textured; may be toned to various warm shades; often exhibits silvering; may fade; paper fibers not visible.

References

1. History of Photographic Techniques, uk.encarta.msn.com/encyclopedia_781533746/Photographic_Techniques_History_of.html#s4

2. The American Museum of Photography, "A Brief History of the Carte de Visite, www.photographymuseum.com/histsw.htm

3. www.forensicgenealogy.info/contest_36_results.html. See also Gettysburg's Unknown Soldier: The Life, Death, and Celebrity of Amos

Humiston, Mark Dunkelman, (Westport, Conn.: Praeger, 1999).

4. A History of Photography by Robert Leggat, www.rleggat.com/photohistory/history/cart-de-.htm

5. O. Henry Mace, *Collector's Guide to Early Photographs*, Krause Publications, 1999, p. 134.

6. www.city-gallery.com/learning/types/cabinet_card/index.php

7. City Gallery, Carte de Visite Matrix, www.city-gallery.com/files/pdf/cdv_matrix.pdf

8. Carte de Visite, www.gclark.com/phototree/main/history/hist_cdv.htm

9. www.city-gallery.com/learning/guide/cabinet-date.php

10. www..cycleback.com/earlyphotos/three.html

11. Reference 6, op cit.

12. Reference 9, op cit.

13. www.pipeline.com/~ciociola/baryla/m&m.htm

14. www.pipeline.com/~ciociola/baryla/civilwar.htm

15. www.pipeline.com/~ciociola/baryla/4c-pc.htm

16. Tax Stamps on Antique Photography photos,

reviews.ebay.com/Tax-Stamps-on-Antique-Photography-photos_W0QQugidZ10000000000942929

17. www.rockaloid.com/faq.html

18. en.wikipedia.org/wiki/Gelatin

19. The American Experience, The Wizard of Photography, Eastman Patents a Dry-Plate Process, www.pbs.org/wgbh/amex/eastman/peopleevents/pande18.html

20. Northwest Document Center's Preservation Leaflets, www.nedcc.org/resources/leaflets/5Photographs/02TypesOfPhotos.php

Age Progression

Are the age progression techniques used in criminal forensics useful to the genealogist? The answer is yes and no.

Age progression is a technique with which forensic scientists model what a missing person may look like at a later date based on his appearance when he disappeared. The technique can be applied to missing children as well as criminals who are in hiding. It is natural to try to apply age progression in genealogy to compare an unknown picture with a known one of an ancestor at a different age to establish if they are of the same person. Unfortunately, while age progression in genealogy could rule out a possible match between the individuals in two pictures, it cannot make a definite identification.

An accurate age progression in criminal forensics relies on information about the aging process of family members and other factors such as the known psychology of the missing person. For example, the apprehension of John Emil List 18 years after he murdered his mother, his wife, and their three children, resulted from an age-progressed image that was extremely accurate. A bust was sculpted requiring an in-depth study of the aging patterns of his parents, in addition to a comprehensive psychological analysis of him. When he was arrested, the likeness of the age-progressed bust to John Emil List's appearance was photo-identical.

There is no quick and easy software package to age-progress an image of a person in a photograph. The process takes much practice and skill. Even if the age progression of a photograph is performed by someone with the expertise to produce accurate results given sufficient information, genealogists often lack the additional data necessary to differentiate between two people who might look alike, such as two brothers, a father and his son, or even two unrelated people.

Although age progression has very little value to genealogists, it is still possible to make an educated guess about whether two photos could be of the same person based on physical features such as a person's hairline. Even if a man has lost some of his hair, his hairline tends to retain its original shape, with the part in the same place. The shape of the hair as it falls on the

Submitted by Marcia Snyder.

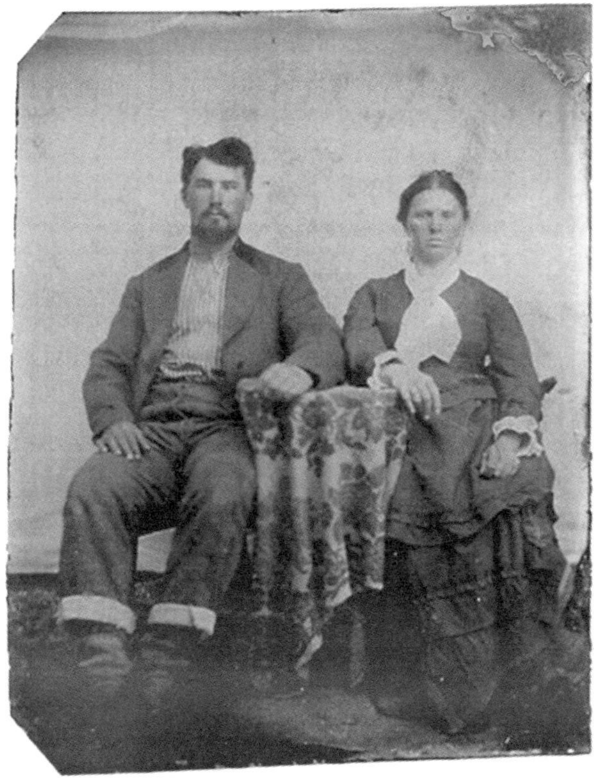

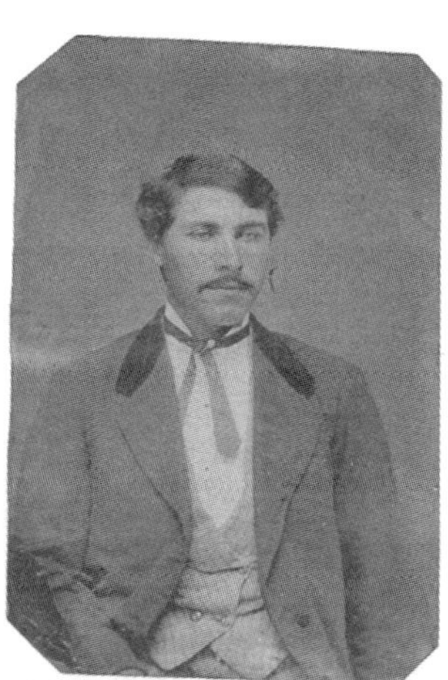

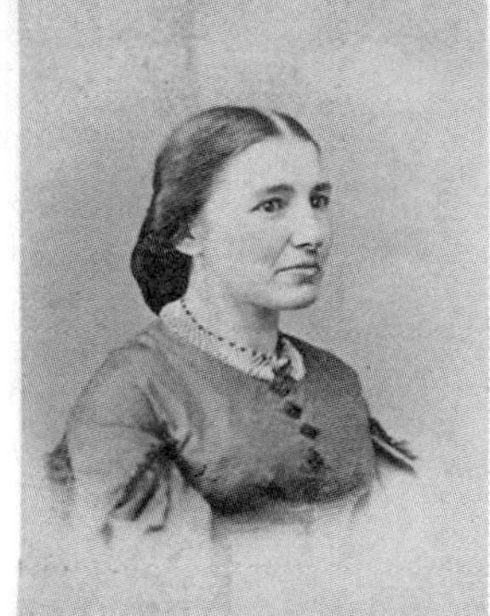

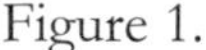

Figure 1.

forehead is another potential identifying trait, as are unusual features such as the shape of the earlobe or a heavy chin. (Plastic surgery was not an issue until recently.)

The three photos shown in Figure 1 are examples of identification by the comparison of physical traits. While there is no conclusive proof that the portraits are of the same people, the photos share certain elements that indicate they probably are. In both photos both sides of the man's hairline are rounded, meeting at his part on the left, high on his head. He has thick hair on both sides of the part, with a lock of hair draped across the right side of his forehead. His moustache does not cover his top lip, revealing a triangle of skin below his nose. The men in the pictures could be wearing the same jacket.

Similar statements can be made about the women in the pictures. The part in the hair of each woman is well defined in the middle of the head, with a thick bundle of hair drawn back from the face on the left. Probability is in favor of the two men and the two women being the same people.

As an example of a case where a match can be ruled out, see Figure 2. The man in the photo by himself cannot be the same as the one on the right

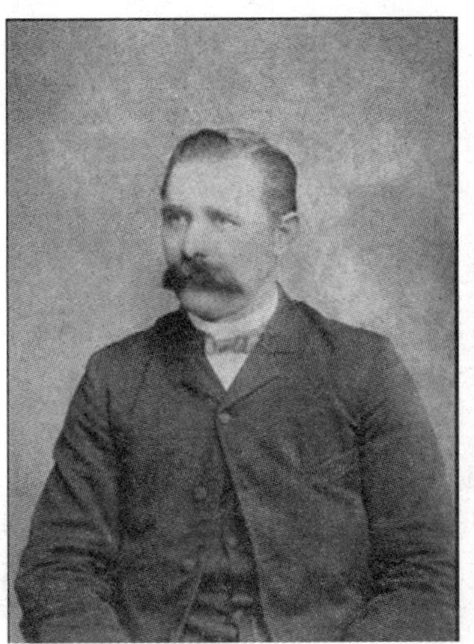

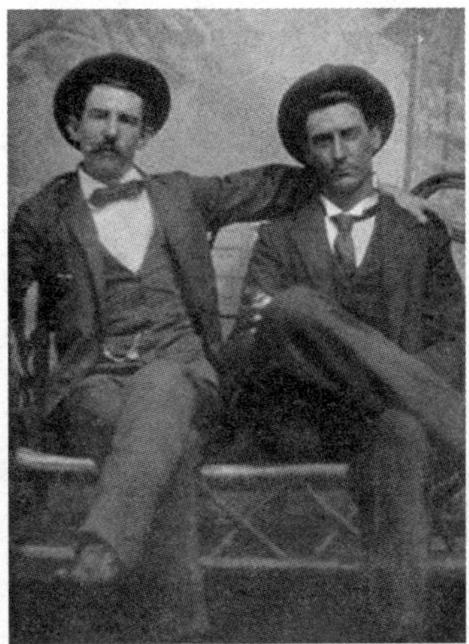

Figure 2.

of the pair of friends. Although they show similarities, the friend on the right does not show the overbite the older man exhibits, nor is the younger man's jaw as wide. The younger man has shadows below his deepset eyes, unlike the older man. We conclude that they cannot be the same person.

On the other hand, there are no conclusive differences between the older man and the friend on the left. Both have similar hairlines, similar moustache shapes, and similar brow ridges. Both are wearing bow ties. (Have you ever met a man who switches back and forth between bow ties and conventional ties?) We conclude that they could be the same person.

Comparing the similarities in photographs might lead you astray. See Figure 3. The man on the left is John Henderson Gray, the father of Lucinda, an old friend who lives in Australia.

Lucinda's father told her many things about his life in the United States before he emigrated to Australia in the 1920s. His father was named Edward, his mother was Mary Teressa, and he had a slightly older brother named Charles. He went to high school in El Paso where he stayed in a boarding house with a couple whose last name was Fish. As a young man, he was a cattleman and in the oil business; he even told her that had his picture taken with Huey P. Long on the steps of the Capitol building. He went to the University of Illinois in Chicago for three years, when he quit school to enlist in the Navy at Great Lakes, IL. Yet in spite of all of the detailed information she has about him, Lucinda has no idea of her father's true identity.

Jake Henderson Gray was born in the United States in about 1893. When he was a young man, he got into trouble and had to quickly leave the country. He arrived in Australia via Germany in the summer of 1926 without a passport and changed his name. He was evidently in touch with his family after he reached Australia, as he was aware that both of his parents died within a couple of years of his departure from the U.S. Lu is sure her father was from Texas, as he sounded just like Willie Nelson and her birth certificate says he was born in El Paso. Her father died June 30, 1970 without ever having revealed his true identity to anyone, including his wife and their four children.

Without already knowing his original last name, it has been impossible for Lucinda to find out who her father really was. Even a Y-DNA test on her brother has not produced any matches. I have helped her search many online census records using various combinations of family names and possible dates. But so far we have not had any luck identifying him.

Recently while she was searching through *Flying Officers of the United States Navy 1917-1919* by Josephus Daniels, Secretary of the Navy during this time period[1], she came across the photo on the right of Figure 3. The man is identified as James Henry Walsh b. 1893, Rhode Island.

The likeness with Lu's dad is striking. J. Henry's ears, though smaller, are the same shape, as are the shapes of the aviator's nose and mouth. Both have long faces with an extended chin. If you allow for the age difference

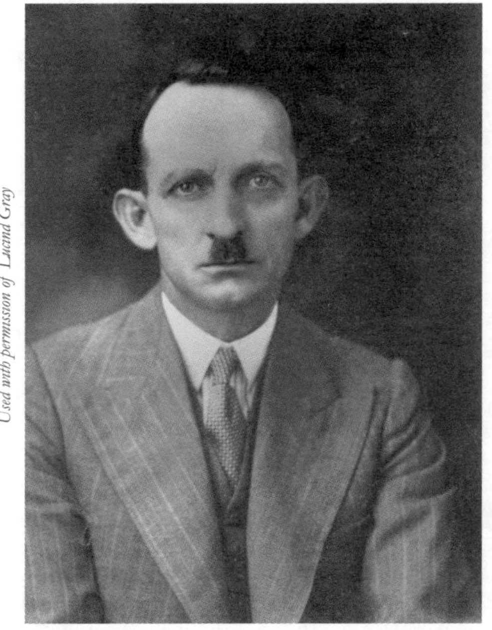

Used with permission of Lucind Gray

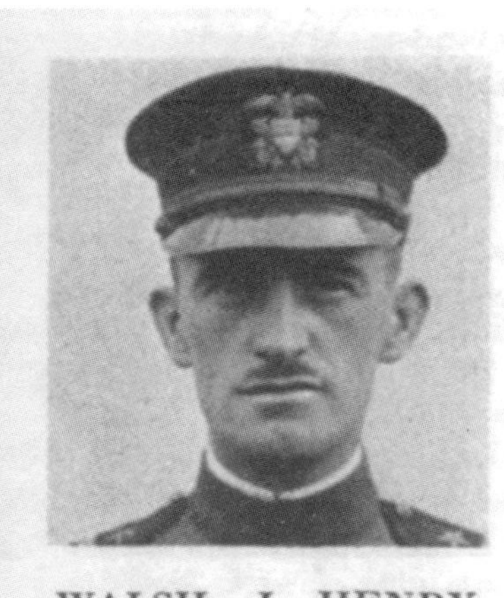

WALSH, J. HENRY
Lieutenant
166 Washington Ave., Prov., R. I. Squantum, Mass., Hampton Roads, Anacostia, D. C. USNRF. N. A. No. 525. HTA.

Figure 3.

between the men, trim the hair around her dad's ears so it is military length and put a cap on him, J. Henderson Gray would probably resemble J. Henry Walsh even more closely.

Alas, John Henry Walsh is not John Henderson Gray, no matter how much they resemble each other. On researching the photograph further, Lu came across Walsh's biography in *Contact! Naval Aviator Careers 1-2000* by Reginald Wright Arthur[2]. John Henry Walsh was born September 1, 1891 in Providence, RI. He enlisted in the Rhode Island naval militia December 30, 1915. He was given an honorable discharge on September 30, 1921, and died in Cranston, RI on September 12, 2965. They two men are not the same person!

An interesting exercise for the reader involving matching the individuals in two pictures, consider the age old mystery of the identity of the model for the Mona Lisa by Leonardo da Vinci. Some historians believe she could have been Leonardo in drag. You can judge for yourself.

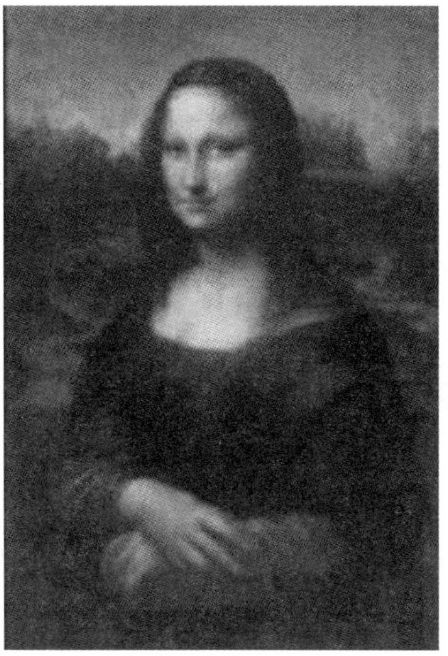

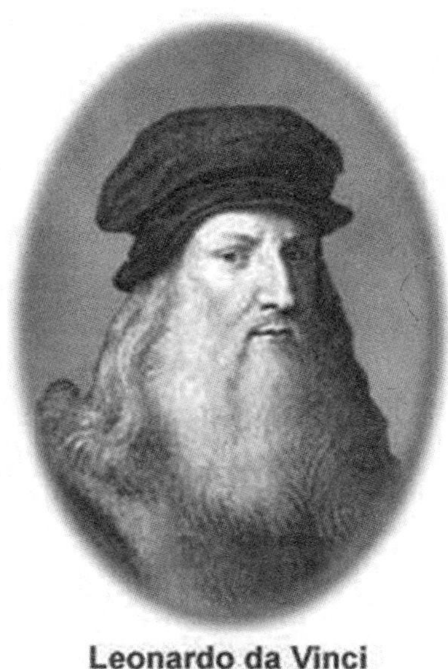

Leonardo da Vinci
(1452-1519)

Figure 4.

References

1. Flying Officers of the Unite States Navy 1917-1919, Schiffer Publishing, Ltd., Atglen, PA, 1997, p 85.

2. Contact! Naval Aviator Careers 1-2000, Reginald Wright Arthur, Naval Aviator Register, Washington, D. C., 1967, p. 165.

Case Study

Photographic Misidentification

Henry Brooks Adams (1838-1918) was a noted American historian, journalist, and author. He was the great grandson of John Adams, second President of the United States and a signator of the U.S. Constitution, and the grandson of John Quincy Adams, the fifth President of the United States.

Henry Adams' most noted work was the semi-autobiographical *The Education of Henry Adams* for which he was posthumously awarded the Pulitzer Prize in 1919. (Figure 1.) It ranked first on the Modern Library's 1998 list of 100

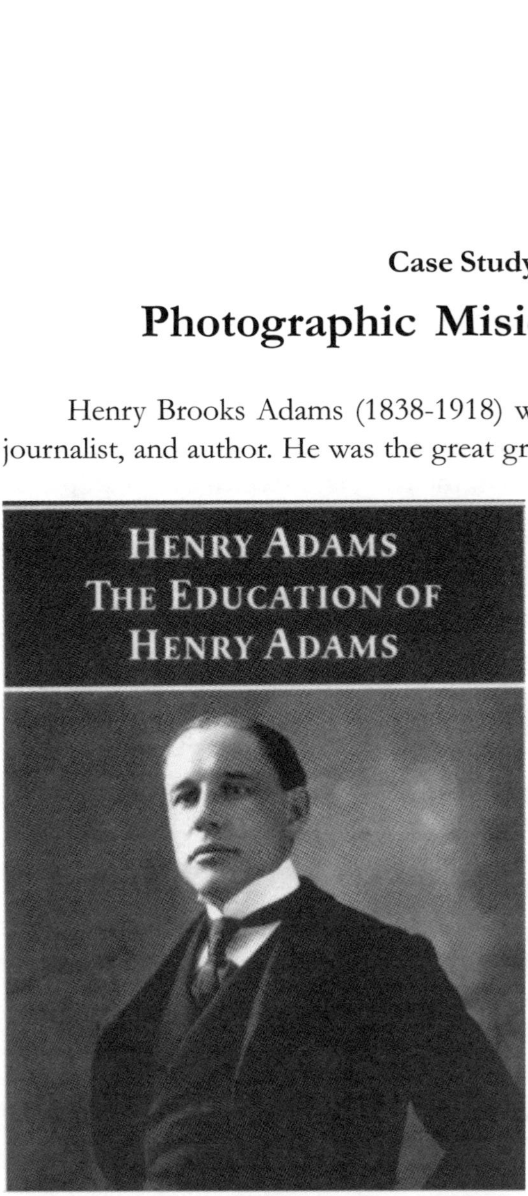

Figure 1.
The Education of Henry Adams,
OxfordUniversity Press, 1999.

Used by permission of Ira B. Nadel.

Best Nonfiction Books and was named the best book of the twentieth century by the Intercollegiate Studies Institute, a conservative organization that promotes classical education[1].

As a noted forensic expert in photograph identification, I was asked to examine the photo that appears on the cover of the publication *The Education of Henry Adams* by Oxford University Press. I was asked for my opinion about whether the man who appears on the cover of the book is Henry Adams (1838-1918) or if there has been a misidentification of the photo.

My response is that there has been a misidentification. The man on the cover is definitely not Henry Adams. My opinion is based on primarily on the type of photograph and the facial features of the man in the picture.

Until about 1880, all photographic paper consisted of two layers, a thick paper mount used to support an albumen coating containing light-sensitive silver salts[2]. In all albumen prints, the rough features of the underlying paper fibers are visible through the coating. A typical albumen photo yellows with age, and exhibits a pattern of fine cracks that appear as the albumen layer dehydrates over a long period of time.

Beginning in about 1880, three-layer photographic paper was produced, consisting of a paper support, a baryta layer, and a top layer of a gelatin or collodion suspension of light-sensitive silver salts. The baryta layer, a mixture of gelatin and finely ground barium sulfate was laid on the paper before it received the emulsion to prevent the emulsion from sinking into the paper fibers. It also provided protection from the impurities of the paper (chiefly metallic particles), better adhesion of the emulsion to the paper support, and better definition of the image[3].

Collodion and gelatin prints are characterized by their warmer color tones, ranging from sepia and purple (glossy) to gold, platinum and black (matte) tones. Three layer prints do not exhibit the rough surface of albumen prints due to the presence of the baryta layer. Print papers with matte, glossy, and textured surfaces were produced.

The photograph on the cover of the Oxford University press book is of the latter type, as evidenced by its warm black and white tonality. This type of photograph did not exist in the 1850s and 1860s when Henry Adams would have been in his young adulthood, as is the man in the photograph. The man on the cover of the book could not be Henry Adams.

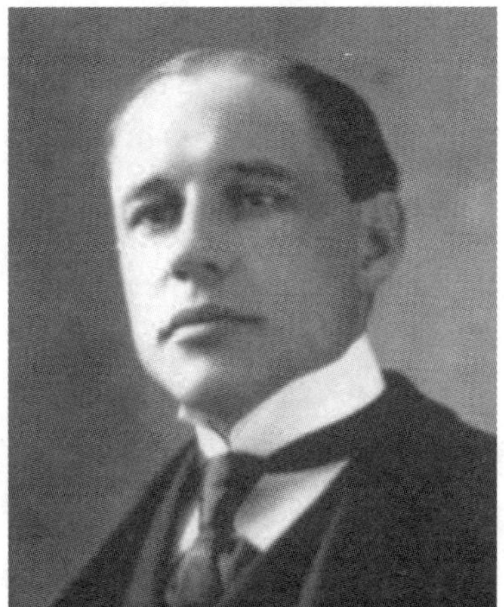

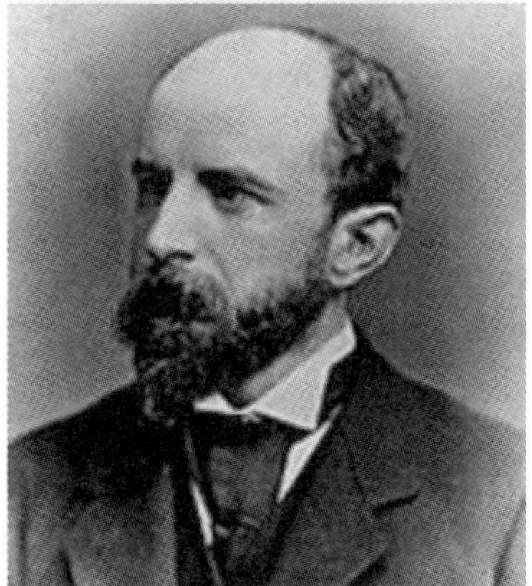

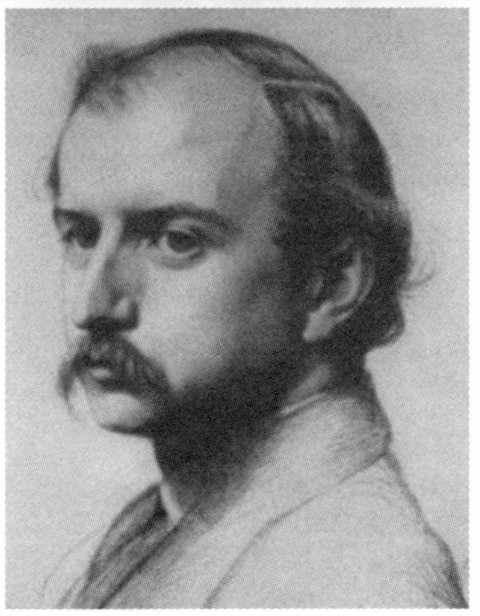

Forensic photo identification is based on matching someone's physical features in a known picture of that person, with those of a picture of an unknown person, to determine if they are the same or different individuals. At best this is a rule-out process. If the features do not match, the photographs are not of the same person. If the features match, the two people might be the same person, but without further information it is nearly impossible to say for certain. Supplemental information that forensic scientists draw on to make a positive identification can include the date the picture was taken, the whereabouts of the person at that time, his approximate age, and very importantly, what other family members look like. A positive identification based only on the similarities of the

Figure 2. Top: Portrait on the cover of *The Education of Henry Adams*; Center: Undated potrait of Henry Adams reversed left to right; Bottom: Sketch of Adams from Smithsonian Magazine article November 2006.

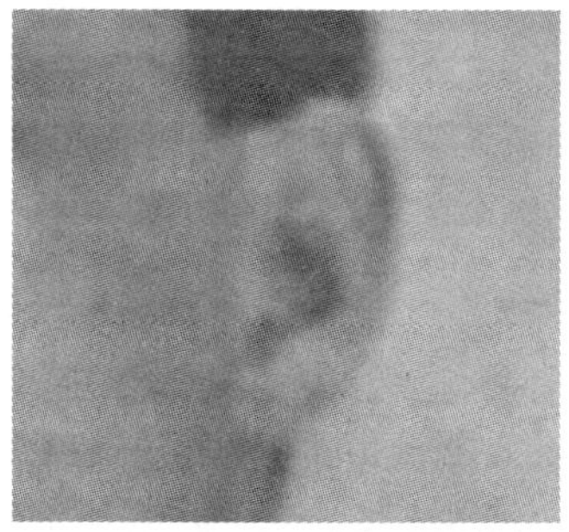

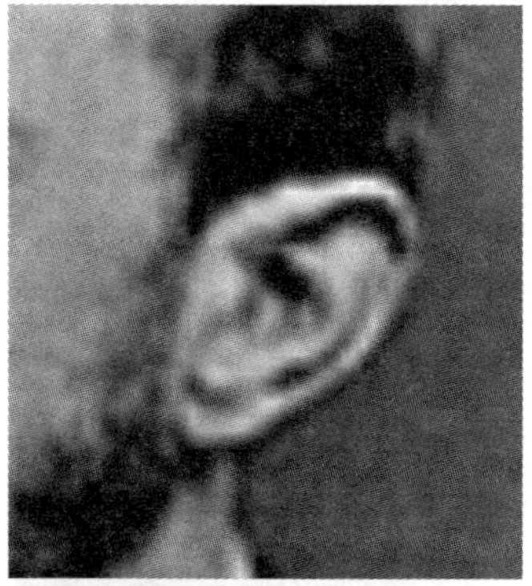

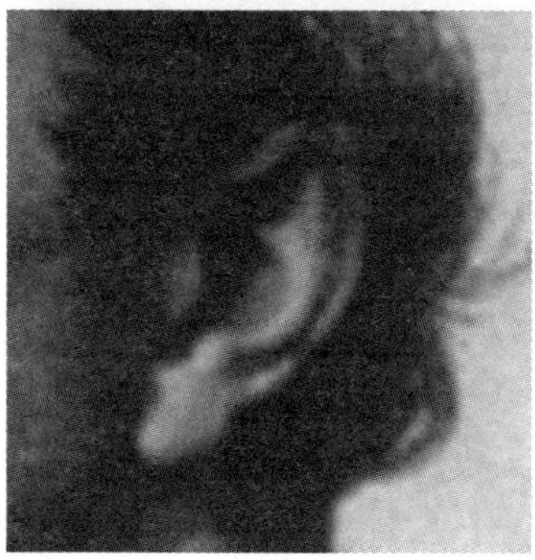

Figure 3. Earlobes taken from the pictures in Figure 2.

physical features of an unknown with a known person is risky.

Fundamental facial features that are used to rule out a possible identity for an unknown person include the shape of the hairline, the position of the part in the hair, the shape of the earlobes, and the shape of the browridge above the eyes . For the sake of the present comparison, several photos of Henry Adams are included in Figure 2.

The hairline in the sketch of Henry Adams that appeared in the Smithsonian Magazine article in November 2006, is different from that of the young man shown on the book cover. Adams' has a hairline that has receded to the top of his head that comes down well below the tip of his ear. He also has a tuft of hair remaining on his forehead. The hairline of the man in the cover photograph, however, has cleanly receded no farther than the top of his forehead, and ends at the top of his ear. While it can be argued that Adams could have styled his hair a certain way to pose for the photograph, it would have been impossible for him to replace hair he had already lost to bring his hairline forward to the top of his forehead.

A second clue is provided by the location of the part in the hair of each man. The Smithsonian sketch shows Adams parting his hair on his left side, while the man in the cover photograph has his part down the center.

Close-ups of the earlobes shown in the three portraits appear in Figure 3. There are two types of earlobes, unattached (Figure 4, top) and unattached (Figure 4, bottom). The man on the book cover seems to have attached earlobes while Adams's portraits indicate his were unattached, with fleshy lobes. Adams' ears are also more pointed towards the back of his head with more folds around the circumference.

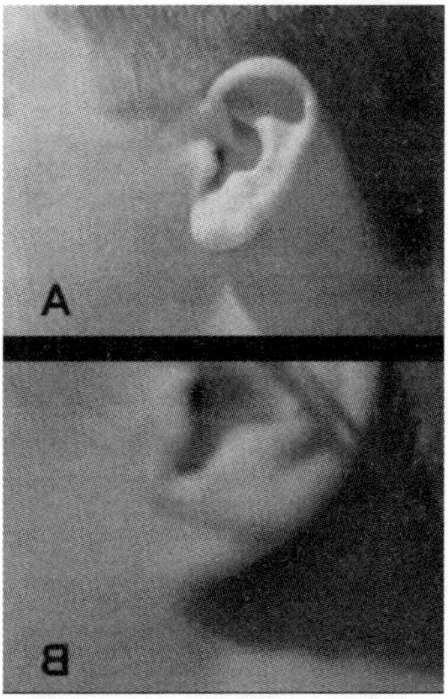

Figure 4. Top: Unattached earlobes; Bottom: Attached earlobes.

Perhaps the most decisive feature that indicates the man on the cover has been misidentified is the shape of the browridge above his eyes. Close-ups taken from the three portraits are shown in Figure 5.

There are noticeable differences between the brow ridge displayed by the unknown man and that shown in Adams' portraits. Mr. X has relatively short, thick eyebrows that follow a short rounded ridge. They begin and end roughly over the edges of his eyes, leaving a wide space across his nose. There is a noticeable gap above his eyelids that runs the full length of his eyebrows.

This contrasts with the shape of the ridge of Adams' brow. Adams' portraits show a longer, less arched ridge, that extends far beyond the tips of his eyes. His ridge dips as it extends toward his nose, giving him a frown. The interior corners of his eyes are overshadowed by the dip of his brow.

Because of these differences in facial features, the man on the cover could not be Henry Adams.

It's common to attempt to date a photograph by the clothing worn by the people in the picture. However, this is usually an inaccurate method of photo analysis. In general, styles of clothing change very slowly and the adoption of new styles is highly irregular both chronologically and geo-

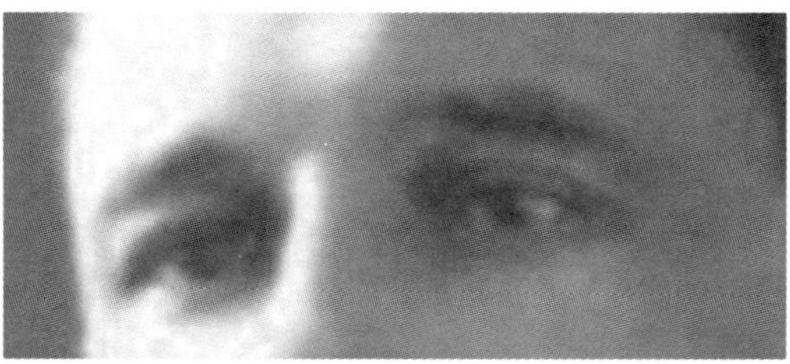
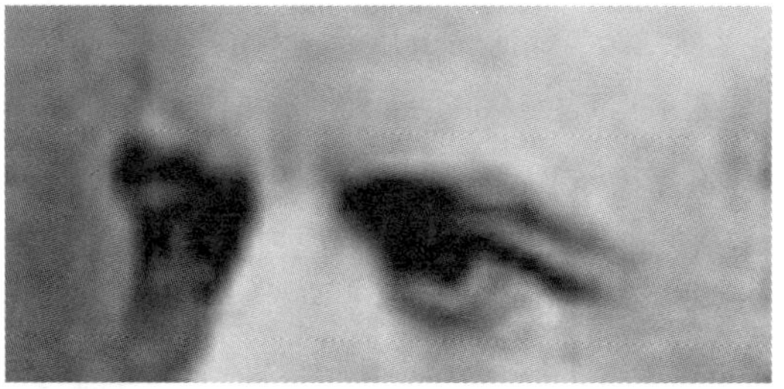
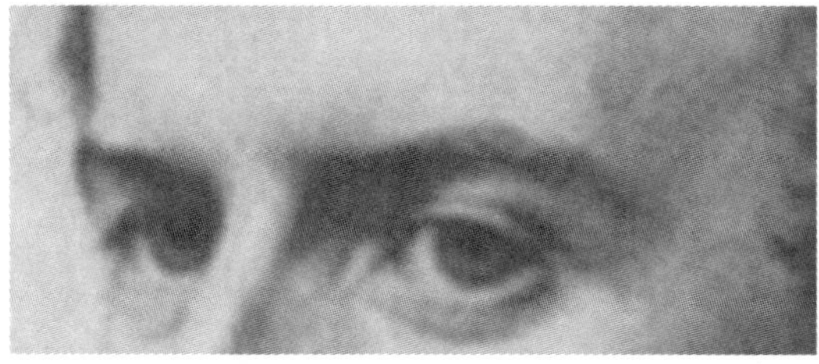
Figure 5. Eyebrow ridges taken from the pictures in Figure 2.

graphically. Individual features such as collars, sleeves, and ties change on their own schedule so that what might be labeled a "style" is usually a composite of these elements all in different stages of development. An additional concern is that people tend to use the clothes they have for a long time without updating their wardrobe, and clothing is often handed down to the next generation. Many women pose for pictures in their mothers' or their grandmother's wedding dresses, for example.

In conclusion, the photograph that appears on the cover of Oxford University Press' *The Education of Henry Adams* is not Henry Adams. The type of photograph that appears on the cover did not exist at the time Adams was a young man. There are also great differences between the facial features of the man on the cover and those of Henry Adams.

References

1. en.wikipedia.org/wiki/Henry_Brooks_Adams

2. Northeast Documentation Conservation Center, Preservation Leaflets, PHOTOGRAPHS, 5.2 Types of Photographs, Gary Albright, Conservator in Private Practice and Monique Fischer, Sr Photograph Conservator; www.nedcc.org/resources/leaflets/5Photographs/02TypesOfPhotos.php

3. Differences in Image Tonality Produced by Different Toning Protocols for Matte Collodion Photographs, Sylvie Penichon, Journal of the American Institute of Conservation 1999, Vol. 38, No. 2, Article 2 (pp. 124 to 143).

The Dead Horse Investigation

Crouching Horse, Hidden Locomotive

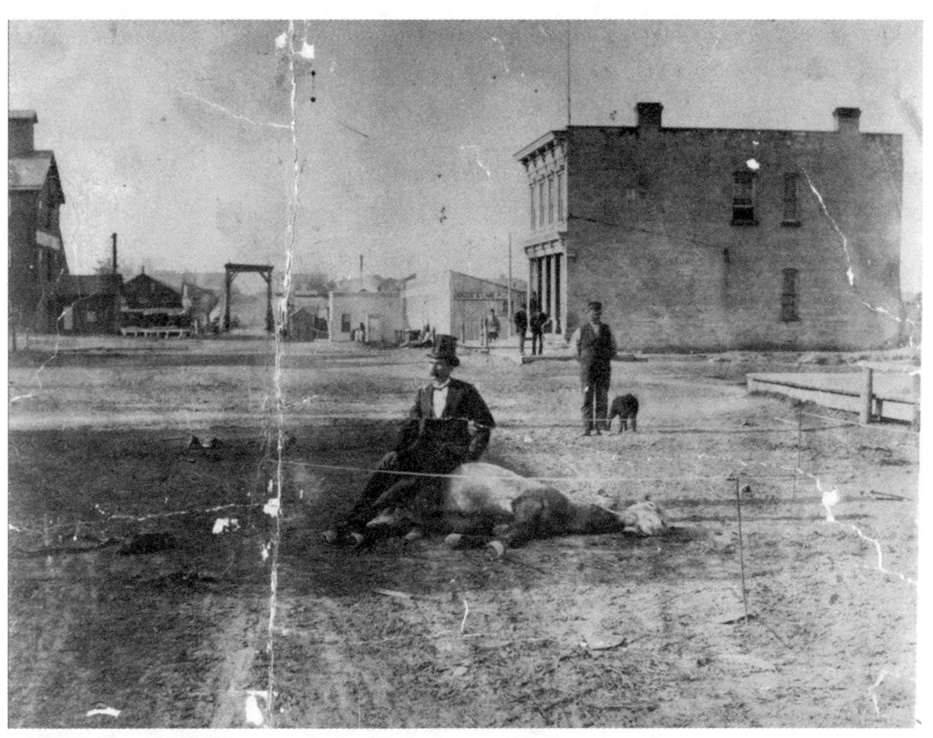

The appearance of the Dead Horse picture in the Sheboygan, WI Press in December 2005 produced much speculation on who the man in the top hat and tails was and why he was photographed sitting on a dead horse in the middle of S. 8th St. in Sheboygan. Many theories were advanced to account for the unusual scene. These included a tornado that occurred while a horse show was in town in 1901, and the possibility that a Sheboygan tannery was staking its claim to a horse that had died in the street.

The mystery of the man's identity, along with his reasons for sitting on the dead horse, remains unsolved. However, with the help of historical map expert Sharon Sergeant of Ancestral Manor, along with a bit of Sheboygan history provided by the Sheboygan County Historical Research Center (SCHRC), we determined that the day of the year the picture was taken was either May 2 or August 10. The year has to be between 1865 and 1880, but we can narrow that down considerable by assuming the streets were deserted because it was a Sunday. In this case the only possibilities are May 2, 1869, and August 10, 1869, 1875, and 1880. The time of day was 4:52 pm.

How did we do it? Elementary, my dear Watson.

Putting Things Into Perspective

All speculation aside, the direction and length of the shadows are the most important clues to the "when" of the photograph. Fortunately, we were able to get a reasonably accurate measurement of the shadows thanks to an ultra high resolution scan that was sent to us by Beth Dibble, director of the SCHRC.

Since 8th St. (then Griffith St.) runs north-south, all the shadows in the picture - those of Mr. Top-Hat-and-Tails, his dead horse, the buildings, and the man with his dog - stretch directly across the street, pointing to the east. This means that Mr. Top Hat and Tails was facing into the sun, which was due west in the sky. This simplified the calculation of when the photo was taken.

Another lucky break was that there is a sundial in the picture. Do you see it?

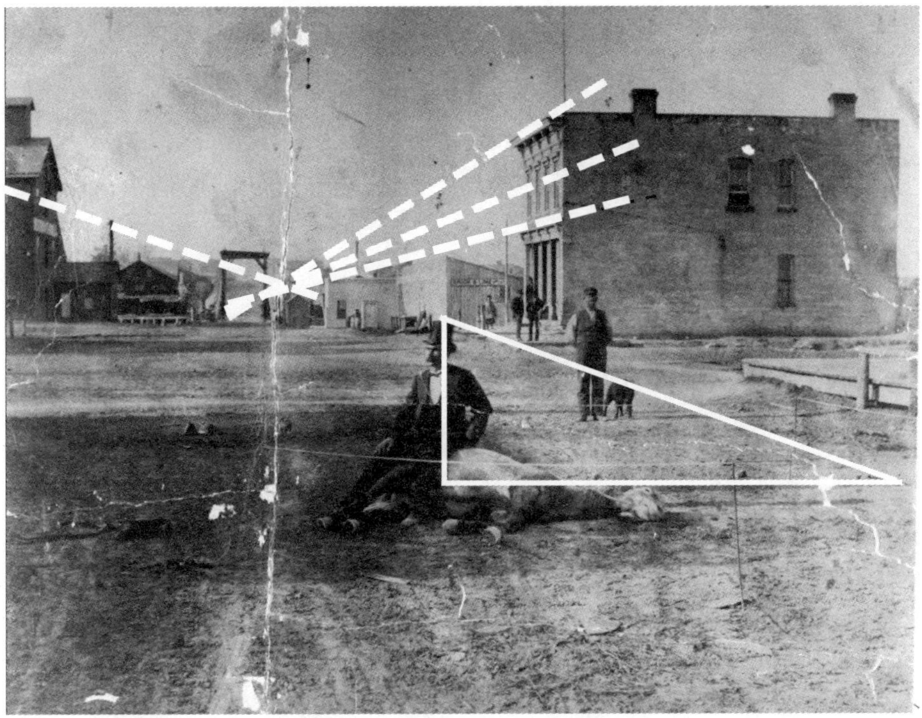

Figure 1. Mr. Tie-and-Tails can be used as a sundial to calculate the time of day. The vanishing point is slightly to the right of the bridge gantry.

It's Mr. Dapper himself!. The man and his shadow form two sides of a right triangle. (Figure 1.) The altitude of the sun can be calculated using a right triangle with hypotenuse running from the left edge of the top hat to the tip of its shadow on the ground[1]. The left edge of the hat is used because it is the edge that cast the shadow, as we could see using our ultra high resolution version of the photo. Using this method, we calculated the angle of the sun to be 22.85°.

In making the measurement, we took into account that the picture has a tear which artificially increases the apparent length of the shadow. Luckily, there is a vertical rod or stick in the photo that spans the tear and that can be used to calculate the amount the two parts of the picture are offset from each other. This offset can be used to obtain a correct length for the shadow. See Figure 2.

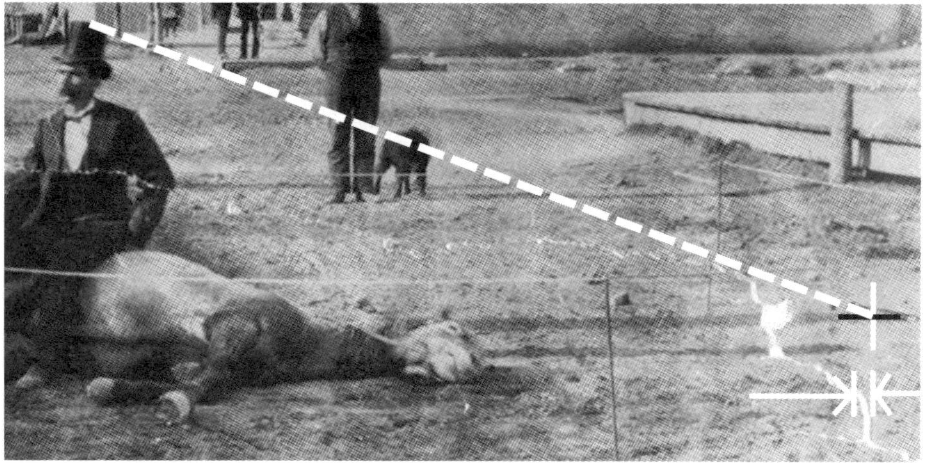

Figure 2. The length of the shadow cast by the man and his hat can be used to determine the elevation of the sun in the sky. Arrows indicate the amount the shadow was corrected by because of a tear in the photograph.

The other two ingredients in the recipe for dating the photograph are the azimuth of the sun in the sky, and the latitude and longitude of the intersection. The azimuth is defined as the angle of the sun relative to north at 0 °. East is considered as 90°, south as 180°, and west as 270°.

It is apparent from the shadows that the sun is approximately due west, but even though we used an ultra high resolution version of the photo, it is hard to know how close to due west it is. (Figure 3.) For one thing, only half the street is visible, so that landmarks such as the opposite street corners or buildings are not available to use for setting up a coordinate system. However, for the present purposes, we assumed that the sun was exactly due west as the starting point for our analysis. If further information appears to indicate otherwise, we can always recalculate the time of day and the day of the year using the updated information.

To determine the possible days of the year the picture could have been taken, we used the Great Circles Studio Calculator on the website www.gcstudio.com/suncalc.html[2]. We were searching for the days of the year when the sun was at 22.85° elevation and 270° azimuth. At this point,

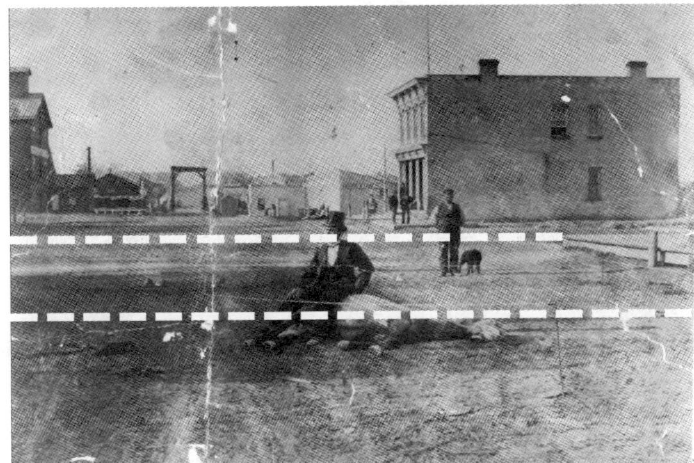

Figure 3. The dotted lines defining east-west are parallel to the shadows, which lie almost directly across the street.

the year was unimportant, since the sun traces the same path every year.

The calculator requires the latitude and longitude of a location, and given a date interval, it will return the position of the sun in the sky over that interval. We needed the reverse information, that is, given a position of the sun in the sky, what days of the year and times of the day correspond to that position?

Since the calculator can not run backwards, using the latitude and longitude of Sheboygan (43° 44' 35" N, 87° 42' 46") we input various days of the year until we found a date and time when the elevation and azimuth of the sun corresponded to our measurements of the picture. The sun is at 22.85° elevation and 270° azimuth on May 2 and August 10. The calculator told us that the sun is at this position at 4:52 pm on both days every year. There are two possible days because the sun passes the same point as it climbs higher in the sky during the spring and as it drops lower during the fall. In other words, what goes up must come down.

Can we distinguish between these two possible dates?

The average temperature[3] in Sheboygan for May 2 is 51° and for August 10 is 72°. Sometimes the weather, and therefore the time of year, is indicated by how warmly the people in a picture are dressed. However, in this case the average temperatures are too similar to make a judgment about the time of year based on clothing. In this case, it is impossible to choose between the two dates based on clothing alone.

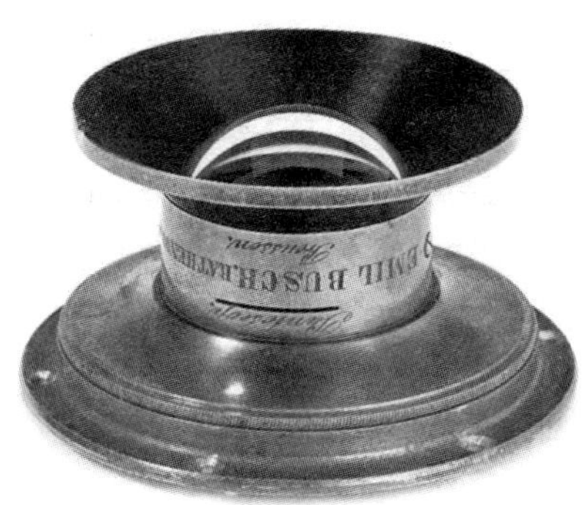

Figure 4. Emil Busch's Pantoscop.

What is the earliest date the picture could have been taken? This is where our backgrounds in optics came in handy. We observed that the photograph was snapped using a wide angle lens. How did we know this? For one thing, the width of the street was 80 ft. To take in half of the street using a normal lens, the camera would have been about 80 ft from the horse. But this is clearly not where the camera was. A wide angle lens explains the discrepancy.

The first wide angle lens, known as the Pantoscop, was produced in 1865 in Rathenow, Germany by Emil Busch[4]. See Figure 4. Although it was first used in 1867 by Albrecht Meydenbauer for photogrammic documentation of buildings and cityscapes[5], even in the 1880s it was not in common use.

The earliest date the picture could have been taken was therefore 1865, although it was probably produced after 1867, and likely later. The first mention we could find of a wide angle lens in U.S. newspapers was a news item in the April 26, 1880 edition of the Chester, PA *Chester Daily Times* describing the use of a wide angle lens in a legal dispute over the building of a new tavern[6].

Although the defendant tried to use photographs to impress the judge with the grand appearance of his new establishment, his strategy backfired. He hired a photographer to photograph both the tavern and the plaintiff's much smaller house across the street. But the photographer used a wide angle lens, probably because he could not get far enough away to capture the larger tavern with a normal lens.

Unfortunately, a wide angle lens severely distorts perspective, making objects in the foreground much bigger and objects farther back much smaller than they are. The photographer made the mistake of photographing the tavern on the diagonal from the corner. The perspective distortions made it look comical and grotesque. On the other hand, he photographed the smaller plaintive's house from directly across the street, so that the same distortions made the house look much larger and grandiose. The reporter pointed out the potential value of photographic evidence for legal proceedings even though the plaintiff won the case.

One other interesting observation is that the vanishing point is not located at the center of the picture, but rather to the immediate right of the gantry. This was probably the center of the field of view of the plate camera used to take the picture. The photograph was undoubtedly made as a contact print, so that it must be the same size as the original glass negative. The unexposed plate was therefore positioned off-center in the camera, taking advantage of the large image created by the wide angle lens to better compose the picture. It's a coincidence that the long vertical white line to the right of the gantry runs through the vanishing point. At first, it was thought that this line represented a fold down the center of a larger photograph that had been subsequently cropped. But according to the Sheboygan Research Center, this line along with the other smaller white lines meandering through the image, is where the original negative was broken. Apparently the picture was contact printed from the reassembled pieces of the shattered negative.

Now what about the latest date for the photograph? Important clues were provided by Sharon Sergeant through her research into Sheboygan's history. By studying the gantry over the entrance to the S. 8th St. bridge, she identified it as a truss swinging bridge, with the gantry used the anchor for the trusses. According to *One Hundred Years of Sheboygan, 1846-1946*, by J. E. Leberman, the bridge was constructed in 1846 and rebuilt in 1869, 1881, and 1893. Sharon found a sketch of the bridge from 1888 in *Sheboygan centennial celebration, 1853-1953: official souvenir program and historic booklet, August 9th thru 15th, 1953* that clearly shows a bridge of a different design without a gantry. See Figure 5. The gantry must have been removed before 1888 during one of the earlier renovations, giving a latest date for the photo of 1881.

The estimate of the latest date can be improved upon through information provided by old maps and census records. According to Sharon, the 1884 Sanborn Fire Insurance Map shows that the northwest and southwest corners of the intersection of Griffith (now S. 8th) and Indiana Aves. was occupied by saloons. See Figure 6. This is confirmed by the 1880 census records. But the shadow that is falling on the man is not being cast by the building on the corner, but rather by the building next to it, second from the corner. The corner is empty. This dates the picture to before the 1880 census.

Of additional interest are the two very long shadows extending from the base of the shadow cast by this building second from the corner. One of these shadows extends behind the man with the dog, with the other located just upstreet from the horse's head. Both shadows extend nearly across the width of S. 8th St. Compared with the height of the other buildings in the picture, the posts that cast these shadows were 1½ stories high. This corresponds to the height of the building at this location shown on the 1884 Sanborn map. These posts could have been part of its frame as the building was being constructed in the 1870s.

A question that plagued the dead horse investigation community for a long time relates to the railroad tracks that should cross in front of the gantry. Library of Congress maps and Sheboygan historical publications document that the railroad was completed through Sheboygan in the early 1860s, and later Sanborn maps indicate the tracks ran across S. 8th St. near the river. Sheboygan was an important depot for the Fond du Lac and Sheboygan railroad in the mid 1870s[7]. An article in the *Oshkosh Daily*

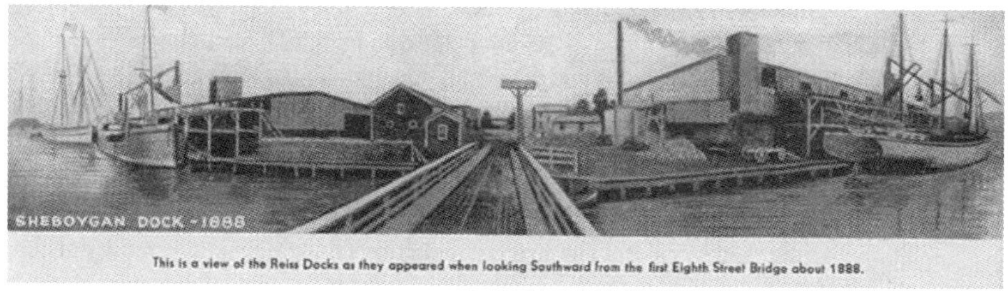

Figure 5. View of the gantry across the Sheboygan River as of 1888[6].

Northwesterner on Friday, October 15, 1875 reported that the Williamson, McKenzie & Crawford Co. had unloaded fifteen thousand tons of coal and wood from vessels into railcars at Sheboygan for transport to Fond du Lac, where the cargo was shipped out by barge via the Wolf River and Lake Winnebago. Railroad tracks should appear crossing the road in front of the gantry assuming the picture was taken between 1867 and 1880. Yet no tracks are apparent in the photograph. Several theories have been advanced to explain their absence, from a natural disaster destroying the tracks, to a period when the tracks were removed for repair.

However, the reason why no one spotted evidence of a railroad crossing near the river is that no one looked hard enough. Believe it or not, there is a full-sized steam-belching locomotive in the picture. It's just well camouflaged. Before reading further, can you spot it?

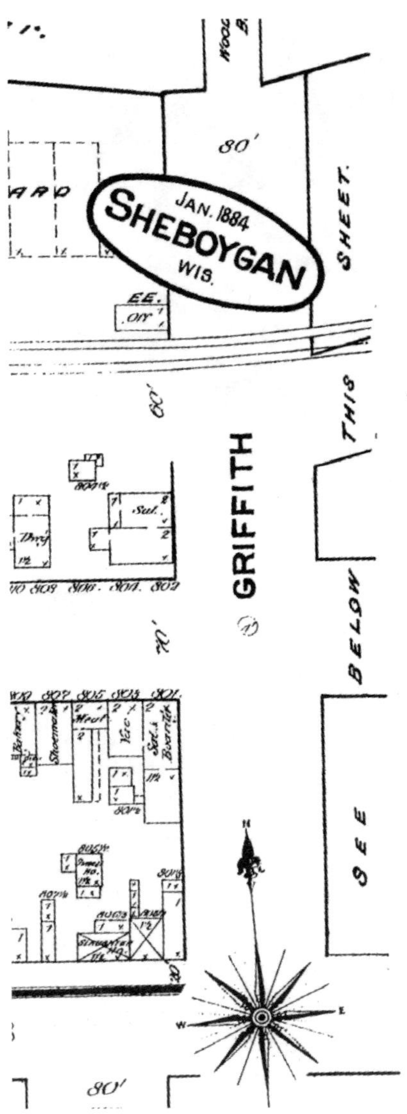

Figure 6. 1884 Sanborn Fire Insurance Map showing the intersection of Griffith Ave (now 8th Ave) and Indiana Ave. Note saloons on the northwest and southwest corners. Circle indicates 1 1/2 story building.

Camouflaged Locomotive

Have a look at the A-frame building facing the camera to the left of the gantry. It has three windows in a row, the left one of which is eclipsed by the shed in front of it.

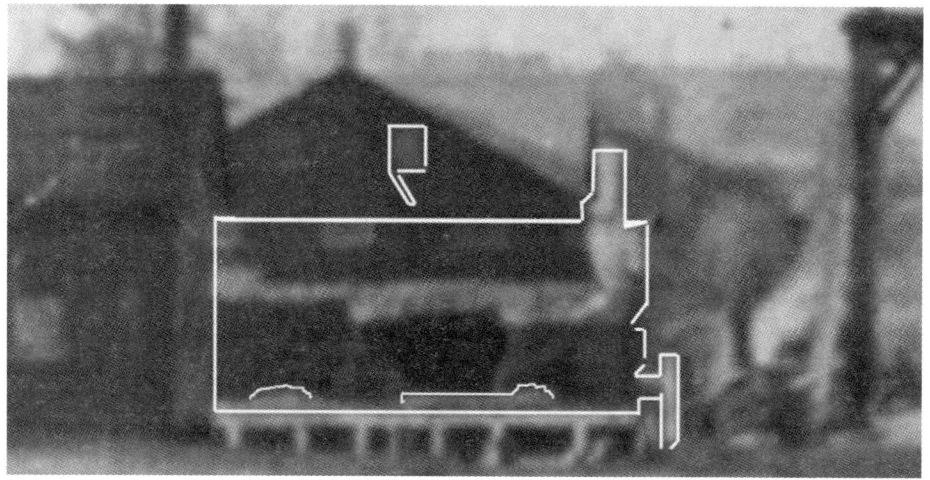

Figure 7. See the locomotive?

The right edge of the house's sloped roof appears cut off by a white chimney. There is a thick white line that zigzags below the windows from the shed to the chimney.

Actually, it's not a chimney. It's the smokestack of a locomotive. The zigzagging white line is the joint between the top and the bottom halves of the locomotive frame. Two thinner white lines just above the wooden platform are the drive shafts connecting the drive wheels. (You can see the tops of these two wheels above the platform if you look hard enough.) The white square located near the top right of the A-frame building is the semaphore on the other side of the track that was used to signal the train. There is steam from engine billowing in front of the locomotive. The shed in front of the tracks and the A-frame house behind the tracks are probably train depots. It's really not a surprise that the locomotive is hard to see, considering the distortion in perspective created by the wide angle lens. The outline of the locomotive is shown in Figure 7.

To make sure we were not imagining things after working so hard on this picture, we investigated the type of locomotive and compared its relative size to other items in the photo. We also consulted two locomotive historians.

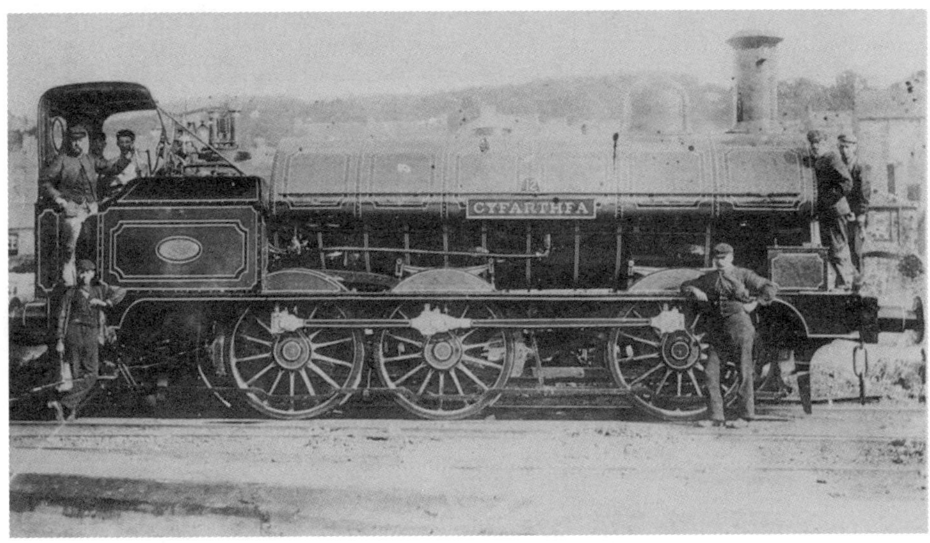

Figure 8. Steam locomotive of the Cyfarthfa Iron Works[8].

Figure 8 shows a locomotive called the Cyfarthfa that we discovered a picture of a Penydarren steam engine used by the Cyfarthfa Iron Works in Australia, built in 1870[8]. It resembles our mystery engine with its short smoke-stack, and long body. Like our mystery engine, it has a platform on the front instead of a cowcatcher.

To check the proportions of our mystery engine, we compared it to the size of the door on the shed to the right of the gantry, since would represent the approximate height of a person. The results of our compari-

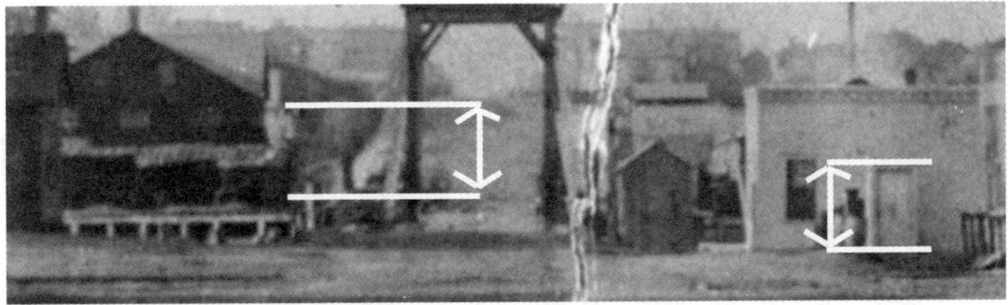

Figure 9. Comparing the size of the mystery engine with the height of a person.

son, seen in Figure 9, show that if a man were to stand on the front platform of our mystery engine, his head would be a little higher than the top of the boiler. This is the same relative height of the Cyfarthfa compared to the men standing on her platform.

Still the experts we consulted were not in agreement about whether the image was that of a locomotive or not. We consulted with Lee Witten, Secretary of the Golden Spike Chapter of the Railway and Locomotive historical Society in Ogden, UT, and with Bob Kreiger, the Vice President of the Union Pacific Historical Society in Cheyenne, WY.

Lee was not convinced he saw a locomotive in the picture. According to Lee:

The picture of the Australian locomotive does not look like anything that an American railroad would have used at that time, at least from what I've seen and read but that's not a conclusive argument on my part. Even if it was like the Australian one, the pattern of the shadows and that zigzag line simply don't jive with what you would expect of a cylindrical boiler with domes on it. I'm just not totally convinced its a locomotive.

On the other hand, Bob not only believed he saw a locomotive, he even thought he knew the type:

Tho very difficult to see it would appear by its vague shape to be a small 0-6-0 tank engine used for moving cars about at a yard or docks. No way to know which railroad.

City Directories

Back to the year the picture was taken.

Sheboygan did not have many city directories in the 1860s and 1870s. There were only two available through the SCHRC, one from 1868 and a second one from 1875. They were somewhat useful in pinning down a date, but they required a bit of interpretation. Evidently Sheboygan did not have street addresses in the 1870s, so that people and businesses were listed in the directory as living on or near an intersection. This made it difficult to establish exactly which businesses were on the corner of 8th (Griffith) Ave. and Indiana.

An additional difficulty in using the directories was that the neighborhood shown in the picture was an industrial area of town, with few vintage photographs taken of it, and little documentation on when roads and buildings were constructed. It is well known that the Italianate building shown in the photo on the northeast corner of the intersection was the Evergreen Hotel. It was a city landmark for many years, but the early history of the building is somewhat obscure. One clue could be the shack-shaped lines on the side of this building. It appears as if a shack had originally been attached to the building but had been removed sometime in the past, presumably to construct Indiana Ave. But no records have been found about this either.

The 1868 city directory only listed three businesses on the corner of 8th (Griffith) Ave. and Indiana Ave. The tall building with the pointed roof that is hiding part of the locomotive was probably the grain elevator located near the river. See Table 1. With the smaller structure on top, it looks like a grain elevator. It makes sense that a locomotive would be parked next to it. Perhaps the trains was loading its cars with grain when the picture was taken.

Unfortunately, the 1868 city directory does not give us any new information. We already know that the north east and northwest corners of the intersection were occupied before the picture was taken, but we have no earliest date. We also know that the two southern corners were not built up

Table 1.

1868 Sheboygan City Directory			
Saloon	Heyn	August	Griffith nwc Indiana Ave.
Boots & Shoes	Heinecke	Gustav	Griffith nec Indiana Ave.
Groceries	Heinecke	Gustav	Griffith nec Indiana Ave.
Grain Elevator	Bertschy	John	Griffith nwc River

until later, but there are no records to indicate when.

The 1875 Sheboygan city directory does not give too much additional information. In this year, there were five businesses listed at the intersection, but the directory does not designate which corner any of them occupied. See Table 2. Since it is possible that more than one business occupied the same building, the fact that there are five businesses listed does not give any hints about how many and which corners were occupied at the time.

Without further information, there is very little additional research that can be done. We have researched the buildings in the residential area in the distance on the north side of the bridge, hoping to fin a building permit or a property deed to indicate the construction of one of the structures we can see in the background. We have also researched train schedules hoping to discover a train that had a scheduled stop at Sheboygan at 4:52 either May 2 of August 10 between 1865 and 1880. But we have turned up nothing. Nada!

We have considered the possibility that the photo was taken on a Sunday. Even though the neighborhood was industrial, and the SCHRC believes that the building on the northeast corner of the intersection was probably a saloon as far back as our earliest date of 1865, the street appears deserted. Perhaps the weekday crowd was absent because they were at church or spending time with their families on their day of rest. The perpetual calendar at www.wiskit.com/calendar.html tells us that there are only a few

Table 2.

1875 Sheboygan City Directory			
Dry Goods	Koehn	F	c Griffith and Indiana av
Grocer	Hobert	J	c Griffith and Indiana av
Hotel	Lakeview House John Messner, Prop		c. Indiana av and Griffith
Meat Mkt	Koll	C	c Griffith and Indiana av
Saloon	Oetking	F	c. Indiana av and Griffith

possible dates where May 2 or August 10 occurred on a Sunday during our time range of 1865 through 1880. May 2 was a Sunday only once, in 1869. August 10 was a Sunday in 1869, 1875, and 1880.

I'd vote for May 2 as the date, simply to put the mystery to rest, and not based on any clever trick we haven't tried. So don't accuse me of beating a dead horse.

And who took the picture? Perhaps we will never know. The photographer must have been knowledgable about the latest photographic equipment, and must have had the means to purchase a very expensive lens. He must also have had the know-how to use it. The historical finger points to either Wolfgang Morganeier, a German photographer in the 1870s, or to his two apprentices, George and Edward Groh. But as they say in math textbooks, the proof is left as an exercise for the reader.

Hmmm.....maybe the horse was hit by the train.....

References

1. Thanks to Roger Bailey and Steve Lelievre of the sundial community for their help with understanding the calculations that were required here.

2. www.gcstudio.com/suncalc.html

3. www.weather.com/weather/wxclimatology/daily/53081?climoMonth=5

4. www.camerapedia.org/wiki/Emil_Busch

5. www.hasler.net/Meydenb.pdf

6. The Chester Daily Times, Vol. 8, No. 1124, April 26, 1880, p. 1, c. 5.

6. *Sheboygan centennial celebration, 1853-1953: official souvenir program and historic booklet, August 9th thru 15th, 1953*

7. Joerns Brothers / *Illustrated historical atlas of Sheboygan County,* (1902), The State of Wisconsin Collection, Travel and transportation, p. 17

8. www.epolitix.com/EN/MPWebsites/Dai+Havard/cadd7449-f6b8-40ac-9e17-6b1fd8649977.htm

If you have enjoyed this book, check out our website www.forensicgenealogy.info for our weekly photo-quizzes. You might also like to purchase our other two books *Forensic Genealogy* and *DNA & Genealogy*, and our *30 Best Photoquizzes* CD. If you have a photo you'd like us to look at, please send it to me at colleen@forensicgenealogy.info.